COUNTY ANTRIM

A

TOPOGRAPHICAL DICTIONARY

OF THE PARISHES, VILLAGES AND TOWNS
OF COUNTY ANTRIM IN THE 1830s

ILLUSTRATED WITH
CONTEMPORARY MAPS AND ENGRAVINGS

BY SAMUEL LEWIS

PREFACE BY BRIAN M. WALKER

BELFAST
PUBLISHED BY FRIARS BUSH PRESS
2002

I

THIS SELECTED EDITION
PUBLISHED 2002
BY FRIAR'S BUSH PRESS
160 BALLYLESSON ROAD
BELFAST BT8 8JU
NORTHERN IRELAND

FIRST PUBLISHED 1837
BY S. LEWIS & CO.
87 ALDERSGATE STREET
LONDON

ISBN 0-946872-61-9

PRINTED BY W.G.BAIRD
CAULSIDE DRIVE
ANTRIM BT41 2RS

SCANNING OF TEXT BY CDDA, 1-4 COLLEGE PARK EAST, BELFAST BT7 1LQ

COVER DESIGN AND BOOK LAYOUT BY RODNEY MILLER ASSOCIATES,
21 ORMEAU AVENUE, BELFAST BT2 8HD

PREFACE

This volume brings together three important contemporary sources of information about life and society in County Antrim in the 1830s. The text is taken from the monumental two-volumed topographical dictionary of Ireland, published by Samuel Lewis in 1837. Thanks to modern scanning methods it has been possible to lift directly and then reformat the County Antrim material from his books which covered all of Ireland in alphabetical order in a grand total of 1405 double columned pages. Maps of the main County Antrim towns have been photographed from the first edition Ordnance Survey maps for the county, which were published in 1834, and are integrated into the text. A considerable number of engravings, mostly from the 1830s, has also been included. In the case of all three components of this book – the topographical text, the maps and the engravings, the period of the 1830s witnessed new heights in the availability and worth of such sources. Brought together here in this particular form, the material presents a special view of the parishes, villages and towns of County Antrim in the period before the great changes of Victorian Ireland. It gives a compelling record of agriculture, industry, population, buildings and antiquities in the county over one hundred and sixty years ago.

Samuel Lewis, publisher

Our knowledge about the life of Samuel Lewis is fairly limited. We do know, however, that during the 1830s and 1840s he ran a publishing business in London, first at 87 Aldersgate Street and secondly at 13 Finsbury Place South. He died in 1865. More is known about the outcome of his publishing efforts, in particular the very successful series of topographical dictionaries for which he was responsible. His 4 volumed topographical dictionary for England appeared in 1831 (7th edition 1849) to be followed a year later by a similar two volumed work for Wales(4th edition 1849). In 1837 he produced a two volumed dictionary for Ireland (2nd edition 1842), accompanied by an atlas of the counties of Ireland. Finally, he published a three volumed topographical dictionary for Scotland in 1846.[1]

Production of the Irish dictionary involved a vast entreprenurial enterprise.[2] Starting in early 1833 agents were dispatched to all parts of Ireland to gather information for the work and also to obtain advance subscribers. The dictionary was priced at two guineas per volume while the atlas was also available for two guineas. As was explained in the preface to the first volume, compared to England and Wales there was less available for Ireland in the form of county histories and other such work, so it was important to gain extensive personal information. His principle sources of information were local landowners and clergy. When the dictionary appeared finally in 1837 the list of subscribers(including many of his informants) ran to a total of nearly 10,000 names, including large numbers in Belfast or County Antrim.

The publication of the Irish dictionary led to considerable controversy, caused not by the content of the volumes but by objections from some of those listed as subscribers to being included on the list. A number of legal cases ensued over questions of liability for payment for the two books. There seems to have been relatively little debate over the accuracy of the contents. The 1842 revised edition made some corrections but also updated the figures in accordance with the 1841 census and replaced educational material with extra material on the railways. The entries reprinted here for County Antrim are from the first edition and so relate to the 1830s.

This dictionary by Lewis gives a unique coverage of life in Ireland, parish by parish and town by town. No-one before had produced such an extensive survey. At the same time as the appearance of these volumes by Lewis an enterprise was underway to record Irish society and economy as part of the Ordnance Survey (O.S.) with the writing of memoirs to accompany the production of the first O.S. maps for Ireland. This project collapsed finally in 1840, however, after only the northern counties had been investigated, and just one volume was published for the parish of Templemore in County Londonderry. Only in the last decade of the twentieth century have these memoirs been published.[3] Lewis's material has a special value in the case of Belfast because he covered the town extensively which the O.S. memoirs did not. These volumes are very valuable for us today not just because Lewis gathered important personal information at local level but also because he availed of much of the statistical and factual information which was now becoming available for Ireland, often through parliamentary papers and reports. In particular, he used the 1831 census report, new educational data and O.S.acreage figures.

At the same time,we must be aware of some of the perspectives and weaknesses of the material. A man of his time, Lewis approached his work from the standpoint of a society run by the gentry. The parishes are those of the Church of Ireland which was the established church. We must appreciate that some of his accounts of Irish pre history and archaeology would be questioned by historians and archaeologists today. His information on these matters reflects the state of knowledge about them at the time, which changed considerably in the course of the nineteenth century, thanks to the work of people such as John O'Donovan. For example his references to 'druidical altars', and some of his accounts of the origins of the early people of Ireland would not now be accepted. Those interested in the composition of placenames should check Lewis's interpretation with modern works on the subject.[4] It should also be noted that Lewis gives distances in Irish miles.(10 Irish miles equal a little over 12 miles British)

Maps and map makers
The year 1834 witnessed the publication of the first 6 inch O.S.maps for County Antrim. Run by officers of the Royal Engineers, and starting in the 1820s a complete mapping survey of the whole country was carried out under the auspices of the Ordnance Survey of Ireland, based at Phoenix Park in Dublin.[5] This led to the appearance in 1833 of the first six inches to the mile maps for County Londonderry, to be followed by similar maps for all the Irish counties over the next nine years. This surveying project was a vast undertaking which involved considerable expenditure and manpower. The result was a very extensive cartographic record for Ireland, which had no equivalent in the world at the time. In 1780 J.Lendrick produced a fine four section map for County Antrim, but this was now superceded by the O.S. production.

In this volume plans of the 8 main towns in County Antrim have been copied from the original 6 inch O.S. maps for the county. For sake of greater clarity the town maps have been reproduced at 140 per cent. It must be remembered that while all the County Antrim O.S.maps were published in 1834, the actual surveying could have been done in the previous one or two years. We have also included a map of County Antrim from Lewis's atlas. One of the advantages of this map is that it gives the location of the parishes, and while it does not show the parish boundaries, nonetheless, it can be helpful to give people some idea of which parish their area is located in. The maps in the atlas were based on drawings reduced from the Ordnance Survey and other surveys.

Artists and engravers

The period from the early 1820s to the early 1840s witnessed an upsurge in the appearance of topographical views of Ireland, partly due to technological advances such as the advent of line engraving on steel in the early 1820s. The bulk of the illustrations in this book come from the 1830s, although some are as early as 1823 and others are as late as 1843. The publication of the weekly *Dublin Penny Journal*, 1832-6, with its many wood engravings, was an important new departure in the level of illustrated material available at a low cost. The journal carried topographical articles and illustrations on many parts of Ireland. Besides *The Dublin Penny Journal,* there now appeared a large number of illustrated books, covering special areas or all of Ireland. Well known artists, such as George Petrie (who worked for the Ordnance Survey for a time in the 1830s), were employed to provide drawings to be engraved for these volumes.

Of special interest in this activity is the work of a number of northern artists. Views by the Belfast born Andrew Nicholl (1804-86) appeared frequently, both in *The Dublin Penny Journal* and in various published tours and guides. We should note the prints of John Thomson (died 1847), who can be regarded as one of the first local print makers in Belfast.[6] A native of Arbroath, Scotland, Thomson came to Ireland in 1798 as a Tay Fencible and eventually settled in Belfast where he became an engraver of plates for labels and stamps for the linen trade. His work was used to illustrate George Benn's *Historical account of Belfast,* published in Belfast in 1823. John Molloy (1798-1877) was an art master in Belfast, who was responsible for views of large private houses in the Belfast neighbourhood, which were engraved and published in 1832 in Belfast and London in a book entitled *Belfast scenery in thirty views.*[7]

In recent times engravings such as these have often been used to illustrate texts, but usually there has been little attempt to name the artist and engraver involved or to accurately date the picture. In this volume, however, an effort has been made to identify both the artist and engraver responsible for a particular piece of work. This has not been possible in every case and where the full information has not been given this is because it is not available. In the case of John Thomson's work it is likely that he was both the artist and the engraver, although on his prints he is described only as the engraver. The title of the book, and the date and place of publication, has been given with each print so that we can establish a date for the particular view.

Brian M. Walker   **Belfast, 2002**

References

[1] See Frederick Boase, (ed) *Modern English biography,* vol. 2 (London, 1965), p.417.

[2] This enterprise is discussed well by Tim Cadogan in his introduction to *Lewis's Cork* (Cork, 1998).

[3] Angelique Day and Patrick Mc Williams, *Ordnance survey memoirs of Ireland,* vols 1-40 (Belfast, 1990-8).

[4] See the two Co.Antrim volumes in the series *Placenames of Northern Ireland,* general editor Gerald Stockman.

[5] See J.H. Andrews, *A paper landscape: the Ordnance Survey in nineteenth century Ireland* (Oxford, 1993; second edition, Dublin,2002).

[6] See R.M. Young, *The town book of the corporation of Belfast, 1613-1816* (Belfast, 1892), p.340.

[7] See modern commentary by Hugh Dixon and Fred Heatley in *Belfast scenery in thirty views, 1832* (reprint Belfast, 1983)

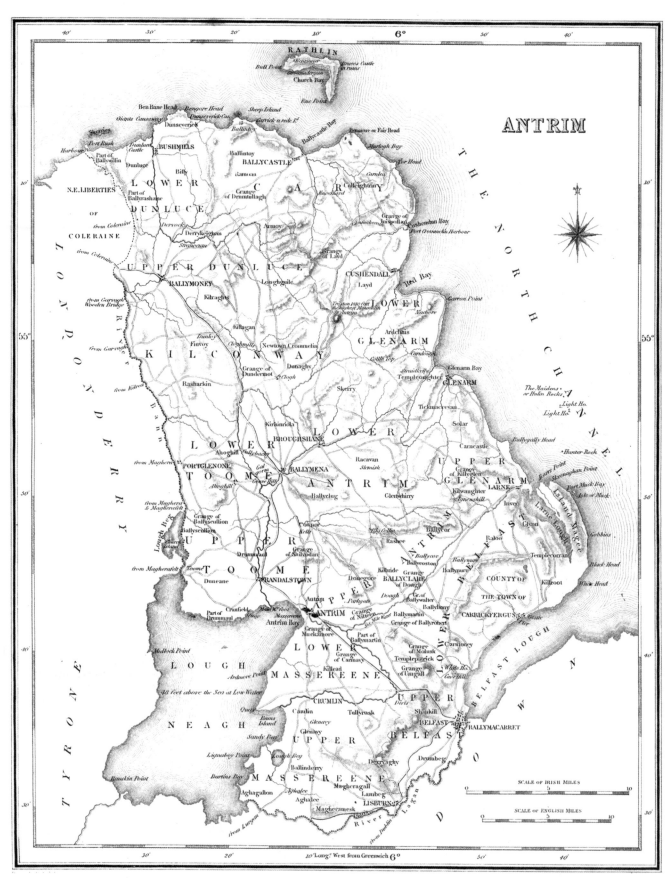

Antrim. Drawn by R. Creighton and engraved by I. Dower. From Lewis's Atlas, *(London, 1837)*

COUNTY ANTRIM

A

TOPOGRAPHICAL DICTIONARY

ANTRIM (County of), a maritime county in the province of ULSTER, bounded on the north by the Northern Ocean, or Deucaledonian Sea; on the north-east and east, by the North Channel; on the south-east, by the lough or bay of Belfast and the river Lagan, separating it from the county of Down, which likewise borders it on the south; on the south-west, by Lough Neagh; on the west, by Lough Beg and the river Bann, which separate it from the county of Londonderry; and on the north-west, by the liberties of Coleraine. It extends from 54° 26' to 55° 12' 16" (N. Lat.), and from 5° 47' to 6° 52' (W. Lon.); and, exclusively of the extensive parish of Carrickfergus (which is a county of a town in itself), comprises, according to the Ordnance survey, 761,877¾ statute acres, of which 466,564 are cultivated land, 53,487½ are under water, and the remainder unimproved mountain and bog. The population, in 1821, was 262,860; and in 1831, 316,909.

In the ancient division of the island the southern and south-western parts of this county were included in the territory called *Dalaradiæ*, or *Ulidia*, the western and north-western were designated *Dalrieda*, and the name of the whole was *Endruim* or *Andruim*, signifying the "habitation upon the waters," and strikingly descriptive of its situation. It was afterwards divided into the three districts of *North* or *Lower Clan-Hugh-Boy*, *Claneboy*, or *Clandeboy*; the *Glynnes*; and the *Reuta*, *Route*, or *Rowte*. North or Lower Clandeboy, so called to distinguish it from South or Upper Clandeboy, now included in the adjacent county of Down, extended from Carrickfergus bay and the river Lagan to Lough Neagh, and consisted of the tract now forming the baronies of Belfast, Massareene, and Antrim: the Glynnes, so called from the intersection of its surface by many rocky dells, extended from Larne, northward along the coast, to Ballycastle, being backed by the mountains on the west, and containing the present baronies of Glenarm, and part of that of Carey: the Route included nearly all the rest of the county to the west and north, forming the more ancient *Dalrieda*, and, in the reign of Elizabeth, occasionally called "Mac Sorley Boy's Country." Within the limits of Clandeboy was a minor division, called "Bryen Carrogh's Country," won from the rest by the Scots. At what precise period Antrim was erected into a county is uncertain: it was divided into

baronies in 1584, by the lord-deputy, Sir John Perrot, but this arrangement was not until some time afterwards strictly observed.

The earliest inhabitants of this part of Ireland on record were a race of its ancient Celtic possessors, designated by Ptolemy *Darnii* or *Darini*; and it deserves notice that Nennius mentions the "regions of Dalrieda" as the ultimate settlement of the Scythian colony in Ireland. According to the Irish annalists, Murdoch Mac Erch, chief of the Hibernian Dalaradians, early in the fourth century, by a series of conquests extended his dominions in the north of Antrim and the adjacent districts, while his brother Fergus succeeded in establishing a colony in North Britain. The first intruders upon these earliest settlers were probably the Danish marauders, to whose desolating descents this coast was for several ages peculiarly exposed. Subsequently the northern Scots harassed the inhabitants by numerous plundering inroads, and ultimately accomplished permanent settlements here, maintaining for a long time a constant intercourse with their roving countrymen of the isles. A right of supremacy over the lords of this territory was claimed by the powerful family of the northern O'Nials (now written O'Neill), who were at length deprived of the southern part of this county by the family of Savage and other English adventurers. Early in the 14th century, Edward Bruce, the Scottish chieftain, gained possession of this district by the reduction of Carrickfergus, which had long resisted the most vigorous assaults of his troops. The English, however, shortly afterwards recovered their dominion; but in 1333, William de Burgho, Earl of Ulster, being assassinated at Carrickfergus by his own servants, and his countess, with her infant daughter, seeking safety by escaping into England, the sept of O'Nial rose suddenly in arms, and, falling furiously upon the English settlers, succeeded, notwithstanding a brave and obstinate defence, in either totally extirpating them, or reducing them within very narrow bounds. The conquerors then allotted amongst themselves the extensive possessions thus recaptured from the English, and the entire district received the name of the Upper and Lower Clan-Hugh-Boy, from their leader, Hugh-Boy O'Nial. During the successful operations of Sir John Perrot, lord-deputy in the reign of Elizabeth, to reduce the province

1

of Ulster into allegiance to the English government, he was compelled to lay siege to Dunluce castle, on the northern coast of Antrim, which surrendered on honourable terms: this fortress having been subsequently lost through treachery, in 1585, was again given up to the English by Sorley Boy O'Donnell or Mac Donnell, the proprietor of a great extent of the surrounding country, to whom it was returned in charge.

This county is in the diocese of Connor, except part of the parish of Ballyscullion in the diocese of Derry, Lambeg in that of Down, and Aghalee in that of Dromore. For purposes of civil jurisdiction it is divided into the baronies of Upper Belfast, Lower Belfast, Upper Massareene, Lower Massareene, Upper Antrim, Lower Antrim, Upper Toome, Lower Toome, Upper Glenarm, Lower Glenarm, Upper Dunluce, Lower Dunluce, Kilconway, and Carey. It contains the borough, market, and sea-port town of Belfast; the borough and market-town of Lisburn; the ancient disfranchised borough and market-towns of Antrim and Randalstown; the sea-port and market-towns of Ballycastle, Larne, and Portrush; the market and post-towns of Ballymena, Ballymoney, Broughshane, and Glenarm; and the post-towns of Ballinderry, Ballyclare, Bushmills, Crumlin, Cushendall, Dervock, Glenavy, Portglenone, and Toome. Connor, the ancient seat of the diocese, is now merely a village: the largest villages are Ballykennedy, Templepatrick, Whitehouse, Dunmurry, Kells (each of which has a penny post), Doagh, Dunethery, Eden, Massareene, and Parkgate. Prior to the Union, this county sent ten members to the Irish parliament,—two knights of the shire, and two representatives for each of the boroughs of Antrim, Belfast, Lisburn, and Randalstown: from that period until 1832 it returned four members to the Imperial parliament,—two for the county, and one each for the boroughs of Belfast and Lisburn; but, by the act to amend the representation, passed in that year (2 Wm. IV., c. 88), an additional member has been given to Belfast. The county constituency (as registered in October, 1836,) consists of 598 £50, 562 £20, and 2246 £10 freeholders; 6 £50 and 19 £20 rent-chargers; and 59 £20 and 337 £10 leaseholders; making a total of 3827 registered voters. The election for the county takes place at Carrickfergus. It is included in the north-east circuit: the assizes are held at Carrickfergus, and the general quarter sessions at Belfast, Antrim, Carrickfergus, Ballymena, and Ballymoney, at which the assistant barrister presides. The county court-house and gaol is situated at Carrickfergus, the house of correction at Belfast, and there are bridewells at Antrim, Ballymena, and Ballymoney. The number of persons charged with criminal offences and committed to these prisons, in the year 1835, was 202; and the commitments under civil bill decrees amounted to 106. The local government is vested in a lieutenant and thirteen deputy-lieutenants, who are all justices of the peace: the entire number of magistrates is 84, including the mayor of the town and county of the town of Carrickfergus, and the "sovereign" of Belfast, who are *ex-officio* magistrates of the county; besides whom there are the usual county officers, including two coroners. There are 29 constabulary police stations, having a force of a stipendiary magistrate, sub-inspector, pay-master, 6 chief and 33 subordinate constables, and 165 men, with 8 horses, the expense of whose maintenance is defrayed equally by grand jury presentments and by Government.

Along the coast are 16 coast-guard stations,—8 in the district of Ballycastle, having a force of 8 officers and 54 men,—and 8 in the district of Carrickfergus, with a force of 8 officers and 51 men; each district is under the control of a resident inspecting commander. The district lunatic asylum and the county fever hospital are at Belfast, the county infirmary is at Lisburn, and there are two dispensaries at Belfast, and others at Crumlin, Ballymoney, Ballymena, Larne, Doagh, Randalstown, Whitehouse, Antrim, Connor, Ahoghill, Loughguile, Bushmills, Ballycastle, Broughshane, and Cushendall, supported by equal grand jury presentments and private subscriptions. The amount of grand jury presentments, for 1835, was £41,002. 16. 1., of which £5230. 7. 10. was for the public roads of the county at large; £14,072. 4. 4. for the public roads, being the baronial charge; £7666. 8. 2. in repayment of loans advanced by Government, £3802. 11. 8. for police, and £10,231. 4. 1. for public establishments, officers' salaries, buildings, &c. In military arrangements this county is included in the north-eastern district: there are barracks for artillery and infantry at Belfast; and Carrickfergus Castle, in which the ordnance stores are deposited, is appropriated as a barrack for detachments from Belfast.

The most striking features of the surface of this county are its mountains, which stretch in a regular outline from the southern to the northern extremity, terminating on the shore in abrupt and almost perpendicular declivities: they attain their greatest elevation near the coast, and have a gradual descent inland; so that many of the principal streams have their source near the sea, and run directly thence towards Lough Neagh: exclusively of the valleys embosomed amid them, these mountains are computed to occupy about one-third of the superficial area of the county. Between this range and the shore, in some places, are tracts of very fertile land, especially from Belfast to Carrickfergus, and thence to Larne, near which the mountains project in rugged grandeur so as nearly to overhang the sea. From Glenarm round to Bengore Head this succession of rocky headlands presents numerous striking and picturesque views broken by narrow valleys watered by mountain torrents, which give a diversified character to the romantic scenery by which this part of the coast is distinguished. The most remarkable ranges of cliffs are those of perpendicular basaltic columns, which extend for many miles, and form a coast of surpassing magnificence: their arrangement is most strikingly displayed in Fair Head and the Giant's Causeway, which project several hundred feet into the sea, at the northern extremity of the county. On the western side of the mountain range the valleys expand to a considerable width, and are of great fertility: that of the Six-mile-water, stretching towards the town of Antrim, is particularly distinguished for its beauty and high state of cultivation. The valley of the Lagan merits especial notice for its beautiful undulating surface, its richness, the enlivening aspect of its bleach-greens, and the numerous excellent habitations, with their gardens and plantations, which impart an air of cheerfulness and industry to this interesting vale. The general inclination of the surface of the mountainous region becomes less rapid as it approaches the river Bann: the flattest parts of this elevated tract are composed of turf bogs, which occupy a great space, but are mostly susceptible of improvement. In the southern part of the barony of

Toome, along the shore of Lough Neagh to the east of Shane's Castle, the surface consists of numerous detached swells, and presents a remarkably pleasing aspect. Thence southward, along the shore of Lough Neagh to the confines of the county, lies the most extensive level tract within its limits, which for fertility and cultivation is nowhere surpassed. Detached basaltic eminences, in some instances attaining a mountainous elevation, are conspicuous in several parts of the county, of which Slemish, to the south-east of Broughshane, and 1437 feet high, is the most remarkable : and in divers places, but generally in the lower tracts, are scattered gravelly knolls, which from Antrim to Kells are particularly striking. Off the northern extremity of the county, nearly seven miles distant from the town of Ballycastle, lies the island of Rathlin, about $6\frac{1}{2}$ miles in length by $1\frac{1}{2}$ in breadth, the shores of which are principally composed of precipitous basaltic and limestone rocks, rearing their heads in sublime grandeur above the waves of a wild and turbulent ocean. Off this part of the coast are some small islets, and a few others lie off the eastern shore, and in Lough Neagh.

Lough Neagh, which is the largest lake in the British islands, is chiefly in this county, but extends into several others :—it is traditionally stated to have been formed in the year 62, by an irruption of the sea, but is obviously formed by the confluence of the Blackwater, Upper Bann, and five other rivers. This lake is about 20 British miles in length from north-east to south-west, about 12 miles in extreme breadth from east to west, 80 miles in circumference, and comprises about 154 square miles : its greatest depth in the middle is 45 feet. According to the Ordnance survey, it is 48 feet above the level of the sea at low water, and contains $98,255\frac{1}{2}$ statute acres, of which 50,025 are in this county, $27,355\frac{1}{2}$ in Tyrone, $15,556\frac{1}{4}$ in Armagh, 5160 in Londonderry, and 138 in Down. The only outlet is the Lower Bann, which being obstructed by weirs and rocks prevents the free egress of the waters, and causes the surrounding country to be injuriously inundated in winter. In some places the waters possess medicinal properties, which they are supposed to derive from the adjacent shore. They have also petrifying powers, but these are supposed to exist in the soil, as petrifactions are only found in the lake near the shore of this county, while they are found at considerable heights and depths and at some distance from the coast inland. Valuable hones are made of the petrified wood, and in the white sand on the shore very hard and beautiful stones, known by the name of Lough Neagh pebbles, are found : they are chiefly chalcedony, generally yellow or veined with red, susceptible of a fine polish, and highly valued for seals and necklaces. Besides the fish usually caught in fresh water lakes, Lough Neagh has the char, a species of trout called the dollaghern, and the pullan or fresh water herring. Swans, teal, widgeon, herons, bitterns, and several other kinds of birds frequent its shores. Canals connect it with Belfast, Newry, and Coal island, and a steam-boat is employed in towing trading vessels across its surface, which, although sometimes violently agitated, is scarcely ever visited by tempests, from the absence of mountains from its borders. This vast expanse of water was frozen in 1739 and 1784, and in 1814 the ice was sufficiently thick for Col. Heyland to ride from Crumlin water foot to Ram's Island, which is the only one of any importance in the lake, and contains the remains of

a round tower. Sir Arthur Chichester, in 1604, received from James I. a grant of the fisheries and of the office of Admiral of Lough Neagh, which have been held by his successors and are now vested in the Marquess of Donegal. Lough Neagh gives the title of Baron to Viscount Masareene. North of this lake, and connected with it by a narrow channel about a mile long, over which is the handsome bridge of Toome, is Lough Beg, or " the small lake," containing $3144\frac{3}{4}$ acres, of which 1624 are in this county, and $1520\frac{3}{4}$ in Derry. This lake, which is generally 15 inches lower than Lough Neagh, contains four small islands, and its banks are more diversified and pleasing than those of the larger lake.

The soils are of considerable variety : that of the plains and valleys is a strong loam upon clay, capable of being rendered very fertile, and in many parts interspersed with whinstones lying on or near the surface, the removal of which is necessary preparatory to tillage. On the rising grounds this kind of soil assumes a different quality, the vegetable mould diminishing in quantity, and being lighter in texture and colour ; and the substratum deteriorates into a brown or yellow *till.* Still nearer the mountains this change becomes more apparent from the coarse and scanty produce, rocks and stones in many parts occupying nearly the entire surface, and the soil gradually acquiring a mixture of peat, and thus forming extensive moors. To the north of the Lagan, at a short distance from Belfast, commences a sandy loam which extends, with occasional interruptions, to the Maze-course, and under good management is very productive : on the shores of Lough Neagh are likewise some tracts of a similar soil : and small stripes of sand are found on different parts of the sea shore. Gravelly soils prevail on the irregularly disposed swells above mentioned, which are composed of water-worn stones of various dimensions, with a loamy covering. There are several detached tracts of soils of various texture, of a superior quality, resting on a substratum of limestone ; one of the most extensive lies in the parishes of Maheragall and Soldierstown. Besides the turf, a prevailing soil upon the mountains is a peculiar loam without either cohesion or strength, which appears to be only a rust or oxyde of the softer parts of the iron-stone, and under tillage yields exceedingly scanty crops of grain, but an abundance of straw, and tolerably good crops of potatoes : its herbage forms excellent pasturage.

The main feature in the tillage system of a great part of Antrim is the potatoe fallow, to which it owes nearly as much as Norfolk does to the turnip fallow. The principal wheat district extends along the shore of Lough Neagh and the course of the Lagan river, stretching as far north as Cairdcastle, in approaching which its extent is greatly reduced by the projection of the mountainous districts. Much barley of the four-rowed or Bere species is grown on the dry and gravelly swells ; but the cultivation of oats is most extensive, the straw being used as fodder for cattle, and the meal, together with potatoes, the chief food of the great body of the people. The other crops of common cultivation are potatoes and flax : turnips have been grown by some agriculturists since 1774, and the quantity is yearly increasing. In some districts the grass lands are extensive and productive, although a considerable portion formerly employed as grazing pastures is now under tillage : the mountains and high lands also are constantly stocked

Forth Bridge on the river Lagan, near Lambeg. From The Dublin Penny Journal, *vol. 4, 1836.*

with either the cattle of the proprietors, or those taken in from distant owners. Much butter is made throughout the county, and is packed in firkins containing from 60 to 80lb., and sold at Belfast, whence a considerable quantity is exported. Carrickfergus and Antrim have long been celebrated for cheese, some of which rivals in quality that of Cheshire.

The principal manure, besides that of the farm-yard, is lime, the produce of the county; but the quarries being situated at its extremities, it requires much labour and expense to convey it into the interior. Near the coast, shells and sea-sand are applied; and sea-sand is also used even where it contains few shells. Great improvement has of late years been made in the agricultural implements, by introducing the best Scotch and English modes of construction. The soil being particularly favourable to the growth of the white thorn, the numerous hedges planted with it greatly enrich the appearance of the lower districts: the mountain fences consist either of loose stones collected from the surface of the ground, or of drains (called shoughs) with banks of earth. The breed of cattle has been very much improved within the last few years, particularly in the more fertile districts; the most esteemed English and Scottish breeds have been introduced, and by judicious crosses stock of the most valuable kind are becoming

general. In several parts is a Bengal breed, imported by Sir Fras. McNaghten, Bart., from which several crosses have been tried, but they appear too tender to endure the cold of winter. Generally, little attention is paid to the improvement of the breed of sheep, though on the rich lands of Muckamore and Massareene it has been very much improved: the old native sheep are principally found in and near the barony of Carey. A very hardy and strong, though small, race of horses, partly bred in the county and partly imported from Scotland, is employed on the northern and north-eastern coast, and among the mountains; and in Rathlin island is a breed similar to these, but still smaller. In other parts of the county the horses are of a good size and valuable kinds, but are chiefly introduced by dealers from other counties. The long-legged flat-sided hogs formerly reared have been superseded by the best English breeds: the bacon and pork of more than 100,000 are annually exported from Belfast.

There is but little natural wood in the county, the greater portion being that which surrounds Shane's Castle, and the scattered trees on the steep banks of a few rivers. Numerous, and in some instances extensive, plantations have, however, been made in various parts; and, though there are still many wide naked tracts, there are others well clothed with wood, especially ad-

4

joining Lough Neagh, the vicinities of Moneyglass and Drumraymond, the valleys of the Six-mile-water, Kells-water, and the Braid, the whole extent from Lisburn to Carrickfergus, the neighbourhood of Bella hill and Castle Dobbs, of Larne, Glenarm, Benvarden, O'Hara-brook, Ballynacre, Leslie hill, and Lisanoure. The greatest tracts of waste land are the highest portions of the mountain range: even the irreclaimable bogs of these elevated tracts produce a coarse herbage, and many of the bogs which overspread to a considerable extent the plains between the mountains and the Bann are likewise covered with verdure. Towards the southern part of the county most of the bogs have been exhausted. Coal is furnished to the northern and eastern coasts from the mines of Ballycastle, but the chief supply is from England, Wales, and Scotland.

The geology of Antrim presents a great variety of the most interesting features, and its mineral productions are of considerable importance. With the exception of a diversified district on the eastern coast and the entire vale of the Lagan, nearly the whole is occupied by basaltic beds, presenting abrupt declivities on the eastern and northern coasts, which are truly magnificent. These secondary beds consist of enormous unstratified masses, the average depth of which is about 300 feet, though in the north, at Knock-laid, it is 980 feet; the base of that mountain is composed of mica slate. The island of Rathlin is principally occupied by these basaltic beds, which are classified by Dr. Berger under the following heads: — tabular basalt, columnar basalt, green-stone, grey-stone, porphyry, bole or red ochre, wacke, amygdaloidal wacke, and wood coal: and imbedded in them are granular olivine augite, calcareous spar, steatite, zeolite, iron pyrites, glassy feldspar, and chalcedony. The beds of columnar basalt occur almost exclusively towards the northern extremity of the county, and form an amazing display of natural grandeur along the shore. Besides the well-known columnar strata composing the Giant's Causeway and the adjacent cliffs, similar strata are seen in divers parts of the county, particularly near Antrim and Kilroot: the pillars composing the Giant's Causeway (which is minutely described in the article on Billy), are irregular prisms standing in the closest contact, and of various forms, from three to nine sides, the hexagonal equalling in number all the rest. Slievemish, or Slemish, mountain is an enormous mass of greenstone, which likewise occurs in other situations. Porphyry occupies a considerable district to the south of Connor and Kells, and is met with in several other places, particularly near Cushendall. The remarkable substance called wood coal occurs in thin strata at Portnoffer, Kiltymorris, Ballintoy, and elsewhere. All the other rocks of Antrim are beneath the basaltic beds in geological position. The first is hard chalk, sometimes called white limestone, which does not average more than 200 feet in thickness, and occurs on the eastern and southern sides of the county, and on the southern coast of Rathlin island. Mulattoe, or green sandstone next occurs in the neighbourhood of Belfast, to the north of Carrickfergus, near Larne, at Garron Point, &c.; and under this are found lias beds on the coast between Garron Point and Larne, and in other places. These, together with the chalk and basalt, are based upon beds of reddish and reddish-brown sandstone of various textures, which are found under the entire south-eastern border of the county, in several detached spots along the eastern coast, and in considerable tracts from Red bay to Ballycastle: the upper strata form a marl, in which are veins of gypsum. The coal district of Ballycastle comprises an extent of about two miles along the coast; the beds crop out above the level of the sea, dipping to the south-east about one foot in nine, and alternate with others of sandstone and slate clay, being themselves of a slaty quality. The only rocks lying under the strata of the great coal district, besides the primitive rocks of mica-slate, &c., already mentioned, are those of "old red sandstone," between the bays of Cushendall and Cushendun. All the above-mentioned strata are occasionally intersected and dislocated by remarkable dykes of basalt or whinstone, varying from three inches to sixteen feet in width. Sometimes very minute dykes or veins of greenstone penetrate these enormous beds of basalt, and are particularly observable near Portrush, where they are seen in the face of the cliff not more than an inch broad. Chert is also found in abundance and variety at Portrush. Fullers' earth exists in the basaltic district, in which also a rough tripoli is found at Agnew's Hill, and a vein of steatite or French chalk in the path to the Gobbins. In Belfast Lough, lying under the level of the ordinary tides, but generally left bare at the ebb, is a stratum of submarine peat and timber, in which nuts are singularly petrified on the east and west sides of the Lough. Numerous organic remains are also found in the beds of chalk, &c.; large and beautiful crystals in the basaltic region, particularly near the Giant's Causeway, where agates, opal, and chalcedony are met with in different situations. Of all this variety of subterranean productions, the coal has been procured to the greatest extent. The collieries of Ballycastle, once flourishing, are now but little worked; they were formerly twelve in number, and exported from 10,000 to 15,000 tons annually. Gypsum or alabaster is dug in different places, and the various species of stone are quarried in spots convenient for building and other purposes.

As this county is situated in the centre of the district in which the linen and cotton manufactures are most vigorously carried on, a brief historical view of the progress of these branches of industry, the most valuable in the island, may here be introduced. The linen manufacture, of which Belfast is the grand mart, is most extensively carried on at Lisburn and the surrounding country: it is of remote antiquity in Ireland, but appears to have been first particularly encouraged in the north about 1637, by Lord Strafford, who induced the Scottish and English settlers, then recently established in Ulster, to cultivate flax, offering them every facility in exporting the yarn. But this rising trade was for some time entirely destroyed by the civil war which speedily followed, and its revival effectually prevented by the competition of the French and Dutch in the English market. In 1678, an act prohibiting the importation of linen from France was passed, which was soon afterwards disannulled by Jas. II., who afforded great encouragement to the French manufacturers. The first parliament of Wm. III. declared the importation of French linens highly injurious to the interests of the three kingdoms; and the progress of the woollen trade in Ireland having alarmed the English manufacturers, the king was prevailed upon to suppress it, and re-establish in lieu the manufacture of linen, which was accordingly so much encouraged as to induce many of the Hugonots to emigrate hither from France, several of whom had carried on the trade extensively in their native country. Amongst these emigrants was Mr. Crommelin, who received from Government a grant of £800 per annum, as an equivalent for the interest of capital to be expended by him in establishing the linen manufacture at Lisburn, with a patent for its improvement, and an additional salary of £200, on condition that, with the assistance of three other persons, also remunerated from the public purse, he should instruct the Irish farmers in the cultivation of flax, which had been altogether neglected for upwards of half a century. These and similar efforts, aided by protecting legislative enactments, produced the most important results : a board of trustees of the linen and hempen manufactures was established under an act passed in 1711, at which period the value of the exports did not exceed £6000 per annum. But in the early part of the reign of Geo. I., a linen-hall having been erected in Dublin, and a Board of Management appointed, authorised by parliament annually to employ a large specific sum in the importation and gratuitous distribution of flax seed, and in awarding premiums for the extension and improvement of the trade, the annual imports, before the year 1730, had increased in value to upwards of £400,000 ; in twenty years more they exceeded one million sterling ; and of such importance was the success of this staple manufacture deemed, that £12,000 was annually granted by parliament for its better protection. During this rapid growth, numerous abuses crept in, and the most obnoxious frauds were practised by the weavers in the length and quality of their webs ; for the suppression of which several acts were passed in vain, until the provisions of the act of the 33rd of Geo. II. were enforced, on the southern border of this county, by Lord Hillsborough and Mr. Williamson, whose persevering activity rendering it impossible for the weavers any longer to evade the law, while the bleachers and merchants were convinced of the advantages to be derived from its observance, the sealing of brown linen by deputed responsible officers, to attest its quantity and quality, became general throughout the whole province, and continues to be practised with equal strictness at present. In 1784, the value of brown linens sold in the markets of Ulster was £1,214,560 ; and for several years prior and subsequent to the Union, the total exports amounted in value to upwards of £2,600,000, of which nearly one-half was the produce of the county of Antrim. Some conception of the present extent of the manufacture may be derived from the fact that at one only of the numerous bleach-greens about 80,000 pieces of linen are finished annually, and at many others nearly the same number. Prior to the accession of Geo. II., every branch of the manufacture was performed by the same parties. Machinery was first invented and applied in the operation of washing, rubbing and beetling at Ballydrain, in the parish of Belfast, in 1725, and, as the manufacture extended, the process of bleaching became a separate business ; the bleacher became merchant, bought the brown linens in the open market, and has made this business one of the most important branches of the trade. Owing to the improvements in machinery, and the aid afforded by the application of chymical preparations, the present number of bleach-greens is not so great as formerly, notwithstanding the vast increase in the produce of the manufacture. So late as 1761, the only acid used in bleaching was buttermilk : in 1764, Dr. James Ferguson,

An unidentified County Antrim bleach green. Drawn by J. H. Burgess and engravd by Walmsley. From S. C. Hall, Ireland: its scenery, character, & c., *vol. 3 (London, 1841).*

of Belfast, received from the Linen Board a premium of £300 for the successful application of lime, and in 1770 he introduced the use of sulphuric acid ; ten years subsequently, potash was first used, and, in 1795, chloride of lime was introduced : the articles now generally used are barilla, American ashes, chloride of lime, and vitriol. The fine material which first induced competition and the offer of a bounty was cambrics : the attention of the Board was next directed to the production of damasks and diapers, and many looms were given to the weavers in the counties of Down and Antrim ; and so great a degree of perfection has the weaving of damasks attained, that the Lisburn and Ardoyne manufactures adorn the tables of most of the sovereigns of Europe. Every species of fabric, from the coarsest canvas to the finest cambric, is now manufactured here, from flax which is cultivated and prepared in all its stages in the province of Ulster.

The cotton trade, which has become of so great importance in the North of Ireland, was introduced in 1777, merely as a source of employment for the children in the poor-house at Belfast, by Mr. Robt. Joy and Thos. McCabe, who, unable to secure individual co-operation, offered the machinery, which was then of the most improved description, to the managers of the charitable institution at prime cost. But the latter refusing to embark in a speculation altogether novel in Ireland, Messrs. Joy, McCabe, and McCracken formed themselves into a company, erected buildings, introduced new machinery, and generously opened their works to the public, at a time when it was endeavoured in England to keep the nature of the improved machinery a secret. In 1779 they commenced the manufacture of calico, dimities, and Marseilles quilting ; and introduced the use of the fly shuttle. This branch of the trade soon acquiring considerable celebrity, many persons were induced to embark in it : the first mill for spinning twist by water was erected at Whitehouse, near Belfast, in 1784, from which period may be dated the fixed establishment of the cotton manufacture ; and so rapid was thenceforward its progress that, in 1800, in Belfast and the surrounding country within a circuit of ten miles, it furnished employment to upwards of 13,000 individuals, or, including those indirectly connected with it, to 27,000. In 1811, the number of bags of cotton wool imported into Belfast was 14,320, and the number exported, 3007 ; leaving for home consumption 11,313,

Belfast Lough from Cave Hill. Drawn by W. H. Bartlett and engraved by R. Wallis. From W. H. Bartlett, Scenery and antiquities of Ireland, *vol. 3 (London, c. 1842).*

worth £226,260, and, when manufactured, worth about one million sterling. The number of spinners in the mills, at the same period, was estimated at 22,000 ; of weavers, including attendants on looms, 25,000 ; and engaged in bleaching, embroidery, making looms, reels, &c., about 5000 more. The manufacture has been since still further extended, and every description of cotton fabric is now produced. In addition to the two above-named important branches of manufacture, there are, in this county, at Belfast, canvas and rope manufactories, and extensive paper-mills in various places. Woollen stockings are woven in several of the towns ; soap and candles are made for exportation and home consumption ; the manufacture of chloride of lime and vitriol, for which there is a great demand in the bleach-greens, has long been carried on at Lisburn and Belfast ; and the manufacture of leather, though not so extensive as formerly, is still considerable throughout the county. At Belfast are several large iron-foundries and glass-manufactories ; and at Lisburn are works for turning and fluting iron. Hence the commerce of this county is very extensive : the exports are linens, linen yarn, cotton goods, all kinds of grain, pork, bacon, hams, beef, butter, eggs, lard, potatoes, soap, and candles ; and the imports consist of the raw materials for the cotton manufacture, also coal and the various foreign articles of consumption required by the numerous population. There is an extensive salmon fishery along the coast at Carrickarede, between Ballintoy and Ken-

bane Head: and this fish is also caught at different places along the entire coast north of Glenarm, and also in the rivers Bann and Bush : all the other rivers, except the Lagan, are likewise frequented by salmon ; and all abound with eels, which are taken at weirs in the Bann. There is a great variety of other valuable fish off the coast ; of testaceous fish this shore affords the lobster and the crab, and oysters of superior size and flavour are found in Carrickfergus bay ; the seal is common.

The two largest rivers are the Lagan and the Bann, both of which rise in the county of Down : at Belfast the Lagan spreads into the wide æstuary called the bay of Belfast, or Belfast Lough, and above it, with the aid of several cuts, has been made navigable to Lisburn, forming part of the navigation between Belfast and Lough Neagh : the Bann flows through Lough Neagh and Lough Beg, and continues its course to Coleraine, below which it falls into the sea. Most of the rivers strictly belonging to the county rise in the mountains on the coast, and owing to the rapidity and shortness of their currents are unnavigable. The Bush runs westward from the mountains of Lisanoure to Benvarden, and then northward to the sea at Port Ballintrae : the Main flows southward into Lough Neagh, and has three copious tributaries, the Ravel, the Braid, and the Glen-wherry : the Six-mile-water also falls into Lough Neagh, at Antrim, and the Camlin, or Crumlin, and Glenavy rivers at Sandy-bay. The rapidity of these and the smaller rivers renders their banks peculiarly advanta-

7

geous sites for bleach-greens, cotton-mills, and flour and corn-mills, of which the last are especially numerous. The only artificial line of navigation is the Belfast Canal, or Lagan Navigation. The Lagan Navigation Company were incorporated by an act of the 27th of Geo. III., empowering them to levy a duty of one penny per gallon on beer, and fourpence per gallon on spirits, in the excise district of Lisburn; but these duties having recently been repealed, an equivalent sum was annually paid to the Company by Government, until the year 1835, when their right ceased: it is navigable for vessels of fifty tons' burden, and the entire length from Lough Neagh to the quays of Belfast is twenty-two miles: its construction was powerfully aided by the noble family of Chichester, and the expense amounted to £62,000, raised by debentures. The roads of late years have been gradually improved, the materials existing within the county for making and repairing them being of the best quality. An important and very difficult work, called the Antrim Coast Road, from Larne to Bally-castle, has been lately executed under the immediate control of the Board of Public Works, opening an improved communication with a fine tract of country comprehended between the coast and the range of mountains from Carrickfergus to Ballycastle, and hitherto cut off from any reasonable means of intercourse by the badness of the roads over those mountains, some of which were conducted for miles at slopes varying from one yard in six to one in twelve. Many projects had been formed, at different times, for an improved line, but were abandoned on account of the great expense involved in the execution of them; but at length a plan with a moderate estimate was sanctioned by the Commissioners, and they and the grand jury granted about £18,000 for carrying it into effect. The new road proceeds from Larne close along the shore to Black Cave, where it winds round the promontory of Ballygalley Head, passing by Glenarm, Cairnlough, Garron Head, and Waterfoot, to Cushendall, where it strikes off inland to its northern terminus at Ballycastle, taking in the few portions of the old line that were available. The greatest difficulties encountered in its formation arose from the necessity of conducting the road, in part of its line, under a considerable extent of rock, some hundreds of feet in height, having its base washed by the open sea; and from its passing along portions of very steep hills of moving clay bank. The former obstacle presented itself at the bold headland of Glenarm deer-park, where about 30,000 cubic yards of rock were, by blasting with great care and judgment, hurled in immense masses down upon the shore; and the road, 21 feet in clear width and 10 feet above the highest tides, has been floored partly on the loose and partly on the solid rock. The latter occurred more particularly at the base of the hill of Cloony, and was by far the more serious obstacle, from the slippery nature of the clay banks and their tendency to move over the road. To counteract this inconvenience the engineer proposed, after having thrown down very large masses of detached rock, which were found strewed over the face of the bank (so as to form a sufficient flooring), to construct a revetment wall, from the summit of which any gradual accumulation of the slippery bank might from time to time be removed. Very solid piers of heavy rough blocks were deeply bedded into the bank, 30 feet apart, to be connected by substantial walls having a vertical curvilinear batter combined with an arched

horizontal curve, to which the piers form the abutments. The entire distance being also concave, affords a powerful combination of resistance against the pressure. The old road passes over the hill at an elevation of nearly 200 feet above the sea, with slopes of one in six and upwards; while the new line along the coast is nearly level. A new line of road has been opened from Belfast to Lisburn; another from Belfast to Antrim, which is to be immediately continued to Ballymoney, Ballymena, and Coleraine; and a third recently from Belfast to Crumlin. A new line has been made from Ballymoney to Dervock, crossing a large and valuable tract of bog; and others are in progress leading respectively from Whitewell-brae to Ballyclare and Ballymena, from Belfast to Carrickfergus and Larne, from Glenavy to Moira, from Doagh to Ballymena, and from Ballymena to Cushendall. But the most important and expensive is the mail coach road from Belfast to Derry, now in progress. The lines from Belfast to Carrickfergus and Larne, and from Antrim to Coleraine (the latter being the Derry road), have been undertaken with the sanction of the Commissioners of Public Works. A double line of railway is in progress from Belfast to Cave Hill, which was the first undertaken in Ireland, but for want of funds was abandoned for some years; the operations have, however, been resumed. Railways are also contemplated from Belfast to Carrickfergus, from Belfast to Armagh (being the Dublin line), and from Armagh to Portrush; the last will only pass about two miles through this county.

The remains of antiquity of earliest date consist of cairns or barrows, cromlechs, raths or intrenchments, and mounts differing in magnitude and form. The most remarkable of the cairns is that on Colin mountain, about three miles north of Lisburn; there is also one on Slieve True, to the west of Carrickfergus, and two on Colinward. Near Cairngrainey, to the north-east of the old road from Belfast to Templepatrick, is the cromlech most worthy of especial notice: it has several table stones resting on numerous upright ones; and near it is a large mount, also several fortified posts different from all others in the county. There is likewise a large cromlech at Mount Druid, near Ballintoy; another at the northern extremity of Island Magee; and Hole Stone, to the east of the road from Antrim to Glenavy, appears to be a relic of the druids. Of mounts, forts, and intrenchments, there is every variety which exists in Ireland; and so numerous are they, that the parishes of Killead and Muckamore alone contain two hundred and thirty, defended by one or more ramparts; and ten mounts, two of them containing caves, of which that called Donald's Mount is a fine specimen of this kind of earthwork. Among the most remarkable of the rest are, one at Donegore, one at Kilconway, one at the Clough-water, one at Dunethery, the last of which is planted with trees; one with a square outwork at Dunmacaltar, in the parish of Culfeightrin; Dunmaul fort, near Nappan; one at Cushendall, having a castle within its defences, and probably a Danish relic; one at Drumfane on the Braid, one at Camlent-Oldchurch, and another in a bog near Ballykennedy: one near Connor has outworks exactly resembling that at Dromore, and in another near Carrickfergus have been found several curious Danish trumpets. Stone hatchets or celts of various sizes have been discovered in several places, but in the greatest numbers near Ballintoy; arrow heads of flint, spear heads of brass, and numerous miscellaneous relics have been found. There have also been discovered a Roman torques, a coin of Valentinian, fibulæ, and other Roman antiquities, supposed to be relics of the spoil obtained by the Irish Scots in their plunder of South Britain, in alliance with the Picts. Of the singular round towers, the original purpose of which has been a fertile source of almost innumerable conjectures, there are at present four in this county; viz., one at Antrim, one on Ram's Island in Lough Neagh, a fragment of one near the old church at Trummery (between Lisburn and Moira), and one in the churchyard of Armoy.

Archdall enumerates forty-eight religious establishments, as having existed in this county, but adds, that twenty of them are now unknown, and scarcely can the existence of half the entire number be now established by positive evidence. There are still interesting remains of those of Bonamargy, Kells, Glenarm, Glynn near Larne, Muckamore, and White Abbey, to the west of the road from Belfast to Carrickfergus; and extensive ruins of other religious edifices, in the several townlands of Dundesert, Ballykennedy, and Carmavy, in the parish of Killead. Of ancient fortresses, that of Carrickfergus, which has always been the strongest and most important, is the only one in complete preservation: there are interesting ruins of Green Castle, to the west of the road between Belfast and Carrickfergus; Olderfleet Castle, situated at the extremity of the peninsula which forms one side of the harbour of Larne; Castle Chichester, near the entrance to the peninsula of Island Magee; Red Bay Castle; and the Castle of Court Martin, near Cushendall. Near the northern coast are likewise several old castles, some of which are very difficult of access, and must have been fortresses of great strength prior to the use of artillery: of these the principal are Dunluce, remarkable for its amazing extent and romantic situation, also Dunseverick, Kenbane, Doonaninny, and Castle Carey; in Rathlin Island are the remains of Bruce's Castle. Inland there are also many remains of fortified residences, of which Shane's Castle, the venerable seat of the O'Nials, was destroyed by fire in 1816: Castle Upton is the only mansion of this kind at present habitable. Lisanoure, the beautiful seat of George Macartney, Esq., on the banks of Lough Guile, is so called from an old fort in the vicinity. Near the summit of White Mountain, two miles north of Lisburn, are the extensive remains of Castle Robin; and at Portmore, near the Little Lough in Ballinderry, are similar remains. Among the mansions of the nobility and gentry, few are splendid, though many are of considerable elegance; they are noticed under the heads of the parishes in which they are respectively situated. There are numerous mineral springs: one near Ballycastle is chalybeate, another aluminous and vitriolic, and a third, on Knocklaid mountain, chalybeate; at Kilroot there is a nitrous water of a purgative quality; and near Carrickfergus are two salt springs, one at Bella hill, and the other in Island Magee. There are also various natural caverns, of which the most remarkable are those of the picturesque mountain called Cave Hill; a curious and extensive cavity at Black-cave-head, to the north of Larne; a cave of larger dimensions under Red Bay Castle; one under Dunluce Castle; the cave at Port Coon, near the Giant's Causeway; and those of Cushendun and the white rocks, near Dunluce; besides which there are numerous artificial caves.

AGHAGALLEN, or AUGHAGALLON, a parish, in the Upper half-barony of Massareene, county of Antrim, and province of Ulster, 2 miles (N. W. by N.) from Moira, on the road from that place to Antrim; containing 3574 inhabitants. It is bounded on the west by Lough Neagh, and comprises, according to the Ordnance survey, 7885 statute acres, of which 2415 acres are in the lough: the land is chiefly under an improved system of tillage; there are about 300 acres of bog, but no waste. Many of the inhabitants are engaged in weaving linen and cotton, and some in spinning. The parish is intersected by the Lagan canal from Lough Neagh to Belfast. It is a vicarage, in the diocese of Connor, and is part of the union of Magheramesk; the rectory is impropriate in the Marquess of Hertford. The tithes amount to £66. 10., of which £26. 10. is payable to the impropriator, and the remainder to the vicar. The church has long been in ruins. In the R. C. divisions it is the head of a union or district, called also the union of Ballinderry, which comprises the parishes of Aghagallen, Aghalee, Ballinderry, and Magheramesk, and contains two chapels, one of which is in this parish. The parochial school is principally supported by the vicar; and there are three private schools and a Sunday school.

AGHALEE, or AGHANALEE, a parish, in the Upper half-barony of Massareene, county of Antrim, and province of Ulster, 1 mile (N. by W.) from Moira, on the road from that place to Antrim; containing 1411 inhabitants. This place obtained the name of Soldiers'-town from its having had, during the war in 1641, a barrack in the village, in which were quartered two troops of horse and foot belonging to the royal army. The parish is bounded on the west by Lough Neagh, and comprises, according to the Ordnance survey, 2499½ statute acres: the land is fertile and in a very high state of cultivation; there is neither bog nor waste land. Limestone abounds, and great quantities are shipped off by the Lagan canal from Lough Neagh to Belfast. Broommount House is the property and residence of Stafford Gorman, Esq. Many of the working class are employed at their own houses in weaving linen and cotton for the manufacturers of Belfast. The parish is in the diocese of Dromore; the rectory is impropriate in the Marquess of Hertford; the vicarage forms part of the union of Magheramesk. The tithes amount to £100. 16., of which £21. 16. is payable to the impropriator, and the remainder to the vicar. The church of the union, situated here, is a small plain edifice in substantial repair. The glebe-house, about half a mile from the church, was built in 1826; and the glebe contains 13a., 3r., 9p., valued at £12. 8. 6. per annum. In the R. C. divisions it forms part of the union or district of Aghagallen, or Ballinderry. The parochial school, near the church, is principally supported by the vicar; and there are two other public and two private schools. A finely wrought and flexible piece of gold, shaped like a gorget, was found near this place a few years since.

AHOGHILL, a parish, partly in the barony of Lower Antrim, partly in that of Kilconway, partly in that of Upper Toome, but chiefly in the barony of Lower Toome, county of Antrim, and province of Ulster, 4 miles (E. S. E.) from Portglenone; containing 14,920 inhabitants, of which number, 421 are in the village. The district around this place appears, from the numerous remains of forts and the great number of *tumuli* and human bones found, to have been the scene of much early warfare. During the war of 1688, the ford of the river Bann at Portglenone was regarded as a very important pass between the counties of Antrim and Derry; and Sir I. Magill and Capt. Edmonston were, in 1689, despatched to defend it against the Irish army on their march towards the Bann, in order to enter the county of Derry. In 1760, when the French under Thurot made a descent on Carrickfergus, the inhabitants of this place rose in a body for the defence of the country: a well-appointed force marched to Belfast, numerous parties proceeded to Carrickfergus, while others patroled the country nightly, and these irregular levies had a powerful effect in repelling the invaders. About the year 1771, an organised system of outrage pervaded the whole of this parish, in common with other parts of the county: the persons who thus combined, called themselves "Steel Men," or "Hearts of Steel," and executed their revenge by houghing cattle and perpetrating other outrages; they attacked the house of Paul McLarnon, Esq., who, in defending himself, was shot. In 1778, a corps was raised by John Dickey, Esq., of Cullybackey, and called the Cullybackey Volunteers; a similar corps was embodied the following year by T. Hill, Esq., of Drumra, called the Portglenone Volunteers, to which was afterwards added a second corps by — Simpson, Esq.; and a corps, called the Ahoghill Volunteers, was raised by Alexander McManus, of Mount Davies.

The parish, anciently called *Maghrahoghill*, of which the derivation is unknown, is bounded by the river Bann, which flows out of Lough Neagh in a direction from south to north, and is intersected by the river Maine, which flows into that lough in a direction from north to south. It was formerly more extensive than at present, having included Portglenone, which, in 1825, was, together with 21 townlands, severed from it and formed into a distinct parish. According to the Ordnance survey, including Portglenone, it comprises 35,419 statute acres, of which 14,954 are applotted under the tithe act, and 145¾ are covered with water. The system of agriculture is in a very indifferent state; there is a considerable quantity of waste land, with some extensive bogs, which might be drained. The surface is hilly, and many of the eminences being planted, render the valley through which the Maine flows beautiful and interesting. The village is neatly built, and the neighbourhood, is enlivened with several gentlemen's seats. The castle of Galgorm, a seat of the Earl of Mountcashel, is a handsome square embattled edifice, erected in the 17th century by the celebrated Dr. Colville; the rooms are wainscoted with Irish oak from the woods of Largy and Grange. The other principal seats in the parish and neighbourhood are Mount Davies, the residence of Alex. McManus, Esq.; Low Park, of J. Dickey, Esq.; Ballybollan, the property of Ambrose O'Rourke, Esq.; Lisnafillen, of W. Gihon, Esq., of Ballymena; Fenaghy, the residence of S. Cuningham, Esq.; Leighnmore, the property of J. Dickey, Esq.; and Drumona, built by Alex. Brown, Esq. The linen trade appears to have been introduced here by the ancestor of John Dickey, Esq., of Low Park, and now in its several branches affords employment to the greater number of the inhabitants. There are several bleach-greens on the river Maine: and a good monthly market is held in the village, for the sale of linens, on the Friday before Ballymony market. Fairs for cattle and pigs are held on

June 4th, Aug. 26th, Oct. 12th, and Dec. 5th. The manorial court of Fortescue, anciently Straboy, has jurisdiction extending to debts not exceeding £5 late currency; and the manorial court of Cashel is held monthly at Portglenone, for the recovery of debts to the same amount. Two courts leet are held annually; and petty sessions are held every alternate Friday.

The living is a rectory, in the diocese of Connor, and in the patronage of the Crown: the tithes amount to £1015. 7. 8. The church is an ancient edifice; the walls have within the last few years been raised and covered with a new roof. The glebe-house was built by a gift of £100 and a loan of £1500 from the late Board, of First Fruits, in 1815; the glebe comprises 138½ acres. In the R. C. divisions this is the head of a union or district, comprising also Portglenone, and containing three chapels, one about half a mile from the village, another at Aughnahoy, and a third at Portglenone. There are places of worship for Presbyterians in connection with the Synod of Ulster at Ahoghill and Cullybackey, both of the third class: in the former are also two places of worship for Seceders of the Ahoghill Presbytery, each of the second class, and in the latter is one for Covenanters; there is also a place of worship for Independents, and a Moravian meeting-house at Gracehill. There are 15 schools in different parts of the parish, in which are about 400 boys and 330 girls; and there are also 12 private schools, in which are about 300 boys and 150 girls; and 16 Sunday schools. John Guy, in 1813, bequeathed £12 per ann. to the Moravian establishment, which sum is now, by the death of his adopted heir, augmented to £45 per annum. There are some remains of Rory Oge Mac Quillan's castle of Straboy, and some tumuli at Moyessit.

ANTRIM, a market and post-town, and a parish (formerly a parliamentary borough), partly in the barony of UPPER ANTRIM, and partly in that of UPPER TOOME, county of ANTRIM, and province of ULSTER, 13 miles (N. W. by W.) from Belfast, and 94 miles (N.) from Dublin; containing 5415 inhabitants, of which number, 2655 are in the town. This place was anciently called *Entruim, Entrumnia*, or *Entrum Neagh*, signifying, according to some writers, "the habitation upon the waters," probably from its contiguity to Lough Neagh. The earliest notice of it occurs in the year 495, when Aodh, a disciple of St. Patrick, founded a monastery here, which was destroyed during the Danish incursions, and of which no further mention appears till the foundation of Woodburn Abbey, to which it became an appendage. A sanguinary battle between the native Irish and the English took place near the town, when Sir Robert Savage, one of the earliest English settlers, is said with a small party of his forces to have killed more than 3000 of the Irish army. In the 13th of Jas. I., the town and sixteen townlands of the parish, together with the advowson of the living and the rectorial tithes, were granted to Sir Arthur Chichester. A naval engagement took place on Lough Neagh, in 1643, when Col. Conolly and Capt. Longford gave battle to a party of Irish marauders, who at that time had possession of the fort of Charlemont, near the shore of Clanbrassil, on which occasion the Irish were defeated, and their fleet brought by the victors in triumph up to the town. In 1649 the town was burnt by Gen. Monroe; and in 1688 a party of Lord Blayney's troops, being separated from the main body of the army, crossed the

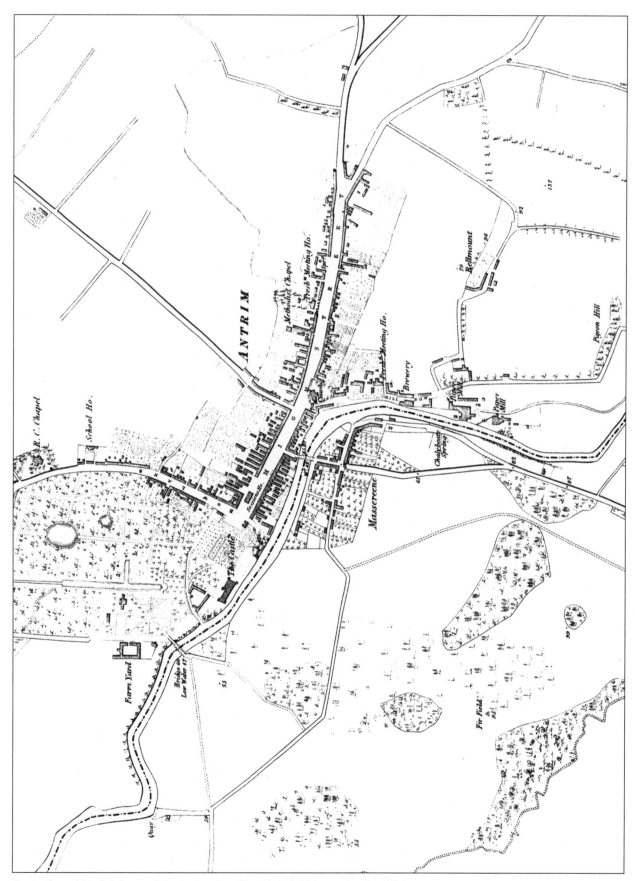

Antrim. Part of 6 inch O.S. map of Co. Antrim, sheet 50, published 1834 (reproduced at 140%).

11

river Bann at Toome, and were made prisoners in a skirmish near this place. During the disturbances of 1798 it was the principal scene of the hostilities which took place in the county: the insurgents had planned an attack on the 7th of June, by marching their forces in four columns respectively by the Belfast, Carrickfergus, Ballymena and Shane's Castle roads; but their design becoming known to the military commanders of the district, troops were hastily assembled in the town, and the inhabitants were also mustered for its defence. The conflict was obstinately maintained on both sides, but at length the insurgents fled in all directions, leaving behind them about 3000 pikes and muskets: more than 900 of them were slain in the town and many killed in the pursuit.

The town is situated on the banks of the Six-mile-water river, on the great road from Belfast to Londonderry, and in one of the most fertile and beautiful valleys in the county: it consists of two principal streets, with others branching from them; many of the houses are modern, and well built of stone and roofed with slate, and several are ancient, of timber frame-work and plaister, with gable fronts, of which the upper projects over the lower story: the inhabitants are amply supplied with water from conduits in the streets. The manufacture of paper is carried on to a very great extent; mills for that purpose were first erected about the year 1776, but were burnt down a few years after; they were, however, rebuilt on a very extensive scale, and the first machinery used in the North of Ireland for the making of paper was introduced and is now employed in manufacturing paper of every description. Attached to these and belonging to the same proprietors, Messrs. Ferguson and Fowke, are a large brewery, flour and meal mills, malt-kilns, stores for grain, and other appendages, the whole affording employment to a great number of the industrious poor. At Boghead, one mile distant, and on the same stream, is another paper-mill on a smaller scale: there are also several bleach-greens in the parish; and the weaving of linen, calico, and hosiery is carried on in the dwellings of many of the poor both in the town and neighbourhood. The situation of the town within a quarter of a mile of the north-eastern portion of Lough Neagh, where a small rude pier or quay has been constructed, is favourable to the increase of its trade, from the facility of water conveyance afforded by the lake, the Belfast canal, and the Upper Bann. Several patents granting fairs and markets are extant, of which the earliest, granting to Sir James Hamilton a market on Thursday, is dated Feb. 14th, 1605. The market is still held on Thursday, and there is a market for grain every Tuesday, but, although the town is situated in a fine grain country, the market is very small. Fairs are held on Jan. 1st, May 12th, Aug. 1st, and Nov. 12th; those in May and August are well supplied with black cattle and pigs. Tolls were formerly levied, but were discontinued about fourteen years since, by direction of Viscount Ferrard. This is a chief or baronial station of the constabulary police. Chas. II., in the 17th year of his reign (1666), granted the inhabitants letters patent empowering them to send two members to the Irish parliament, which they continued to do till deprived of the privilege at the time of the Union, when the compensation grant of £15,000 for the abolition of the franchise was assigned in equal shares to Clotworthy, Earl of Massareene, and three members of the Skeffington family. The seneschal of

the manor of Moylinny, within which the town is situated, is appointed by the Marquess of Donegal, and holds a court once in three weeks, under charter of the 21st of Chas. II., granted to Arthur, Earl of Donegal, for determining pleas "not exceeding £20 current money in England," with power of attachment of goods: he also holds a court-leet annually. Petty sessions are held every alternate Tuesday; and the quarter sessions for the county are held here in April and October. The court-house is a large and handsome building nearly in the centre of the town; and part of the market-house is appropriated as a county district bridewell.

The parish comprises, according to the Ordnance survey, 8884¼ statute acres, of which about three-fourths are arable and one-fourth pasture land, and 200 acres are under plantations; there is little waste and no bog. The scenery is diversified and embellished with several gentlemen's seats, and derives much interest from Lough Neagh, which is partly within the limits of the parish. Closely adjoining the town is Antrim Castle, the ancient residence of the Earls of Massareene, and now, by marriage, the property and residence of Viscount Ferrard: it appears to have been originally built in the reign of Chas. II. by Sir John Clotworthy, and has been enlarged and partly rebuilt. It occupies an elevated situation above the precipitous banks of the Six-mile-water, commanding a fine view of the lake and of the surrounding country. Not far from the town are Steeple, the residence of G. J. Clark, Esq.; Ballycraigy, of W. Chaine, Esq.; Spring Farm, of Lewis Reford, Esq.; Birch Hill, of A. Montgomery, Esq.; Greenmount, of W. Thompson, Esq.; Muckamore, of S. Thompson, Esq.; the Cottage, of F. Whittle, Esq.; Moilena, of W. Chaine, jun., Esq.; and Holywell, of H. Joy Holmes, Esq. The living is a vicarage, in the diocese of Connor, and in the patronage of the Marquess of Donegal; the rectory is impropriate in Lord Ferrard. The tithes amount to £598. 2. 10., of which sum, £318. 18. 8. is payable to the impropriator, and the remainder to the vicar. The church, originally built in 1596, was destroyed by fire in 1649, and remained in ruins till 1720, when it was rebuilt; a lofty square embattled tower, surmounted by an elegant octagonal spire of freestone, was added in 1812, for which the late Board of First Fruits granted a loan of £1500. There is a glebe-house, but no glebe. In the R. C. divisions the parish forms part of the union or district of Drumaul, also called Randalstown: the chapel is a spacious and handsome edifice. There are two meeting-houses for Presbyterians; one, in Main-street, in connection with the Synod of Ulster and of the second class, was built in 1613; and the other, in Mill-row, in connection with the presbytery of Antrim and of the third class, was built in 1726. There are also two places of worship for Primitive Wesleyan Methodists, and one for the Society of Friends. A free school on the foundation of Erasmus Smith was established in 1812, and is supported by annual grants of £30 from the trustees and £2 from the rector: the school-house was built at an expense of £800, of which £200 was given by Lord Ferrard. On the same foundation is also a school for girls, to which the trustees contribute £27. 10. per annum; and there are an infants' school, supported by subscriptions amounting to about £15 per ann., and two Sunday schools. The total number of children on the books of these schools, exclusively of the Sunday schools, is about 300; and in the private pay schools are 230

boys and 100 girls. A mendicity society has been established for some years; a temperance society was
formed in 1829; and a branch savings' bank, in connection with the Belfast savings' bank, was established
here in Dec. 1832, in which the deposits during the first
half year amounted to £1369. 9. 3. About half a mile
to the north-east of the church, and in the middle of
the plantations of G. J. Clark, Esq., in a part of the
valley leading to Lough Neagh, is one of the most perfect round towers in the island : it is built of unhewn
stone and mortar, perfectly cylindrical in form, and is
95 feet in height and 49 feet in circumference at the
base ; the summit terminates with a cone 12 feet high ;
the door is on the north side, and at a height of 7 feet
9 inches from the ground ; the walls are 2 feet 9 inches
in thickness, and the tower contains four stories, the
ascent to which appears to have been by a spiral staircase ; each of the three lower stories is lighted by a
square window, and the upper story by four square per-
forations, corresponding with the cardinal points ; immediately above the doorway is a Grecian cross rudely
sculptured in alto relievo on a block of freestone, which
appears to be part of the original building. Around the
base of the tower great quantities of human bones and
some vestiges of the foundations of buildings have been
discovered; the latter are supposed to indicate the site
of the ancient monastery founded by Aodh. In a garden
adjoining the tower is a large detached mass of basalt,
having nearly a level surface, in which are two cavities

or basins, evidently the work of art, of which the larger
is 19 inches in length, 16 inches wide, and 9 inches
deep, and during the driest seasons is constantly filled
with fine clear water. There is a very powerful chalybeate spring in the garden of Frederick Macauley, Esq.
John Abernethy, Esq., the eminent surgeon, was a
native of this place. Antrim gives the title of Earl to
the family of Macdonnel, of which the present repre-
sentative is the Countess of Antrim and Viscountess
Dunluce, in the peerage of Ireland, who succeeded
her father, Randal William, Marquess and sixth Earl
of Antrim, in 1791, in the earldom and viscounty only,
by virtue of a new patent which the earl, having no son,
obtained in 1785, with remainder to his daughters and
their heirs male.

ARDCLINIS, a parish, in the Lower half-barony of
GLENARM, county of ANTRIM, and province of ULSTER,
6 miles (N. by W.) from Glenarm ; containing 1617 inhabitants. This parish is situated on Red bay in the
North Channel, and comprises, according to the
Ordnance survey, 15,691 statute acres, of which 15,144
are applotted under the tithe act and valued at £2055 per
annum. The surface is hilly and irregular, but the land
in cultivation is fertile, and the system of agriculture
is in a very improving state. Much of the waste land
has been planted, especially the hills, imparting to the
coast an interesting and cheerful aspect. The arable and
inhabited portion of the parish consists of one long strip
extending from the village of Carnlough along the sea-

Village of Waterfoot, near Cushendall. Drawn by Andrew Nicholl and engraved by F. G. Bruce. From The Dublin Penny Journal, *vol. 3, 1834.*

coast into Red bay, and up one side of the beautiful glen of Glenariff. On the land side it is enclosed by a steep and lofty mountain, ascended only by narrow paths traversing its acclivities, by which the inhabitants convey their fuel in slide carts. The river Acre rises in the neighbouring mountains, and forms a boundary between this parish and that of Layde ; it abounds with excellent trout, and where it empties itself into the sea is a salmon fishery. The highest part of the mountains is called Carnealapt-Aura, and near Broughshane they are mostly covered with heath and abound with moor game. Glenariff, one of the seven great glens, is flat in the centre ; the river winds through the whole extent of it in a serpentine course, and being on a level with the sea, whenever a high tide meets a flood, it overflows its banks and inundates the glen ; the rise on each side towards the rocks assumes an appearance of circular rising ground. Three-fourths of the superficial extent of the parish are composed of mountainous, marshy, boggy, and unprofitable land. Limestone and basalt are found in great abundance. The scenery is enlivened with several gentlemen's seats, among which are Drumnasole, the residence of F. Turnley, Esq.; Knappan, of Major Higginson ; and Bay Lodge, of Major Williams. Several of the inhabitants are engaged in the fishery carried on in the bay, where there is a small but commodious harbour, and vessels from 14 to 20 tons' burden can enter the river Acre at high water. Fairs are held at Carnlough. The royal military road passes through this parish, the most mountainous of all the parishes on the coast, notwithstanding which the road preserves a perfect level throughout, at an elevation of a few feet above high water mark ; the excavations round Garron Point will be 360 feet in depth. Garron Point is one of the eight coast-guard stations, in the district of Carrickfergus.

The parish is in the diocese of Connor, and the rectory forms part of the union of Agherton and corps of the treasurership in the cathedral church of Connor, in the patronage of the Bishop : the tithes amount to £150. The church has for many years been in ruins, and divine service is performed in the school-room at Drumnasole, near the centre of the parish. In the R. C. divisions it is in the union or district of Layde, or Cushendall ; the chapel at Glenariff is a spacious building, in which divine service is performed every alternate Sunday. There is a place of worship for Methodists, open every alternate Thursday. A large school-house was erected at Drumnasole, at an expense of £1000, by F. Turnley, Esq., and entirely supported by that gentleman till the year 1833, when it was placed under the management of the National Board of Education: there are also other schools, the whole affording instruction to about 230 boys and 170 girls. On the summit of a headland, near Garron Point, are the remains of a large Danish camp, called Dunmaul or Doonmul, which, according to tradition, was occupied by the Danes during their continuance in Ireland, and from which they set sail when they finally quitted the country.

ARMOY, or ARDMOY, a parish, partly in the barony of UPPER DUNLUCE, but chiefly in that of CAREY, county of ANTRIM, and province of ULSTER, 4 miles (S. S. W.) from Ballycastle ; containing 2622 inhabitants, of which number, 129 are in the village. St. Patrick is said to have had a cell at this place, where, in attempting to convert the natives to Christianity, his disciple Uhda was killed. The parish is situated on the river Bush, and is intersected by a small river called the Wellwater, which rises in a bog on the eastern side, and, with its tributary streams, flows through the parish into the river Bush on the western side. The road from Ballycastle to Ballymena passes through it, and is intersected by one from east to west, and by another from north-east to south-west. It comprises, according to the Ordnance survey, 9349 statute acres, of which 826¾ are in Upper Dunluce and 8522¼ in Carey ; about seven-tenths are arable, pasture, and meadow land. The surface is broken by a ridge of mountains which take their names from the townlands to which they are contiguous, and of which the north side affords good pasturage for cattle, and the summits are heathy and barren ; about nine-tenths of the great hill of Knocklayd, the highest in the county, is good arable and pasture land. That portion of the parish which is under tillage is in a very high state of cultivation ; the system of agriculture is rapidly improving, and composts of lime and earth, or moss, are used as manure for potatoes, by which the produce is greatly increased. There are three bogs, called respectively Ballyhenver, Breen, and Belaney, and the small bog of Moninacloygh ; and turf may be had on the sides and summits of all the mountains. Several quarries of excellent white limestone and basalt afford good materials for building, and for repairing the roads. Turnarobert is the residence of the Rev. S. Hunter. The whole of the parish, with the exception of the townlands of Ballycanver, Park, Bunshanloney, and Mulaghduff, and part of the village of Armoy, belongs to the see of Connor. The village is very flourishing and has a penny post to Ballycastle : several handsome houses have been built, new roads have been opened, and bridges constructed over the river Wellwater. Fairs for horses, horned cattle, pigs, corn, and butter, are held on Jan. 25th, Feb. 25th, March 29th, May 25th, Aug. 16th, Nov. 14th, and Dec. 26th.

The living was formerly a vicarage, the rectory being appropriate to the archdeaconry of Connor, from the year 1609 till 1831, when, upon the decease of Dr. Trail, the last archdeacon, it became a rectory under the provisions of Bishop Mant's act ; it is in the diocese of Connor, and in the patronage of the Bishop ; the tithes amount to £225. The church, situated in the centre of the parish, was rebuilt in 1820, for which a loan of £415 was obtained from the late Board of First Fruits: it is a neat plain edifice, and has been lately repaired by a grant of £128 from the Ecclesiastical Commissioners. The glebe-house was built in 1807, at an expense of £376. 10. 4.: the glebe comprises 23 acres, valued at £30 per annum. In the R. C. divisions this parish is united with that of Ballintoy, in each of which there is a chapel: that in Armoy is a small edifice. There is also a place of worship for Presbyterians in connection with the Synod of Ulster, of the third class. The parochial school is in the townland of Doonan ; there are national schools at Breene and in the village of Armoy, and another school at Mulaghduff. In the churchyard are the remains of an ancient round tower, 47½ feet in circumference and 36 feet high ; the present rector has enclosed the upper part with a dome of wood and stone, in which is placed the church bell. Some beautifully clear crystals, called Irish Diamonds, are found on Knocklayd ; and fragments of gneiss, porphyry and mica slate are found in various parts of the parish.

BALLINDERRY, a parish, in the barony of UPPER MASSAREENE, county of ANTRIM, and province of ULSTER, 3½ miles (N.) from Moira; containing 5356 inhabitants. At Portmore, an extensive castle was erected by Lord Conway, in 1664, on the site of a more ancient fortress: it contained accommodation for two troops of horse, with a range of stabling 140 feet in length, 35 feet in breadth, and 40 feet in height; the remains consist only of the ancient garden wall, part of the stables, and the ruins of one of the bastions. During the Protectorate the learned Jeremy Taylor retired to this place, and remained at the seat of Lord Conway till the Restoration, when he was promoted to the bishoprick of Down and Connor. On a small island in the lough are still some remains of a summer-house, in which he is said to have written some of the most important of his works, and in the neighbourhood his memory is still held in great respect. The parish is situated on the road from Antrim to Dublin, and is intersected by the mail coach road from Lurgan to Antrim: it comprises, according to the Ordnance survey, 10,891 statute acres, of which 283½ are in Portmore Lough. The land is almost all arable and in a good state of cultivation; the system of tillage is improving. There is little or no waste land; in the north-east and south-west parts of the parish are some valuable bogs. The weaving of linen and cotton affords employment to a considerable number of persons, but the greater number of the inhabitants are engaged in agriculture. The Lagan canal from Lough Neagh, on the north-west, to Belfast passes within the distance of a mile. The parish is within the jurisdiction of the manorial court of Killultagh, held at Lisburn.

The living is a vicarage, in the diocese of Connor, and in the patronage of the Marquess of Hertford, in whom the rectory is impropriate: the tithes amount to £480, of which £400 is paid to the vicar, and £80 to the impropriator. The church was erected in 1827, through the exertions of Dean Stannus, at an expense of £2200, of which the Marquess of Hertford gave £1000, and the late Board of First Fruits the remainder; it is a handsome edifice, in the later style of English architecture, with a tower and spire 128 feet in height, and is beautifully situated on rising ground near the small village of Upper Ballinderry. There is a glebe of eight acres, but no glebe-house. In the R. C. divisions the parish forms part of the union or district of Aughagallon and Ballinderry: the chapel is a small building. There is a place of worship for Presbyterians in connection with the Synod of Ulster, of the third class; also a Moravian meeting house. In addition to the parochial school, there are schools at Lower Ballinderry, Killultagh, and Legartariffe; all, except the last, were built within the last ten years, chiefly through the benevolent exertions of Dean Stannus, at an expense of £600; they are well conducted, and will accommodate 300 children: there are also several private pay schools. —Murray, Esq., bequeathed £100 British; J. Moore Johnston, Esq., £83. 6. 8.; and Hugh Casement, Esq., £25 Irish currency, to the poor of the parish. The old parish church, which was built after the Restoration of Chas. II., still remains; and on the eastern side of it is a burial-place, called Templecormack, in the centre of which the foundations of a small building may be traced. There are also some remains of an ancient church close to Portmore Lough, at the western extremity of the parish. The manor of Killultagh gives the title of Baron Conway of Killultagh to the Seymour family.

BALLINTOY, a parish, in the barony of CAREY, county of ANTRIM, and province of ULSTER, 4 miles (N.W.) from Ballycastle; containing 4061 inhabitants, of which number, 278 are in the village. This parish is situated on the most northern part of the coast of Antrim, which is here diversified with creeks and bays, and with cliffs and headlands of singular and romantic appearance. It lies opposite to the north-west point of the island of Rathlin, and comprises, according to the Ordnance survey, 12,753¾ acres (including Sheep and Carrickarede islands), of which about one-half is arable, one-third pasture, and the remainder bog. The surface is boldly varied: immediately above the village rises the lofty hill of Knocksoghy, covered with rock and furze; there is also another hill called Croaghmore, which rises to a great height, and may be seen at a great distance; its sides are arable, and on the summit, which is fine pasture, without any heath, are a cairn of stones and some graves. The land about the village and near White Park bay is in a high state of cultivation. Seaweed, of which some is made into kelp, and shell sand and lime are the chief manures. The village contains about 60 houses: the road from Ballycastle to Bushmills passes through the parish, and commands some pleasantly diversified scenery and some highly romantic views, among which are White Park bay and the beautiful windings of the shore studded with detached masses of basaltic rock and limestone. Near it is Mount Druid, the residence of the Rev. Robert Trail, a handsome mansion deriving its name from the Druidical relic on the hill above it. In the hills are found mines of woodcoal, which seems to be peculiar to this part of the coast: it is found in strata generally under basalt, varying from two inches to two feet in thickness, and displays the grain, knots, roots, and branches of timber; it is generally used as domestic fuel, but its disagreeable smell renders it very ineligible for that purpose. These mines belong of right to the Antrim family, who are lords in fee; but their claim has never been asserted to prevent the tenants raising as much coal as they might require. There are extensive quarries of good stone, which is obtained for building and also for repairing the roads; and limestone abounds in the parish. Some of the inhabitants are employed in spinning yarn and weaving, but the greater number are engaged in agriculture. There are salmon fisheries at Portbraddon, Carrickarede, and Laryban, on the coast. The insulated rock of Carrickarede is separated from the main land by a chasm 60 feet wide and more than 80 feet deep; at this place the salmon are intercepted in their retreat to the rivers. The fishing commences early in spring and continues till August: a rude bridge of ropes is every year thrown across the chasm, which remains during the season, and a singular kind of fishery is carried on, which is generally very productive. The other fish taken off this coast are glassen, grey gurnet, cod, lythe, ling, sea trout, mackerel, and turbot: a species of red cod, and a small thick red fish of indifferent quality, called murranroe, are also found here. About 30 boats are employed in the fishery, which are drawn up in the several creeks along the shore; there are also several bays, into one of which, called Port Camply, vessels of light tonnage occasionally sail from the Scottish coast. At Port Ballintoy there is a coast-guard station, which is one of the eight stations that form the district of Ballycastle. Fairs are held in the village for horses, Scotch ponies, cattle, pigs, and pedlery, on June 3rd, Sept. 4th, and Oct. 14th. The parish is within the jurisdiction of the manorial court of Ballycastle, which is held there every month.

The living is a rectory, in the diocese of Connor, and in the patronage of the Bishop: the tithes amount to £415. 7. 8. The church, a plain edifice with a spire, was rebuilt on the site of the ancient structure, in 1813, by aid of a gift of £800 from the late Board of First Fruits; it is romantically situated on a plain on the sea-shore, backed by lofty hills. The glebe-house was built by the present incumbent in 1791, and is situated on a glebe of 40 acres, subject to a rent of £25. 5. late currency. In the R. C. divisions this parish is united to that of Armoy, and contains a small chapel. There is a place of worship for Presbyterians in connection with the Synod of Ulster. A parochial school was founded and endowed by Mrs. Jane Stewart, under whose will the master is appointed by the vestry held at Easter, and has a salary of £15 per annum. At Prollisk and Island Macallen are two schools, supported by a society of which the late Dr. Adams was the originator, which, with the parochial school, afford instruction to about 240 boys and 80 girls; and there are also three private schools, in which are about 90 boys and 30 girls. The splendid ruins of Dunseverick castle, one of the earliest Scottish fortresses, situated on a bold and isolated rock projecting into the sea, at the north-west extremity of the parish, and formerly the seat of the O'Cahans, form an interesting feature on the coast; traces of the outworks are still visible, and the remains of the keep, consisting only of part of the shell crowning the summit of the rock, which has been rendered more inaccessible by clearing away immense masses from the base, in order to make it the more precipitous, derive much interest from the singularity of their situation. At Port Coan, near the Giants' Causeway, is a singular cavern, the sides and roof of which are formed of round pebbles imbedded in a matrix of basalt of great hardness. At the other extremity of the parish, on the sea-coast to the east of the village, and about a mile from the road leading to Ballycastle, are the ruins of Mac Allister's castle, a small fortress erected by the native chieftain whose name it bears, but at what precise period is not known; it is situated on the verge of a frightful chasm, on the lower extremity of an abrupt headland connected with the shore by a narrow isthmus, which is perforated at its base by several caverns, in one of which are some basaltic columns. There are some remains of the ancient church of Templeastragh, the burial-ground of which is still in use.

BALLYCARRY, a village, in the parish of TEMPLE-CORRAN, barony of LOWER BELFAST, county of ANTRIM, and province of ULSTER, 4½ miles (N. E.) from Carrick-fergus; containing 247 inhabitants. This village is pleasantly situated about a mile from the shore of Lough Larne, opposite to Island Magee, and on the road from Carrickfergus to Larne: it comprises about 50 houses, and the inhabitants are partly employed in the spinning of yarn and weaving of linen cloth, and partly in agriculture. There is a penny post to Carrickfergus and Larne; and fairs are held on June 21st, Aug. 19th, and Oct. 31st. Here are the ruins of the ancient parish church, formerly a spacious and handsome cruciform structure.

Carrick-a-rede island and rope bridge. Drawn by T. M. Baynes and engraved by J. Davies. From G. N. Wright, Ireland illustrated *(London, 1831).*

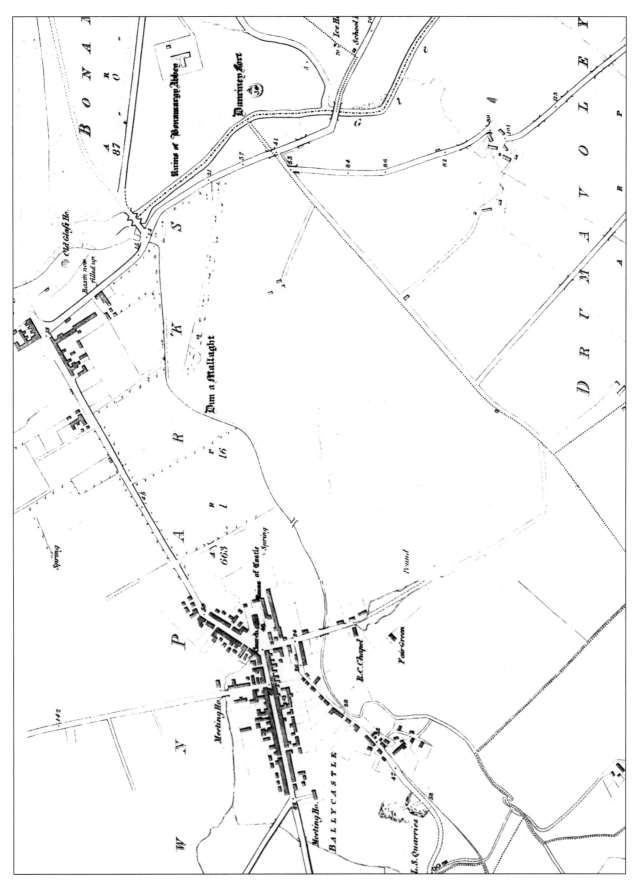

Ballycastle. Part of 6 inch O.S. map of Co. Antrim, sheets 5 & 8, published 1834 (reproduced at 140%)

BALLYCASTLE, a sea-port, market and post-town, in the parish of RAMOAN, barony of CAREY, county of ANTRIM, and province of ULSTER, 9¼ miles (N. E. by E.) from Dervock, and 132 miles (N.) from Dublin : containing 1683 inhabitants. This place, in the Irish language called *Ballycashlain*, or "Castletown," derived that name from a castle built here in 1609 by Randolph, Earl of Antrim, who was directed by Jas. I. to raise "faire castels" at reasonable distances on his vast estates, that the country might be the more speedily civilized and reduced to obedience. The town is advantageously situated on the northern coast, at the head of the fine bay to which it gives name, and in a beautiful valley at the foot of Knocklayd, opposite to the island of Rathlin. It consists of the Upper and Lower Town, of which the latter, called the Quay, is separated from the former by a road bordered with fine trees, which, sheltered by the hills intervening between them and the coast, have attained a stately and luxuriant growth. The houses, amounting, in 1831, to 275 in number, are in general neatly built, and in both portions of the town are several of handsome appearance. Within the distance of half a mile from Ballycastle are the elegant seats of C. McGildowny, Esq., Capt. Boyd, A. and J. McNeale, Esqrs., and several others. It was formerly a place of great manufacturing and commercial importance, abounding with various works upon a large scale, among which were extensive breweries, glass-houses, salt-works, and spacious warehouses ; and in the immediate neighbourhood were extensive collieries, the produce of which formed a material article in its trade. In 1730, endeavours were made in the Irish parliament to erect it into a place of import and export, but were successfully opposed by the Irish Society and the corporation of Londonderry. It had a spacious harbour, in which 74-gun ships could anchor in safety in any weather, and upon the improvement of which £130,000 had been expended ; also a pier and quay, the construction of which cost £30,000. But this high degree of prosperity, which the town attained under the auspices of Hugh Boyd, Esq., began to decline soon after that gentleman's decease, and all that at present remains of its trade is a small fishery carried on by a few boats in the bay. The harbour is now completely choked up ; the pier and quay are a heap of ruins ; the custom-house has been converted into a whiskey shop, the breweries are untenanted, the glass-houses have been converted into a carpenter's shops, and the mansion-house is a parish school. The collieries, which extended nearly a mile in length along the coast, and from which from 10,000 to 15,000 tons were annually exported, subsequently declined ; the estate is now in chancery, and the works, which had been conducted with success from a very remote period, are discontinued. They were situated in the adjoining parish of Culfeightrin, but were always called the Ballycastle collieries, and occupied the northern face of Cross Hill, an eminence nearly 500 feet in height, of which about 150 feet are formed by a cap of columnar basalt resting on alternating of strata sandstone and clay-slate, extending 150 feet in depth, immediately under which is the bed of coal, at an elevation of 200 feet above the level of the beach. No manufactures are carried on at present, with the exception of a few webs of linen, which are woven in the houses of some of the farmers ; a little fishing is carried on in the bay, but the inhabitants are principally employed in agriculture. The market is on Tuesday, and

a great market is held on the first Tuesday in every month ; the fairs are on Easter-Tuesday, the last Tuesdays in May, July, and August, Oct. 25th, and Nov. 22nd, for Raghery ponies, horses, cattle, sheep, pigs, linen yarn, and pedlery. Here is a station of the constabulary police ; also a coast-guard station, which is the head of a district comprising also the stations of Port Rush, Port Ballintrae, Port Ballintoy, Rathlin Island, Tor Head, Cushendun, and Cushendall, and under the charge of a resident inspecting commander. A manorial court is held by the seneschal every month, for the recovery of debts and the determination of pleas to the amount of £20 by attachment and civil bill process ; its jurisdiction extends over the entire barony of Carey, with the exception of Armoy. A court baron is also held in April and October ; and petty sessions are held every alternate Tuesday. There is a very good market-house, and a commodious court-house, in which the courts and petty sessions are held.

A handsome church, in the Grecian style of architecture, with a lofty octagonal spire, was erected in 1756, at the sole expense of H. Boyd, Esq.: the stone for building it was procured from the quarries in the parish, which were then worked on that gentleman's estate. It is a chapelry, in the diocese of Connor, endowed with £60 per ann., of which £20 per ann. is paid by the trustees of Primate Boulter's augmentation fund, and the remainder by the patron, H. Boyd, Esq., descendant of the founder. There is neither glebe-house nor glebe. The R. C. chapel is a small building ; and there are places of worship for Presbyterians and Wesleyan Methodists the former in connection with the Synod of Ulster and of the third class. There are several schools in the town, principally supported by the resident gentry. H. Boyd, Esq,, in 1762, built and endowed with the rental of the townlands of Carnside and Ballylinney, reserving only £40 for the incumbency of Ballycastle, 20 almshouses near the church, for poor men, or the widows of poor men who had worked eight years in the collieries or other works on his estate ; they are still maintained, and are tenanted by the deserving poor of the town under the superintendance of the Primate, the Bishop, and the Chancellor of Connor for the time being, whom he appointed trustees for the management of the lands. There are some ruins of the castle from which the town derived its name ; also some ruins of Bona Margy, a religious house founded in 1509 by Charles Mac Donnell, for monks of the Franciscan order, and one of the latest of those establishments which were founded in Ireland ; the remains of the chapel are the most perfect. This is the burial-place of the Antrim family, who have put a new roof upon a small oratory erected over the ashes of their ancestors, over the window of which is a Latin inscription scarcely legible, importing that it was built in 1621 by Randolph Mac Donnell, Earl of Antrim. In 1811 was found, by the side of a rivulet near the town, a flexible rod of gold composed of twisted bars 38 inches long, hooked at each end, and weighing 20 ounces and a half ; it was undoubtedly a Roman torques, and probably brought hither by some of the Danish or Scottish ravagers of Roman Britain. There is a strong chalybeate spring near the town ; and on the shores are found chalcedony, opal, jasper, and dentrites.

BALLYCLARE, a market and post-town, partly in the parish of BALLYNURE, but chiefly in that of BALLYEASTON, barony of LOWER BELFAST, county of ANTRIM, and province of ULSTER, 93½ miles (N.) from Dublin; containing 824 inhabitants. This place is situated close to the Six-mile-water, and at the extremity of the mail coach road, which branches off from that between Belfast and Antrim. The town, which is neatly built, contains about 180 houses, and is noted for its monthly linen market, and for its horse fairs, which are held on May 24th, July 19th, Aug. 23rd, and Nov. 22nd. There are places of worship for Presbyterians and Wesleyan Methodists, the former in connection with the presbytery of Antrim, and of the second class.

BALLYCLUG, a parish, in the barony of LOWER ANTRIM, county of ANTRIM, and province of ULSTER; containing, with part of the post-town of Ballymena, called the village of Henryville, 3692 inhabitants. This place, with a district extending many miles around it, was the property of the ancient and princely sept of the O'Haras, who settled here during the reign of Hen. II., and whose ancient mansion still occupies the summit of a gently rising eminence near the village of Crebilly. During the insurrection in 1641, Cromwell wrested from them a considerable portion of the manor of Crebilly, or the "Kearte," which he divided among several of his adherents. Some of the timber about Crebilly is of very ancient growth; and there are several traces of the former splendour, and many traditions of the princely hospitality of the chiefs of the O'Hara sept. The parish comprises, according to the Ordnance survey, 8268¾ statute acres, about one-fifth of which is brush-wood and mountain, which is gradually being brought into cultivation; 150 acres are bog, 30 acres are woodland, and the remainder is arable and pasture. The soil is fertile, and the system of agriculture is greatly improved; the cultivation of wheat, for which the land is well adapted, has been recently introduced with success. Fairs are held at Crebilly on the 26th of June and 21st of August, for horses, black cattle, sheep, and pigs; they were formerly the largest in the province, but are now indifferently attended. Courts leet and baron are held annually; and a manorial court for the district of Kearte is held monthly by the seneschal, for the recovery of debts, with jurisdiction over the whole of this parish and parts of the parishes of Connor and Rathcaven. The living is a rectory and vicarage, in the diocese of Connor, formerly belonging to the chancellorship, but episcopally united to the impropriate curacy of Kirkinriola on the death of the late Dr. Trail; the tithes amount to £129. 4. 7½. In the R. C. divisions this parish is united to Ballymena: the chapel, situated at Crebilly, was erected in 1810, near the ancient seat of the O'Haras. A school was built at Caugherty in 1829, one at Ballavaddan in 1800, and a parochial school is now being built under the management and patronage of the rector: there are also two other public schools, and a private and three Sunday schools. Col. O'Hara, in 1759, bequeathed £20 per annum to the poor of this parish, which is regularly distributed according to the will of the testator. There are some remains of the ancient parish church, also of Dunavaddan chapel; besides numerous remains of forts, intrenchments, and Druidical altars, and several moats and tumuli, scattered over the surface of this parish.

BALLYCOR, a parish, in the barony of UPPER ANTRIM, county of ANTRIM, and province of ULSTER, 1 mile (N. by E.) from Ballyclare: the population is returned with the parish of Ballyeaston. This parish, which is situated on the road from Broughshane to Larne, and is bounded on the north and east by the Six-mile-water, comprises 7330 statute acres, according to the Ordnance survey. It is a rectory, in the diocese of Connor, and is partly one of the five parishes which constitute the union and corps of the prebend of Carncastle in the cathedral of Connor, and partly one of the two which form the perpetual curacy of Ballyeaston.

BALLYEASTON, a district parish, in the barony of UPPER ANTRIM, county of ANTRIM, and province of ULSTER, on the road from Ballyclare to Larne; containing with the post-town of Ballyclare and the grange of Doagh, 5892 inhabitants. It consists of the ancient parishes of Ballycor and Rashee, comprising, according to the Ordnance survey, 13,790½ statute acres; about one-half of which are arable. The village, which is 1½ Irish mile (N.) from Ballyclare, is situated at the junction of several roads, near the Six-mile-water, and in 1831 contained 61 houses. The living is a perpetual curacy, in the diocese of Connor, and in the patronage of the Prebendary of Carncastle: the income of the curate is £103. 1. 6½. per ann., of which £69. 4. 7½. arises from tithe, £13. 6. 11. is added by the prebendary, and £20 from Primate Boulter's fund. The church was erected in 1786. There is neither glebe-house nor glebe. In the R. C. divisions it forms part of the union or district of Carrickfergus and Larne. There are four places of worship for Presbyterians; one in connection with the Synod of Ulster, of the first class; one with the Presbytery of Antrim, of the second class; one with the Seceding Synod, also of the second class; and one for Covenanters, which is open every alternate Sunday. There are four schools, in which are about 140 boys and 90 girls; also nine pay schools, in which are about 160 boys and 110 girls. —See BALLYCLARE and DOAGH.

BALLYKENNEDY, or GRACE-HILL, a village, in the parish of AHOGHILL, barony of LOWER TOOME, county of ANTRIM, and province of ULSTER, 1½ mile (W. S. W.) from Ballymena; containing 326 inhabitants. This place is situated on the river Maine, over which is a bridge of four arches, connecting it with the village of Galgorim. It owes its origin to the Rev. John Cennick, who, in 1746, founded here an establishment of Moravians, or United Brethren, who hold under Lord O'Neill, on lease renewable in perpetuity, about 200 plantation acres of land, which are divided in small portions among the brethren. The village consists of 39 family residences, of which the greater number are small cottages, exclusively of the chapel, and the two principal houses for unmarried brethren and sisters respectively, which occupy three sides of a quadrangle, of which the area is ornamented with shrubs. The sisters support themselves by various kinds of needlework, particularly tambour and embroidery, which are much admired, and also superintend an extensive boarding-school for young ladies. The inhabitants of the brethren's house having greatly diminished in number, the greater part of the building has been appropriated as a boarding-school for young gentlemen, conducted by the minister of the establishment and several assistants, and a daily school for boys and girls of the surrounding country. A small linen manufacture and several other trades are carried on. Each family has land sufficient for the keep of a cow and the raising of potatoes. The chapel is a neat and commodious building; the burial-place is on the summit of a rising ground, at a distance from the village. In a bog in this townland is a curious artificial mount; and within its limits may be yet seen the ruins of an ancient church.—See AHOGHILL.

BALLYLINNEY, a parish, in the barony of LOWER BELFAST, county of ANTRIM, and province of ULSTER, 1½ mile (S. S. E.) from Ballyclare, on the road from Belfast to Doagh; containing 2412 inhabitants. It comprises, according to the Ordnance survey, 5684 statute acres (including 320½ in Ballywalter grange), which are generally in a good state of cultivation. The living is a vicarage, in the diocese of Connor, united from time immemorial to the vicarage of Carmoney and the rectory of Ballymartin; the rectory is impropriate in the Marquess of Donegal. The tithes amount to £300, of which £200 is payable to the impropriator, and £100 to the vicar. The church was destroyed by the insurgents under the Earl of Tyrone, and has not been rebuilt; the churchyard is still used as a burial-ground by the parishioners. In the R. C. divisions the parish forms part of the union or district of Larne and Carrickfergus. There are three schools situated respectively at Bruslie, Palentine, and Ballylinney, in which are 114 boys and 95 girls; also two pay schools, in which are 58 boys and 77 girls.

BALLYMARTIN, a parish, in the barony of UPPER BELFAST, county of ANTRIM, and province of ULSTER, 8 miles (N. N. W.) from Belfast; containing 721 inhabitants. This parish is situated on the Six-mile river, by which it is bounded on the north, and comprises, according to the Ordnance survey, 2421¼ statute acres, including a detached portion of 560 acres: the soil is fertile, and the system of agriculture is improving. It is a rectory, in the diocese of Connor, and is part of the union of Carmoney: the tithes amount to £150. There

is neither church nor any place of worship in the parish; the inhabitants are chiefly Presbyterians, and attend the places of worship of that denomination in the neighbourhood. There is a school of 25 boys and 15 girls. The ruins of the ancient church still remain, and the churchyard is used as a burial-ground by most of the inhabitants.

BALLYMENA, or BALLYMANIA, a market and post-town, in the parish of KIRKINRIOLA, barony of LOWER TOOME, county of ANTRIM, and province of ULSTER, 24¾ miles (N. W.) from Belfast, and 105 miles (N.) from Dublin; containing 4067 inhabitants. In the disturbances of 1798 this place was the scene of an obstinate battle between the yeomanry and the United Irishmen of the surrounding district, who, on the 7th of June, entered the town and proceeded to attack the market-house, which was defended by a party of the yeomanry aided by a few of the military and some of the loyal inhabitants; the insurgents having gained possession of the lower part of the market-house, the yeomanry surrendered themselves prisoners of war; but while a party of them was marching out of the market-house, those who were within being instigated by a person named Davis to give the United Irishmen another volley, the fire was returned from the street, and several of the loyalists were killed while descending the steps. Some straggling parties of the enemy brought into the town Captain Ellis, of Innisrush, and Thomas Jones, Esq., of Moneyglass, with a number of the yeomanry, whom they took prisoners at Straid, in this parish, and lodged them in the market-house; and on the day following, several of the yeomanry were marched into the town as prisoners. Great divisions took place in the committee of the United

View of Ballymena. From The Dublin Penny Journal, *vol. 2, 1834.*

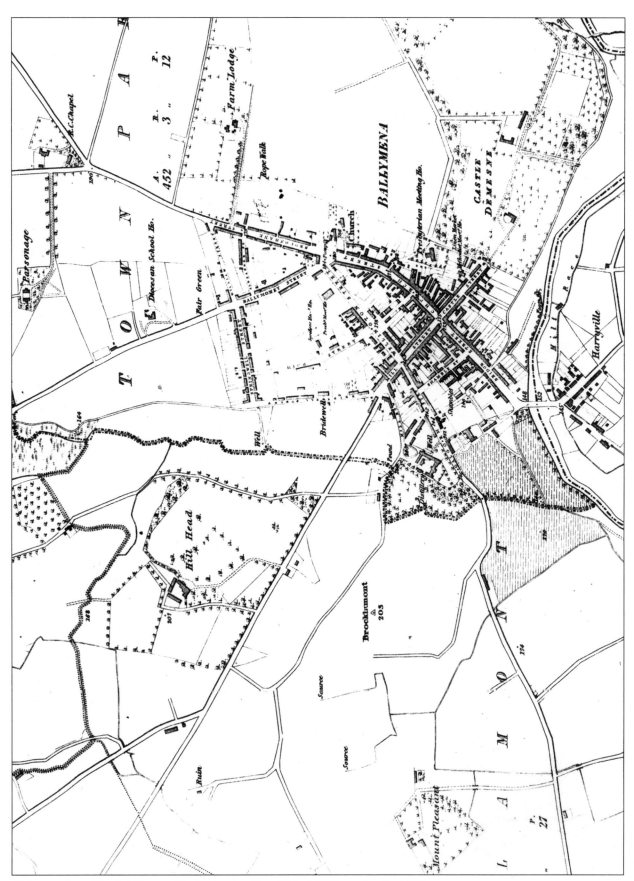

Ballymena. Part of 6 inch O.S. map of Co. Antrim, sheet 32, published 1834 (reproduced at 140%).

21

Irishmen, on the propriety of marching direct to. Antrim, which they had been informed was in the possession of the king's troops; but on hearing of the royal proclamation, offering a free pardon to all, with the exception of officers, who should lay down their arms and disperse, almost all the men from Route were disposed to accept the terms; some, who were determined on making a stand, joined the united camp at Donegore, while others departed homewards, leaving the town to be taken possession of by Col. Clavering and the military, who, after the recapture of Antrim, had encamped at Shanescastle, in the neighbourhood.

The town is pleasantly situated on the river Braid, over which is a large bridge of stone: it owes its rapid rise and present importance to the linen manufacture, which was introduced into the neighbourhood by the Adairs and Dickeys about the year 1732, since which time it has greatly increased in extent, wealth, and importance. It comprises more than 700 houses, in general large and well-built, among which are a few of very ancient character, with gabled fronts. The linen trade is carried on extensively in the neighbourhood, and within a circuit of 5 miles round the town are 14 bleach-greens, at each of which, on an average, about 15,000 pieces are annually bleached, exclusively of considerable quantities of brown and black goods, which are also finished here, and for the manufacture of which there are several large establishments. Several linen merchants unconnected with the bleaching department reside in the town. There is a mill for spinning linen yarn by machinery; and an extensive ale brewery, originally established in 1729, continued in operation for more than a century, and was afterwards purchased by Clotworthy Walkinshaw, Esq., who, in 1831, converted it into a distillery, in which great quantities of barley, grown in the neighbourhood, are annually consumed. Branches of the Provincial Bank of Ireland and of the Belfast and Northern Banking Companies have been established here. The market is on Saturday for the sale of linens, of which 4000 pieces are on an average sold every market-day; there are two weekly markets for grain, pork, and other provisions, of which great quantities are bought and sent to Belfast either for home consumption or for exportation; great numbers of horses, cattle, and pigs are also sold on the market-days. Fairs for every description of live stock are annually held on July 26th and Oct. 21st; but the sales on the market days preceding and following these dates are frequently greater than at the fairs. The market-house is a commodious edifice in the centre of the town, with a steeple 60 feet high. Here is a chief constabulary police station. Courts leet and baron are annually held for the manor; a court under the seneschal is held every month for the recovery of debts; and petty sessions are held every alternate Tuesday. The quarter sessions for the county are held in January and June, alternately with Ballymoney. There is a secure and well-built bridewell, containing seven cells. The parish church, a large plain structure with an embattled tower crowned with pinnacles, is situated in the town; and there are also a R. C. chapel, built in 1820; two places of worship for Presbyterians in connection with the Synod of Ulster, one for Seceders, and one for Wesleyan Methodists. The diocesan school, originally established at Carrickfergus in the reign of Elizabeth, was removed to this place in 1829, when an acre of land was given by William Adair, Esq., on which the building was

erected, at an expense of £900: the master, who is appointed by the Lord-Primate and the Bishop of Connor alternately, derives his stipend from the beneficed clergy of the dioceses of Armagh and Connor, and is allowed to receive private boarders. A free school was founded here in 1813, by John Guy or Guay, who bequeathed £24 per annum to the master, and £50 towards the erection of a school-house, which, with a house for the master, was built in 1818: there are 200 children in the school, who are gratuitously taught reading, writing, and arithmetic, and supplied with books and stationery. In connection with this establishment a female school is now being built, for the instruction of the girls in needlework. A parochial school was established in 1832, in which 170 children are instructed and occasionally clothed by subscription. The Parade school, to which is attached an adult school, was rebuilt in 1833, and is in connection with the London Hibernian Society. The only remains of antiquity are some terraces and foundations of walls of a castle built in the reign of Jas. I.—See KIRKINRIOLA.

BALLYMONEY, a market and post-town, and a parish, partly in the north-east liberties of COLERAINE, county of LONDONDERRY, and partly in the barony of KILCONWAY, but chiefly in that of UPPER DUNLUCE, county of ANTRIM, and province of ULSTER, 35 miles (N. W.) from Belfast, and 119 miles (N. by W.) from Dublin; containing 11,579 inhabitants, of which number, 2222 are in the town. This place was anciently the head of one of those Irish districts called Tuoghs, which were similar to the present baronies; and in a grant from the crown, by which it was given to Alexander Mac Donnel, it was designated *Tuogh Ballymoney*, that is, "the district of the town in the bog," part of it at present being situated on a bog several feet in depth. The parish is bounded on the west by the river Bann, which passes within three miles of the town, and is intersected by the road from Belfast to Derry. The town is built upon an eminence, and from its situation is considered healthy: a new line of mail coach road is now being constructed to pass through it, and in every respect it is rapidly improving. A new road has been opened across the Garry bog leading to Ballycastle and the Giant's Causeway, and a bridge has been lately erected over the river Bann at Agivey, about three miles distant, opening a direct communication with the county and city of Derry, Tyrone, and other places. Races were formerly held here and were in high repute; but they have been discontinued for some years, and a steeple chace for a gold cup has been substituted, which takes place in the middle of December. The trade consists principally in the sale of linens manufactured in the neighbourhood, for which this town is, next to Ballymena, the chief depôt. The linen market has long been established, and is eminent for the superior quality of the goods sold here. Though much less extensive than it was, it is still very considerable: from 15,000 to 20,000 double pieces are annually sold, and on the first Thursday in every month large quantities of seven-eighths linen, of various qualities, are sold here, principally for the London market, under the name of "Coleraines," being purchased and bleached by the persons engaged in that trade. Some years since, the finer pieces sold at very high prices, generally from 7s. to 8s. per yard, and some of the finest webs at 10s. 6d. per yard. There are two markets every month for low-priced brown linens, three quarters of a yard wide, which are sent to Eng-

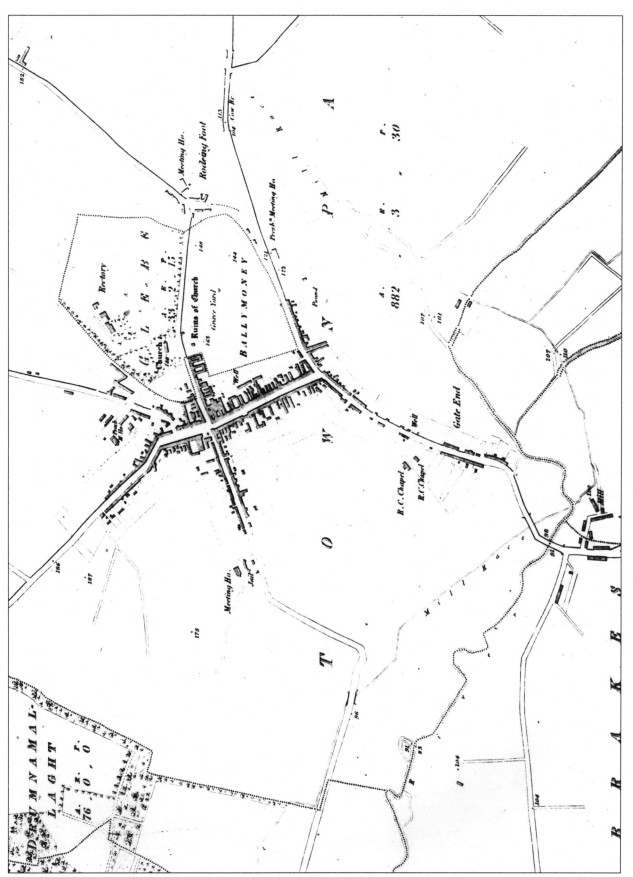

Ballymoney. Part of 6 inch O.S. map of Co. Antrim, sheet 17, published 1834 (reproduced at 140%).

land and America: but the demand for these latter goods have decreased. A very extensive trade is carried on in grain, butter, pork, and general provisions. The market for grain was first established in 1820; but for want of encouragement it languished for a time and was discontinued; in 1831 it was revived, and the new market-place was appropriated to its use, and stores were built by Messrs. McEldeny & Co., for the use of which and for weighing they are entitled to one penny per sack; a considerable quantity of oats is sent to Liverpool, London, and other English markets, and some are consumed in a distillery near the town. The market for provisions was established about the year 1790, and has since been gradually increasing and is now largely supplied: about 4000 carcases of pigs are generally sold during the season, which are principally cured at home for the Liverpool and other English markets; they were formerly all sent to Belfast, and a considerable number are still purchased by the curers of that place. A public crane was established under the provisions of an act of the 52nd of Geo. III. In the market for butter about 10,000 casks are generally disposed of during the season, the greater part of which is shipped off from Portrush, about 9 miles distant, for Liverpool. There are a soap and candle and a tobacco manufactory, a tanyard, and a large brewery in the town; and at Moore Fort, about 3 miles distant, is a very extensive distillery belonging to James Moore, Esq., in which from 50,000 to 60,000 gallons of whiskey are annually made: there is also a mill for spinning flax, and a very extensive flour-mill. A branch of the Belfast banking company has been established here. The trade of the town is susceptible of great increase, from its favourable situation in the centre of a rich tract of country, without any markets nearer to it than Ballymena on the one side, and Coleraine on the other. There is, however, but little facility of water carriage, the river Bann not being navigable above Coleraine, nor below Portna. The general market is on Thursday; and fairs are held annually on May 6th, July 10th, and Oct. 10th. A chief constabulary police station has been fixed here. The manorial court for the barony of Dunluce is held in the town on the first Friday in every month; petty sessions are held every alternate Thursday; and the quarter sessions for the county are held here and at Ballymena alternately. The court-house or town-hall, the property of Lord Mark Kerr, is situated in the centre of the town; and the bridewell, recently built, contains seven cells, with day-rooms and airing-yards adapted to the classification of prisoners, and apartments for the keeper.

The parish comprises, according to the Ordnance survey, 23,108¾ statute acres, of which 21,736½ are in Upper Dunluce, and 753¼ in Kilconway; 18,367 are applotted under the tithe act; about 500 acres are woodland, 2225 bog, 59½ water, and the remainder principally arable land. The soil is fertile, and the system of agriculture greatly improving: the principal crops, till within the last few years, were barley and oats, of which last great quantities are still grown in the neighbourhood; but the cultivation of wheat has been recently introduced, and is rapidly increasing; abundant crops are now raised and begin to form a material portion of the corn trade. Coal and iron-stone are found in abundance at O'Hara Brook; and there are medicinal springs on several parts of the estate. The principal seats are O'Hara Brook, that of C. O'Hara, Esq.; Leslie Hill, of J. Leslie, Esq.; Ballynacree, of Sampson Moore, Esq.;

Moore Fort, of J. Moore, Esq.; Greenville, of J. R. Moore, Esq.; Stranocum, of J. Hutchinson, Esq.; and Vine Cottage, of J. Thompson, Esq. The parish comprises the ancient parishes of Ballymoney, Dunlap, Kilmoil, and Tullagore; it is a rectory, in the diocese of Connor, and is the corps of the precentorship in the cathedral of Connor, which is in the patronage of the Bishop: the tithes amount to £1015. 7. 7½., and the gross income of the precentorship is returned by the Commissioners of Ecclesiastical Inquiry at £1073. 10. 8. per annum. The church, a large plain edifice with a tower and cupola, was built in 1782, near the site of an ancient church, of which there are still some remains. The glebe-house is situated on a glebe of 20 acres. In the R. C. divisions the parish is the head of a union or district, comprising also that of Dunluce, in both of which are chapels in which the parish priest officiates. There are places of worship for Presbyterians in connection with the Synod of Ulster, for those of the Remonstrant Synod, Seceders, and Covenanters; the first is a first class congregation, and that of the Seceding Synod a second class. A school was established in 1813 by the trustees of Erasmus Smith's fund. Sampson Moore, Esq., J. Leslie, Esq., and C. O'Hara, Esq., have each built and endowed schools on their own estates, for the education of the poor; and there are also other schools in different parts of the parish. In these schools are about 200 boys and 100 girls; and there are 13 private schools, in which are about 300 boys and 200 girls, and 11 Sunday schools. A mendicity association for suppressing vagrant mendicity, by giving employment and relief to the poor at their own dwellings, was established in 1821, and a dispensary in 1827. On the estate of Major Rowan is a fine moat, commanding a very extensive view; there is also another at Moore Fort, and one in the townland of Cross. A double patera of gold, weighing 19 ounces and 10 drachms, of elegant form and curious workmanship, was discovered in this parish by a peasant a few years since.

BALLYNURE, a parish, in the barony of LOWER BELFAST, county of ANTRIM, and province of ULSTER, 6 miles (N. W.) from Carrickfergus; containing, with part of the town of Ballyclare, 3549 inhabitants, of which number, 415 are in the village. This parish, which is situated on the Six-mile-water, and on the road from Carrickfergus to Antrim, comprises, according to the Ordnance survey, 8540¾ statute acres. The soil is fertile, and the lands are generally in a good state of cultivation; the system of agriculture is improving; there is some waste land, and a considerable tract of bog. A kind of basaltic stone is quarried and used for building and for repairing the roads. There is an extensive bleach-green; also a large paper-mill, in which the most improved machinery is used for the manufacture of the finer kinds of paper. Fairs for cattle, pigs, and pedlery are held on the 16th of May, Sept. 5th, and Oct. 25th; there are large horse fairs in May and Nov., and also on Christmas-day, at Reagh Hill; and fairs are also held at Ballyclare, which see. In the village is a constabulary police station; and a manorial court is held every third week by the seneschal, for the recovery of debts to the amount of £10. The living is a rectory, in the diocese of Connor, united by charter of the 7th of Jas. I. to the vicarages of Kilroot and Templecorran, together constituting the corps of the prebend of Kilroot in the cathedral of Connor: the tithes amount to £330. The church, a plain small edifice, built about the year 1602, is situated near the western extremity of the parish. There is neither glebe nor glebe-house. In the R. C. divisions the parish forms part of the union or district of Larne and Carrickfergus. There is a place of worship in the village for Presbyterians in connection with the Synod of Ulster, of the second class. There are three schools, which afford instruction to about 240 children; and four pay schools, in which are about 90 boys and 70 girls. The late Mr. Dobbs, of Castle Dobbs, bequeathed £100 for winter clothing for the poor.

BALLYRASHANE, or ST. JOHN'S-TOWN, a parish, partly in the barony of LOWER DUNLUCE, county of ANTRIM, but chiefly in the north-east liberties of COLERAINE, county of LONDONDERRY, and province of ULSTER, 3 miles (N. E.) from Coleraine; containing 2851 inhabitants. This parish is situated on the road from Coleraine to Ballycastle, and comprises, according to the Ordnance survey, 6360¾ statute acres, of which 2689 are in the county of Antrim, and the remainder in the county of Londonderry. The greater portion of the land is fertile and in a high state of cultivation; wheat and barley have been introduced since the year 1829, and are raised with great success. There are detached portions of bog, affording a good supply of fuel. Vast quantities of basalt are raised; and in a geological point of view the parish is very interesting, containing beautiful specimens of amorphous, columnar, and divaricated basalt, which are found here in all their varieties, accompanied with chalcedony, opal, zeolite, and other fossils; it abounds also with botanical specimens of considerable interest. Brookhall, the seat of S. Boyce, Esq., is in this parish. The inhabitants are principally employed in the weaving of linen cloth; and there are some paper-mills for brown and fancy papers, affording employment to about 30 persons. The living is a rectory, in the diocese of Connor, and in the patronage of the Bishop: the tithes amount to £350. The church is a plain small edifice, in the later English style, erected by aid of a grant of £900 from the late Board of First Fruits, in 1826. The glebe-house, nearly adjoining it, was built in 1828: there is no glebe. In the R. C. divisions the parish forms part of the union or district of Coleraine. There are two places of worship for Presbyterians in connection with the Synod of Ulster; one at Kirkstown of the first class, and the other at Ballywatt of the third class. The male and female parochial schools at Lisnarick are supported by the rector, who also contributes annually to the support of a school at Ballyrack; at Ballyvelton is also a school, and there are two private pay schools and two Sunday schools. At Revellagh are the ruins of a castle and fort. There are also some extensive artificial caverns at Ballyvarten, Island Effrick, and Ballynock; the first has four rooms or cells, 5 feet high and 2½ feet wide, having the sides formed of unhewn stones and the roof of large flat stones.

BALLYROBERT, a grange, in the parish of TEMPLEPATRICK, barony of LOWER BELFAST, county of ANTRIM, and province of ULSTER, 2 miles (S.) from Ballyclare: the population is returned with the parish. It is situated on the roads from Carrickfergus to Ballywater and Doagh, and comprises, according to the Ordnance survey, 883½ statute acres.

BALLYSCULLION, a grange, in the barony of TOOME, county of ANTRIM, and province of ULSTER, 4 miles (N. W.) from Randalstown; containing 3351 inhabitants. This place, which is an extra-parochial district, never having paid either church cess or tithe, is situated on the road from Portglenone to Antrim, and is bounded on the north-west by the river Bann; it comprises, according to the Ordnance survey, 4279¼ statute acres. There is no provision for the cure of souls; the members of the Established Church attend divine service in the contiguous parish of Duneane, in the diocese of Connor. In the R. C. divisions it forms part of the union or district of Ballyscullion, in the diocese of Derry; the chapel is a small plain building; there is also a place of worship for Presbyterians.

BALLYSCULLION, a parish, partly in the barony of UPPER TOOME, county of ANTRIM, but chiefly in that of LOUGHINSHOLIN, county of LONDONDERRY, and province of ULSTER; containing, with the post-town of Bellaghy, 6453 inhabitants. This parish, which is intersected by the roads leading respectively from Castle-Dawson to Portglenone, and from Maghera to Bellaghy, comprises, according to the Ordnance survey, 12,750¼ statute acres, of which 10,617¼ are in the county of Londonderry, 2406 are part of Lough Beg, and 72¾ part of the river Bann, which here forms the boundary of the parish, barony, and county. On the plantation of Ulster, these lands were granted by Jas. I. to the Irish Society, and by them transferred to the Vintners' Company of London, who founded the castle and town of Bellaghy, described under its own head. At a very early period a monastery was founded on an island in Lough Beg, about two miles from the shore, then called Ynis Teda, but now Church island, from the parish church having been subsequently erected there: this establishment continued to flourish till the dissolution, and some of the lands which belonged to it are still tithe-free. Two townlands in the parish belong to the see of Derry, and the remainder has been leased in perpetuity by the Vintners' Company to the Marquess of Lothian, the Earl of Clancarty, Lord Strafford, and Sir Thomas Pakenham. There are from 400 to 450 acres of bog, part of which in summer affords coarse pasturage for cattle; a portion of it lying remote from the Bann is of a blackish colour, and capable of cultivation for rye and potatoes; the other part, which from its white colour is called "flour bog," is quite incapable of cultivation till it has been cut away for fuel, when the subsoil appears, varying from 5 to 10 feet in depth. The land is fertile, and under the auspices of the North-West Agricultural Society, of which a branch has been established here, is generally in an excellent state of cultivation; mangel-wurzel, rape, turnips, and other green crops, are being introduced with success. There are indications of coal in several parts, particularly on the Castle-Dawson estate; but there is no prospect of their being explored or worked while the extensive bogs afford so plentiful a supply of fuel. Of the numerous seats the principal are Castle-Dawson, the seat of the Right Hon. G. R. Dawson; Bellaghy Castle, the residence of J. Hill, Esq.; Bellaghy House, of H. B. Hunter, Esq.; Fairview, of R. Henry, Esq.; and Rowensgift, of A. Leckey, Esq. The splendid palace built here by the Earl of Bristol, when Bishop of Derry, one of the most magnificent in the country, was scarcely finished at his Lordship's decease, and was soon after taken down and the materials sold: the only entire portion that has been preserved is the beautiful portico, which was purchased by Dr. Alexander, Bishop of Down and Connor, who presented it to the parish of St. George, Belfast, as an ornament to that church. A small portion of the domestics' apartments and a fragment of one of the picture galleries are all that remain. There are some extensive cotton-mills at Castle-Dawson, also flour, corn, and flax-mills; and about a mile above the town is a small bleach-green. Fairs for cattle, sheep, and pigs are held at Bellaghy on the first Monday in every month; and a manorial court is held monthly, for the recovery of debts not exceeding £2.

The living is a rectory, in the diocese of Derry, and in the patronage of the Bishop: the tithes amount to £350. The church, situated in Bellaghy, is a large and handsome edifice, erected in 1794 on the site of a former church built in 1625: it is in the early English style, with a lofty and beautiful octagonal spire erected at the expense of the Earl of Bristol, and is about to be enlarged by the addition of a north aisle. There is a chapel at Castle-Dawson belonging to the Dawson family, by whom it was built and endowed; it is open to the inhabitants. The glebe-house is about a quarter of a mile from the town on a glebe comprising 70 acres; and there is also a glebe of 84 acres at Moneystachan, in the parish of Tamlaght-O'Crilly, all arable land. In the R. C. divisions this parish comprehends the grange of Ballyscullion, in the diocese of Connor, in which union are two chapels, one at Bellaghy and the other in the grange. At Ballaghy are places of worship for Presbyterians in connection with the Synod of Ulster, Methodists, and Seceders. There is a male and female parochial school, aided by annual donations from the rector and the proprietors of the Bellaghy estate, who built the school-house; and there are five other schools, which afford instruction to about 300 boys and 240 girls; also three private schools, in which are about 100 boys and 20 girls. Here is a dispensary conducted on the most approved plan; and the proprietors of the Bellaghy estate annually distribute blankets and clothes among the poor. The ruins of the old church on Ynis Teda, or Church island, are extensive and highly interesting; and close to them a square tower surmounted by a lofty octangular spire of hewn freestone was erected by the Earl of Bristol, which is a beautiful object in the landscape. A large mis-shapen stone, called Clogh O'Neill, is pointed out as an object of interest; and not far distant is a rock basin, or holy stone, to which numbers annually resort in the hope of deriving benefit from the efficacy of the water in healing diseases.

BALLYWALTER, a grange, in the parish of BALLYLINNY, barony of LOWER BELFAST, county of ANTRIM, and province of ULSTER: the population is returned with the parish. It is situated on the road from Carrickfergus to Doagh, and comprises, according to the Ordnance survey, 320½ statute acres.

BALLYWILLIN, or MILLTOWN, a parish, partly in the barony of LOWER DUNLUCE, county of ANTRIM, but chiefly in the North-East liberties of COLERAINE, county of LONDONDERRY, and province of ULSTER, 3½ miles (N. by E.) from Coleraine, on the road to Portrush; containing 2219 inhabitants. This parish is bounded on the north by the Atlantic ocean, and comprises, according to the Ordnance survey, 4673¼ statute acres, of which 1617 are in the county of Antrim: about 300 are sand and 150 bog; the remainder is arable and pasture. The entire district abounds with fossils and minerals of great variety, and with features of high geolo-

gical interest. The soil, though various, is generally good; and the lands are in an excellent state of cultivation, particularly where not exposed to the drifting of the sand, which accumulates on the coast near Portrush. There is no waste land, except the sand hills near Portrush, which, from the constant blowing of the north and north-west winds, have overspread a large tract of excellent land, which it has been found impossible to reclaim. Much of the bog has been exhausted and brought under cultivation, and there is now barely sufficient for the supply of fuel. There are vast quantities of ironstone; in some places the ore is found nearly in a metallic state, and in nodules of stone used for making the roads have been found nuclei of almost pure metal. Limestone is very abundant, but is not worked; the extensive quarries in the adjoining parish of Dunluce being held under a lease which prohibits the opening of any other upon the estate. Basalt in every variety is found here in a confused mixture of amorphous basalt with veins of red ochre, chert, soap-stone, and zeolite. In other parts there are magnificent columnar masses, the prisms of which are more perfect and more beautiful than those of the Causeway. These columns form part of a bold ridge of hills lying north and south, and displaying some of the finest features of basaltic formation in the island. Beardiville, the seat of Sir F. Macnaghten, Bart., a spacious and handsome mansion, is pleasantly situated and surrounded with extensive and thriving plantations; and at Portrush are several elegant lodges and pleasing villas, which are occupied by their respective proprietors during the bathing season, and one of which belongs to the Bishop of Derry. The Skerries, a cluster of islands about a mile from the shore, and containing, according to the Ordnance survey, 24a. 1r. 9p., belong to this parish. Behind the middle of the largest of them a vessel may ride well sheltered in from 5 to 7 fathoms of water, and on good holding ground.

The living is a rectory, in the diocese of Connor, and in the patronage of the Bishop: it was formerly an appendage to the chancellorship of that see, under a grant by Jas. I., at which time a vicarage was instituted; but it again became a rectory under the provisions of Dr. Mant's act, on the death of Dr. Trail in 1831. The tithes amount to £263. The church is an ancient, spacious, and handsome edifice, in the early English style, and is said to be the only one in the diocese or county, built prior to the Reformation, in which divine service is now performed; it has neither tower nor spire, but being situated on an eminence it is visible at the distance of several leagues at sea. There is a glebe-house, for the erection of which the late Board of First Fruits, in 1828, gave £450 and lent £140. In the R. C. divisions this parish forms part of the union or district of Coleraine. There is a place of worship at Magherabuoy for Presbyterians in connection with the Synod of Ulster, and of the second class, and at Portrush is one for Wesleyan Methodists. The male and female school at Portrush is aided by an annual donation from Miss Rice; the school-house was erected in 1832 by Dr. Adam Clarke. A male and female school is aided by an annual donation from Mr. Lyle. In these schools are about 80 boys and 60 girls; and there are also a pay school, in which are about 40 boys and 10 girls, and a Sunday school. Here are the remains of Ballyreagh, or "the Royal Castle," situated on a promontory having a bold façade of rock rising to the height of 296 feet, the base of which is washed by the Atlantic. Dunmull, originally a druidical circle, afterwards a Danish fort, and now a pasture for sheep, is one of the most curious and extensive vestiges of antiquity in the country; and about half a mile to the north-west of the church are the remains of a druidical circle and altar, with an extensive and well-arranged cave; there is also a druidical altar near Beardiville, in a very perfect state. Fine impressions of the cornua ammonis are found in the chert at Portrush; the cornua and the echenite are found also in the limestone, and every variety of the zeolite and opal in the basaltic or trap formation, with chalcedony, strontium, agate, rock tallow, and veins of fullers' earth.

BELFAST, a sea-port, borough, market-town, and parish, partly in the barony of LOWER, but chiefly in that of UPPER, BELFAST, county of ANTRIM, and province of ULSTER, 8 miles (S. by W.) from Carrickfergus, 13¼ (S. E. by E.) from Antrim, and 80 (N.) from Dublin; containing, in 1821, 44,177, and in 1831, 60,388 inhabitants, of which latter num-

Arms.

ber, 53,287 were in the town and suburbs, and 48,224 in the borough; and within three years after the latter census the population of the parish had increased nearly 7000 more. At a very early period this place obtained, according to some writers, the appellation of *Beala-farsad*, which has been supposed to signify "Hurdles-ford town," and according to others that of *Bela-fearsad*, "the town at the mouth of the river;" which latter is accurately descriptive of its situation on the river Lagan, near its influx into the lough or bay of Belfast. But,

perhaps, a still more probable conjecture is that which ascribes its etymology to the Irish *Ball-Fosaght*, signifying "the town with a ditch or foss," which, from its low situation, were anciently constructed round the town, to protect it from the tide. Previously to the English conquests in the province of Ulster, it appears to have been a fortified station commanding the passage of the river, which is here fordable at low water, and important also from its position on the line between the ancient stations of Carrickfergus and Ardes, respectively in the counties of Antrim and Down, between which the Lagan has ever been regarded as the boundary. The original fort, of which the site is now occupied by St. George's church, was taken and destroyed about the year 1178, by John de Courcy, who soon after erected a noble castle on a more eligible spot. King John marched his army to this place, in 1210; but no notice of any town occurs till the year 1316, when the destruction of the town and castle by Edward Bruce is recorded. The Irish chieftains, having by his aid recovered their ancient possessions, rebuilt the castle, of which, through the intestine divisions in England and their union with the English settlers in Ulster, they kept uninterrupted possession for nearly two centuries, till the reign of Hen. VII., when the Earl of Kildare, at the head of a large army, in 1503, took and destroyed the town and castle; but the latter was soon afterwards repaired by the native chieftains, from which, however, their forces were again driven by the earl, in 1512, and compelled to retire to the mountains. From this period Belfast remained in a ruined and neglected state, till the year 1552, when Sir James Crofts, lord-deputy, repaired and garrisoned the castle; and during the same year the Irish of Ulster again appeared in arms, under the command of Hugh Mac Nial Oge, but the English government offered terms of accommodation which that chieftain accepted, and, swearing allegiance to Hen. VIII., he obtained a grant of the castle and town of Belfast,

View of Belfast from the lough. Engraved by John Thomson. From George Benn, History of the town of Belfast *(Belfast, 1823).*

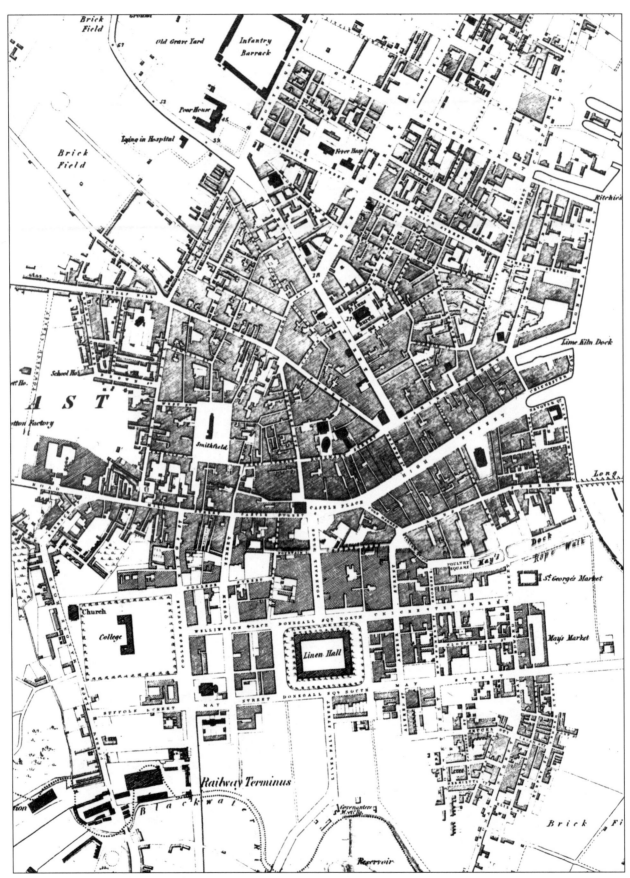

Belfast. Part of 6 inch O.S. map of Co. Antrim, sheet 61, published 1834, amended early 1840s (reproduced at 140%).

with other extensive possessions. After the death of Hugh, who was killed in 1555 by a party of Scottish marauders, his possessions passed to other branches of his family, with the exception of the castle, which was placed in the custody of Randolph Lane, an English governor; in the 13th of Elizabeth it was granted, with its extensive dependencies, to Sir Thomas Smythe and his son, on condition of their keeping a certain number of horse and foot in readiness to meet at Antrim after a brief notice, to attend upon the lord-deputy. In 1573 the Earl of Essex visited the fortress, which the Irish had previously, on different occasions, frequently attempted to take by surprise; and in 1575 the Lord-Deputy Sydney encountered the Irish forces at the ford of this place. About that period, Belfast is said to have had a forest and woods, of which all traces have long since disappeared. After the death of Elizabeth, the garrison, influenced by Hugh O'Nial, Earl of Tyrone, refused submission to the English crown; but, on the defeat of that powerful leader and his adherents, the English gained the ascendency, and Sir Arthur Chichester, lord-deputy in the reign of Jas. I., issued his summons requiring the supplies of horse and foot, according to the tenure by which the castle was held; and no one appearing in answer to this requisition, the castle and demesne became forfeited to the crown, and were given to Sir Arthur in 1612.

Prior to the civil war in 1641, the town had attained a considerable degree of commercial importance, and was the residence of many merchants and men of note; but the inhabitants, being chiefly Presbyterians, suffered severely for refusing to conform to the Established Church; many of them left the kingdom, and those who remained embraced the parliamentarian interest. The immediate local effect of this rebellion was the suspension of all improvements, but the town was saved from assault by the defeat of the rebels near Lisburn; and, while the insurgents were overpowering nearly all the surrounding country, Belfast was maintained in security by the judicious arrangements of Sir Arthur Tyringham, who, according to the records of the corporation, cleared the water-courses, opened the sluices, erected a draw-bridge, and mustered the inhabitants in military array. In 1643 Chas. I. appointed Col. Chichester governor of the castle, and granted £1000 for the better fortification of the town, which, while the people of the surrounding country were joining the Scottish covenanters, alone retained its firm adherence to the royal interest. The royalists in Ulster, anticipating an order from the parliament for a forcible imposition of the Scottish covenant, assembled here to deliberate upon the answer to be returned to Gen. Monroe, commander of the Scottish forces in Ireland, when required to submit to that demand; but the latter, being treacherously informed of their purpose, and favoured by the darkness of the night, marched to Belfast with 2000 men, surprised the town, and compelled them to retire to Lisburn. The inhabitants were now reduced to the greatest distress; Col. Hume, who was made governor of the castle for the parliament, imposed upon them heavy and grievous taxes, and the most daring of the Irish insurgents were constantly harassing them from without. After the decapitation of Chas. I., the presbytery of this place, having strongly expressed their abhorrence of that atrocity, were reproachfully answered by the poet Milton; and the Scottish forces of Ulster having, in common with the covenanters of their native

country, embraced the royal cause, the garrison kept possession of it for the king. But Gen. Monk, in 1648, seized their commander, Gen. Monroe, whom he sent prisoner to England, and having assaulted Belfast, soon reduced it under the control of the parliament, who appointed Col. Maxwell governor. In 1649, the town was taken by a manœuvre of Lord Montgomery; but Cromwell, on his arrival in Ireland, despatched Col. Venables, after the massacre of Drogheda, to reduce it, in which enterprise he succeeded.

On the abdication of Jas. II., the inhabitants fitted out a vessel, and despatched a congratulatory address to the Prince of Orange, whom they afterwards proclaimed king; but, within a few days, James's troops having obtained possession of the place, many of the inhabitants fled to Scotland and elsewhere for safety, and several of the principal families were placed under attainder. On the landing of Duke Schomberg at Bangor, on Oct. 13th, 1689, with an army of 10,000 men, the Irish forces evacuated the town, of which Col. Wharton took possession in the name of King William: a reinforcement of 7000 well-appointed troops from Denmark shortly after joined the forces of Schomberg, which had encamped under the walls; and on June 14th, 1690, the king arrived in person, and issued from this town a proclamation to the army forbidding them to lay waste the country. The king remained here for five days, whence he proceeded to the Boyne by way of Hillsborough, and on his march issued an order to the collector of the customs of Belfast, to pay £1200 per annum to the Presbyterian ministers of Ulster, which grant formed the origin of the more extensive royal bounty at present paid to that body. The castle was destroyed by an accidental fire in 1708, and has not been rebuilt. In 1715, on the threatened invasion of the Pretender, the inhabitants of the town and neighbourhood formed themselves into volunteer corps for the better defence of the country; in 1745 they again had recourse to arms; and in 1760, by their prompt muster, in conjunction with the people of the surrounding country, they saved their town from the French under Thurot, who had landed at Carrickfergus, intending to surprise Belfast; but, overawed by the muster of 12,000 men, posted within two miles of Carrickfergus on the road to Belfast, he hastily re-embarked, after having obtained a considerable supply of brandy, wine, and provisions from the merchants of that town. The formation of the Irish volunteers, induced all the principal young men of Belfast again to accoutre themselves, and they assumed a formidable political attitude, until suppressed with the rest of that body. Notwithstanding the powerful excitement which prevailed towards the close of the 18th century, Belfast, although the centre of motion to the northern union, was preserved in peaceable subjection by the precaution of Government in placing in it a strong military force: but the spirit of disaffection had diffused itself considerably, and seven individuals were executed here for treason. With the exception of commercial difficulties, from which, however, this town suffered less than any other of equal importance in the kingdom, few circumstances have occurred in modern times to retard its progress; and it is now the most flourishing in the island, celebrated alike for its manufactures and commerce, and for the public spirit of its inhabitants in the pursuit of literature and science, and in the support of charitable and other benevolent institutions.

The Long Bridge and Cave Hill, Belfast. Drawn by George Petrie and engraved by William Miller. From P. D. Hardy, The northern tourist, or, stranger's guide to the north & north-west of Ireland *(Dublin, 1830).*

The town is advantageously situated on the western bank of the river Lagan, a long narrow bridge of 21 arches, erected in 1686, connecting it with the suburb of Ballymacarrett, in the county of Down, below which the river expands into the noble estuary called Belfast or Carrickfergus Lough; another bridge over the Lagan into the county of Down has been lately erected, and there is a third at some distance to the south. Its general appearance is cheerful and prepossessing; the principal streets and squares, which are well formed and spacious, are Macadamised, and the footpaths flagged with excellent freestone. The houses are handsomely built of brick and slated, and several new squares, terraces, and ranges of building have been recently erected, making the total number of houses 8022. The town is lighted with gas from works belonging to a company established by act of parliament in 1822. The inhabitants, previously to 1795, were but scantily supplied with water; but the late Marquess of Donegal granted to the trustees of the Incorporated Charitable Society a lease, for 61 years, of all the springs of water on his estate; and in 1805 the Malone springs were purchased, and the water was brought to the town at an expense of £3650. In 1817 an act was obtained, under the authority of which the trustees appointed water applotters, who took upon themselves the whole management, and now receive the rates, paying to the Society £750 per annum.

The town, though situated little more than six feet above high water mark of spring tides, is considered healthy, the air being pure and salubrious; and the surrounding scenery is richly diversified and, in many parts, picturesque. An extended range of mountains, 1100 feet in height, rises at the distance of two miles to the north-west; and within the limits of the parish is Divis mountain, 1567 feet above the level of the sea at low water. The views down the lough in a north-eastern

direction are strikingly beautiful, the shores on both sides being decorated with elegant country seats and plantations. The inhabitants have long been distinguished for their zealous encouragement of literary pursuits, and the first edition of the Bible ever published in Ireland was printed at Belfast in the year 1704. In this town also was established, in 1737, the Belfast News Letter, the first newspaper ever printed in the North of Ireland: there are now several others, also a Mercantile Register and monthly periodicals. The Belfast Society for Promoting Knowledge, established in 1788, is supported by annual subscriptions of one guinea; the library contains more than 8000 volumes, and there are a cabinet of minerals, and a valuable philosophical apparatus. The Literary Society, for improvement in literature, science, antiquities, and the arts, was established in 1801; and the Historic Society, for the study of general history, the British laws and constitution, and the cultivation of oratory, in 1811. The Natural History Society, established in 1821, has recently erected a very handsome building: the lower story is an imitation of the Choragic monuments of Thrasyllus, with a portico, which is an exact copy of that of the octagon tower of Andronicus at Athens; and the upper portions are designed after the model of the temple of Minerva: the interior comprises several spacious, lofty, and elegant apartments, with lecture-rooms, an observatory, and a very valuable museum. The Botanic Gardens were formed in connection with the Natural History Society, by some of the members, who, in 1827, purchased for that purpose about 16 acres of land, on the banks of the Lagan, about a mile from the town, on the Malone road: they are under the direction of a committee of 21, elected from the holders of 500 shares of five guineas each, of whom those holding less than four shares pay also a subscription annually; the society has expended more than £4000 on these gardens, to which

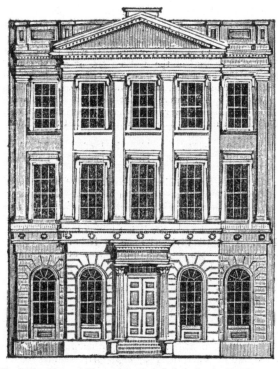

The Belfast Natural History Museum, College Square North.
From The Dublin Penny Journal, *vol. 1, 1832.*

persons may subscribe without being shareholders. A spacious and handsome news-room, to which respectable strangers have free access, on entering their names in a book kept for the purpose, occupies the lower story of the Commercial Buildings : there is another large news-room in one of the wings of the White Linen Hall; a third has been recently opened in connection with the office of the Northern Whig newspaper, and a fourth under the patronage of the Belfast Society. Over the exchange is an elegant suite of assembly-rooms; there are also others in the Commercial Buildings, and there is a neat theatre in Arthur-street. On the north-eastern side of the town are artillery and infantry barracks; and a town-major is regularly appointed, this being nominally a garrison town : it is also a chief constabulary police station for the county.

Belfast owes much of its importance to the increase of the linen trade of Ulster, of which it is now become the grand depôt. In 1830 a very extensive mill was erected for spinning linen yarn upon the same principle as in the chief houses at Leeds, in order to meet the increasing demand of the manufacturers; and, in 1832, a large cotton-mill was adapted to the spinning of the refuse flax of the linen-mill, for the use of the canvas weavers. In these two mills more than 700 persons are employed, and, since their erection, a linen cloth manufactory has been established on a very large scale at Ligoneil, two miles distant, which is the first of the kind in this part of the country. Seven more spinning mills, containing 48,000 spindles, and affording employment to more than 5000 persons, were built in 1834, and several others have been erected since; they are all of brick, roofed with slate, and are mostly five stories high. The celebrated Ardoyne damask manufactory was established in 1825; and the elegance of

the fabric soon extended its reputation, and obtained royal patronage, an extensive order for his Majesty being at present under execution. Linens and sheetings of the stoutest fabric, for the London market, are likewise manufactured in this establishment, the proprietor of which, Michael Andrews, Esq., obtained the gold medal of the Royal Dublin Society for specimens of his productions, shewn at their exhibition of national manufactures, held in Dublin, in May 1835. The business of the linen trade of the whole kingdom was for a long time transacted solely in Dublin, by agents resident there; but the serious inconvenience experienced by the numerous bleachers in the province of Ulster, in consequence of the remoteness of the principal mart, prompted them to the establishment of a linen-hall at Belfast, and in 1785 a spacious and handsome quadrangular building was erected in the centre of Donegal-square, by public subscription, and called the White Linen Hall, which affords great facility for making up assorted cargoes for foreign countries; great quantities are exported to America, the West Indies, and various other places, and nearly all the London merchants are supplied by factors resident here. The Brown Linen Hall, erected about the same time, is an enclosed space on the south side of Donegal-street, containing several detached platforms, where the merchants attend every Friday for the purchase of brown webs from the weavers, who assembled here from the surrounding districts. The webs brought to this mart are principally one yard in width, and of the finest quality; and so great is the quantity purchased by the merchants, who are also bleachers, that in the Belfast district, situated within a distance of six miles of the town to the west and south west and containing in all fourteen bleaching-greens (of which eleven are within the parish of Belfast), 260,000 pieces are annually bleached, exceeding by 87,000 the number of pieces bleached in the same district in the year 1822; the value of the goods finished annually in these establishments is little less than one million sterling.

The cotton manufacture, of which Belfast is the centre and principal seat, was originally introduced here in 1777, by Mr. Robert Joy, father of Chief Baron Joy, and at that time one of the proprietors of the Belfast News Letter. That gentleman had been chiefly instrumental in establishing the incorporated poor-house, which under his auspices became the nursery of this important branch of manufacture, at that time unknown in any other part of Ireland, and which, after struggling with various difficulties, at length attained such rapidity of progress that, in 1800, it afforded employment to 27,000 persons within a circuit of ten miles round Belfast, and is still carried on here to a vast extent in all its branches, more especially in the spinning department, for which alone there are, in the town and neighbourhood, no less than 21 factories. The machinery used in these works is partly impelled by steam, but chiefly by water, for which the streams in the neighbourhood are particularly favourable, by reason of the rapidity of their currents and their numerous falls; and gives motion to about 982,000 spindles and 640 power-looms, which latter are of very recent introduction. The buildings are of very large dimensions, in general from six to eight stories in height, and in some of them from 800 to 2000 persons are employed. The principal articles manufactured are velvets, fustians, jeans, ticking, checks, ginghams, quiltings, calico muslins, and mus-

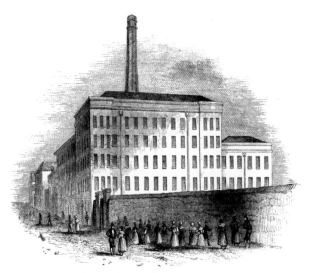

Mulholland's spinning mill, Henry Street, Belfast. Drawn by J. H. Burgess and engraved by Sly. From S. C. Hall, Ireland: its scenery, character, & c., *vol. 3 (London, 1841).*

linets. There are also very extensive print-fields, bleach-greens, dye-works, and establishments for every department of the manufacture, which in the aggregate affords employment to 36,225 persons; but is at present in a declining state, several of the works having been recently suspended, and others applied to different purposes. Connected with these establishments are various manufactories for machinery, iron-forges, and works for the preparation of oil of vitriol and other chymical products used in bleaching, dyeing, and printing, together employing about 1000 persons; engraving also, as connected with the printing of cotton goods, is carried on extensively. An iron-foundry was first established here in 1792; in 1798 the Lagan foundry, in Ballymacarrett, was erected, where steam-engines are now made; and in 1811 the Belfast foundry, in Donegal-street, was built, in which the patent rotatory steam-engines, originally invented by one of the proprietors, have been manufactured. In 1834 the manufacture of machinery for spinning flax was first successfully introduced into Ireland, by the proprietors of the Belfast foundry; two other foundries have been since established,—the Phœnix, in York-street, and the Soho foundry, in Townsend-street, where spinning machinery is made; there are also several other foundries on a smaller scale, the whole affording employment to about 600 persons. The making of vitriol was introduced in 1799; at present there are two establishments, in which about 180 persons are employed. The manufacture of flint glass was commenced in 1776, and in a few years several extensive glass-houses were erected; at present there are only two in operation, employing together about 90 persons. There are two distilleries, which annually produce 311,000 gallons of spirits, nearly the whole of which is for home consumption: about 150 men are employed in the process; and at Brookfield, adjoining the town, is another upon an extensive scale. There are twelve extensive ale and porter breweries, from which many thousand barrels are annually exported; some large flour and meal-mills, worked by steam and water; and extensive manufactories for tobacco, soap, candles, starch, glue, and paper, both for home consumption and for exportation. The tanning of leather for exportation was

formerly carried on to a great extent, and at the commencement of the present century there were 36 tanyards in the town and neighbourhood; but it has much declined, and is at present chiefly confined to the home market. The manufacture of ropes and canvas was originally introduced in 1758, to which were added, in 1784, the making of sail-cloth, and, in 1820, the making of sails, which has since grown into celebrity and affords employment to a great number of persons of both sexes. Ship-building was commenced in the year 1791, prior to which time all vessels belonging to the port were built and repaired in England and Scotland; there are now two extensive yards, with graving docks and every requisite appendage, in which more than 200 men are constantly employed, and from which four or five brigs of the first class, and schooners of from 100 to 360 tons' registered burden, are annually launched. Several ships have also been lately built, among which is the Hindoo, of 400 tons' register, for the East India trade.

The trade of the port, comparatively of modern origin, has been rapid in its growth and uniformly increasing in its progress: it originally rose into importance on the purchase by the Crown, in 1637, of the privileges possessed by the corporation of Carrickfergus (of which port Belfast was formerly only a dependency), of importing merchandise at a far lower rate of duty than was paid at any other port. After the completion of this purchase, the custom-house of that place was removed to Belfast, which, however, arose into distinguished notice only with the linen trade, as, at the commencement of the last century, there were only five vessels, of the aggregate burden of 109 tons, belonging to the port; and the amount of custom-house duties, in 1709, was not more than £1215. In 1740 it had not only become well known on the continent as a place of considerable trade, but was in equal repute with the most celebrated commercial towns in Europe; and in 1785 it became the principal depot of the linen trade, from which time its commerce rapidly increased. During the fluctuations of trade by which other places suffered so severely, Belfast experienced comparatively but little diminution of its commerce, and in 1825 derived a considerable addition to its trade in the increase

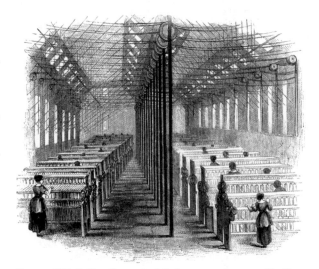

Chartres Mill, Belfast. Drawn by J.H. Burgess and engraved by Sly. From S. C. Hall, Ireland: its scenery, character, & c., *vol. 3 (London, 1841).*

of the cross-channel intercourse, from the introduction of steam navigation. In 1833, the number of vessels which entered inwards at the port was 2445, and which cleared outwards, 1391 ; and the amount of duties paid at the custom-house exceeded £412,000. The trade has been rapidly and uniformly increasing every year ; and in that ending on Jan. 5th, 1836, the number of vessels that entered inwards was 2730, and that cleared outwards, 2047 ; and the amount of duties paid at the custom-house, was £357,645. 2. 10., and of quayage dues at the ballast-office, £9289. 19. 11. The commerce of the port consists of various branches, of which the most important at present is the cross-channel trade, which in 1747 employed only three vessels, collectively of 198 tons' burden ; from that time it appears to have rapidly increased, and, since the more direct and expeditious intercourse with the principal ports of Great Britain, afforded by the introduction of steam navigation, has absorbed a considerable portion of the foreign and colonial trade. The principal exports connected with this branch are linen cloth, manufactured cotton goods, and agricultural produce. Its extensive trade in provisions is of very recent introduction, and affords a striking demonstration of the great improvements in the system of agriculture which have taken place since the commencement of the present century, previously to which considerable quantities of corn were annually imported, and in 1789 the only articles shipped from this port were beef and butter, in very limited quantities. The chief imports by the cross-channel trade are tea, sugar, cotton, wool, and various articles for the use of the manufacturers, bleachers, and dyers ; also British manufactured goods, and articles of general merchandise. The number of vessels that entered inwards from British ports during the year 1835 was 2949, and the number that cleared outwards, 1534 ; of these there were nine steam-boats, of which four were employed in the Glasgow, three in the Liverpool, and two in the London trade. The first steam-boat that crossed the channel to this port was from Liverpool, in 1819, but it was not till 1824 that steam-boats were employed in the transmission of merchandise : the passage by steam navigation to Liverpool is performed, on the average, in 14 hours, to London in 132 hours, to Glasgow in 14 hours, and to Dublin in 14 hours.

The trade with the United States and with British North America is also very considerable : the chief exports are linen cloth, manufactured cotton goods, blue, starch, and whiskey ; the imports are timber and staves, tobacco, cotton, wool, ashes, and flax and clover seeds. In 1835, the number of vessels in this trade which entered inwards was 78, and of those that cleared outwards 76, the latter taking out 2675 emigrants, of whom 1824 were destined for the British American colonies, and 851 for the United States. The trade with the West Indies commenced in 1740, and, of late, several first-class vessels have been built expressly for it ; 9 vessels entered inwards, and 15 cleared outwards, in 1835, in connection with the British West India islands only. The trade with the Baltic, which is on the increase, consists in the importation of tallow, timber, ashes, flax, and hemp. Tallow and hides are also imported from Odessa ; mats, pitch, tar, flax, and flax seed from Archangel ; and wine, fruit, lemon and lime juice, olive and other oils, brimstone, and barilla, from the Mediterranean and the Levant. The total number of vessels employed in the foreign trade, which entered inwards in 1835, was 184, and of those that cleared outwards, 145. The coasting trade is also of great importance ; exclusively of ordinary vessels of different classes, and of the regular steam-packets for goods and passengers to Liverpool, London, Dublin, Greenock, Glasgow, and Stranraer, it employs packets, in the summer season, to the Isle of Man, Whitehaven, North Wales, Port Stewart, Derry, and to several other places on the Irish and Scottish coasts. There is also engaged in this trade a regular establishment of vessels of different classes to London, Maryport, Workington, and Whitehaven, those to the last three ports being chiefly employed in the coal trade ; the imports supply the greater part of the North of Ireland. The number of vessels belonging to the port is 219, of an aggregate burden of 23,681 tons ; but they are very inadequate to the extent of its commerce, of which a very large portion is carried on in ships belonging to other countries.

The port is very advantageously situated for trade at the mouth of the Lagan in Belfast Lough, sometimes called Carrickfergus bay, a noble arm of the sea forming a safe and commodious harbour, well sheltered and easy of access ; the entrance is about six miles in breadth from the point between Groomsport and Ballyholm bay, in the county of Down, and White Head in the county of Antrim ; the length from the latter point to the quays at Belfast is 12 miles, decreasing gradually in breadth towards the bridge, where it is very much contracted by the different quays and landing-places, and the embankments of Ballymacarrett. The preservation and improvement of the port and harbour were vested in the Ballast Corporation, constituted by act of parliament in 1785, which was repealed by an act obtained in 1831, and a new " Corporation for Preserving and Improving the Port and Harbour of Belfast" was created, consisting of " the lord of the castle" and "the sovereign," the parliamentary representatives for the counties of Antrim and Down, and the boroughs of Belfast, Carrickfergus, and Downpatrick, and sixteen other commissioners, of whom four go out of office annually, and their successors are elected subject to the approbation of the lord-lieutenant and privy council. Their annual income, arising from pilotage, tonnage, quayage rates on imports and exports, ballastage, &c., on an average of five years, ending Jan. 5th, 1836, amounted to £8868. 18. 8., and the expenditure to £8789 8. 4. The objects of obtaining the new act, in 1831, were to enable the commissioners to purchase quays and grounds for the improvement of the harbour, and to render the enactments suitable to the present state of the trade of the town, which had increased nearly tenfold since the passing of the former act. Below the bridge a fine range of quays extends along the north-west bank of the river, with two graving docks, which were constructed soon after the port was frequented by large vessels; three of these wet docks extend into the principal streets of the town. A spacious graving dock was completed in the year 1826, at an expense of £26,000, by the Ballast Corporation; and several extensive wet docks, quays, and warehouses are now being constructed below the town, under an act of parliament obtained in 1829, by Messrs. Holmes and Dunbar, who have already expended £35,000 in this undertaking: the first of these docks, completed in 1832, is 400 yards in length and 100 yards in breadth, and is intended for the large ships in the timber trade, and for those in the coal trade till the other docks are constructed. The harbour commissioners, under the act of 1831, contemplate the deepening and enlarging of the harbour, the formation of a new channel from the quays to the Mile-water river, the construction of floating docks with entrance locks, additional quays, and other improvements; but these works are at present delayed. The custom-house, a very indifferent building, is situated on Hanover-quay. The Lagan navigation, extending in a line of 22 miles from the port to Lough Neagh, by way of Lisburn, was constructed under an act of the 27th of Geo. III., confirmed by others to the 54th of the same reign, by which the proprietors were invested with a small duty on beer and spirits in the excise district of Lisburn, since commuted for an annual money payment out of the consolidated fund: the number of debentures issued from 1785 to 1793 was sixty-two, amounting to £62,000. The navigation is continued partly in the bed of the river, and partly by collateral cuts to a mile above Lisburn; but, from its circuitous course and the high rate of the tolls, goods are conveyed by land with greater expedition and at less expense. Divers new roads have been formed in the immediate neighbourhood of the town; and, under an act of parliament obtained in 1832, a railway from the harbour to Cave Hill is now being constructed, in a double line, which is the first work of the kind in the North of Ireland.

The Chamber of Commerce was originally established in 1783; its meetings were suspended from 1794 to 1802, since which time they have been resumed without interruption, greatly to the benefit of trade and the interests of the town. The Old Exchange, situated nearly in the centre of the town, at the end of Donegal-street, is the private property of the Marquess of Donegal; it was formerly the place of public resort for the merchants, but, since the erection of the Commercial Buildings, has been used only for the election of the chief magistrate. The Commercial Buildings were erected in 1822, opposite to the Exchange, at an expense of £20,000, by a proprietary of 200 shareholders incorporated by act of parliament in 1823, and by a committee of whom, annually elected, the affairs of the institution are conducted: the buildings comprise an excellent commercial hotel, a spacious and handsome news-room, over which is an elegant assembly-room, and behind these an area with a piazza

for the use of the merchants; and in connection with them are numerous offices principally occupied by professional men. The north front, of Irish granite, is decorated with eight lofty Ionic columns, and the west front is principally occupied by shops: the merchants assemble in the news-room and hold 'Change on Monday, Wednesday, and Friday. The revenue derived by Government from the post-office, in 1835, was £10,073. The banking establishments are the Northern-Banking Company, established in 1824; the Belfast Banking Company, in 1826; and the Ulster Banking Company, in 1836: all have branches in the different large towns throughout the province. There are also branches of the Bank of Ireland, the Provincial Bank, and the Agricultural and Commercial Bank of Ireland.

Jas. I., in 1605, 1608, and 1611, made grants of markets and fairs, which were all included in one grant to Arthur, Lord Chichester, in 1621, of a market to be held on Friday, and fairs annually on Aug. 1st and 2nd, and Oct. 28th and 29th; this grant was also confirmed by Charles II. to Arthur, Earl of Donegal, in 1668. Though the markets are open daily, the principal market day is Friday: the two fairs are now held on Aug. 12th and Nov. 8th. There are in Smithfield two market-places for meat, two for fish, and one for hay, straw, and hides, besides several others for meat and vegetables in various parts of the town, all of which are well supplied: the market for pork and butter is in the weigh-house and buildings adjoining; the sale of poultry of all kinds, collected from a great distance, forms a regular trade; and the fish market is well supplied with turbot and salmon from the coasts of Antrim and Derry.

Belfast is in some measure indebted for its incorporation to the favour shewn to the Chichester family by Jas. I., who, in 1612, granted to Sir Arthur Chichester, who had previously established a number of Devonshire men in the townland of Malone, the castle and an extensive surrounding territory; and in the following year incorporated the inhabitants by charter. In the 4th of Jas. II., on a seizure of the franchises, a charter, the provisions of which were in most respects similar to those of the former, was granted, but is now considered void. Geo. II., in the 33rd year of his reign, also granted a charter, which, however, is only an inspeximus of the charter of Jas. I. The corporation is styled "The Sovereign, Free Burgesses, and Commonalty of the Borough of Belfast;" and consists of a sovereign, lord of the castle, constable of the castle, twelve other free burgesses, and an unlimited number of freemen, assisted by a town-clerk and two serjeants-at-mace. The sovereign is chosen annually on the 24th of June by the free burgesses, from three of their own body nominated by the lord of the castle (or, in default of such nomination, which seldom occurs, elected by themselves), and is sworn into office before the lord, or in his absence before the constable of the castle, on Michaelmas-day. The lord of the castle is a member of the corporation by tenure of the castle of Belfast; the office is held by the Marquess of Donegal, in whose family it has continued since the date of the charter; the constable is appointed by instrument under seal of the lord of the castle, and becomes a free burgess. The other free burgesses are chosen, as vacancies occur, by the sovereign and the remainder of their body; the town-clerk is elected by the sovereign and burgesses; and the serjeants-at-mace are chosen by the corporation at large. The freedom of the borough is acquired only by gift of

Castle Place, Belfast. Published by J. & F. Harwood, 26 Fenchurch Street, London. 16th June 1843. (Private collection).

High Street, Belfast. Drawn by T. M. Baynes and engraved by J. Davies. From G. N. Wright, Ireland illustrated *(London, 1831).*

the sovereign and free burgesses; at present there are no freemen. The borough returned two representatives to the Irish parliament from the date of its incorporation till the Union, after which it sent one to the Imperial parliament, but its original number was restored by the act of the 2nd of William IV., cap. 88, passed to amend the representation. The right of election was formerly vested exclusively in the free burgesses, but by the act above-named has been extended to the £10 householders: the number of voters registered at the close of 1835 was about 1600: the sovereign is the returning officer. The jurisdiction of the corporation and of the town police is supposed to extend on the north to the Mile-water, and on the south to the Blackstaff, both of which streams fall into the Lagan, which forms its boundary on the east; and on the west is also a boundary, but so imperfectly defined that disputes are constantly arising with respect to the county cess, which within it is levied on the houses, and without it only on the acre. Under the act now regulating the harbour a jurisdiction is given to the judges of assize, justices of the peace for Antrim, and the sovereign of Belfast, over all offences committed within the limits of the port and harbour, or within 500 yards of the quays in the county of Down, as if such offences had been committed within the county of Antrim. The act of the 2nd and 3rd of Wm. IV., cap. 89, assigns a new boundary for elective purposes, which is minutely described in the Appendix. The sovereign is a justice of the peace for the borough, and usually holds the commissions of the peace for the counties of Antrim and Down; he is also clerk of the market, and, *ex officio*, a member of different bodies incorporated under local acts for the improvement of the town and port. The charter granted a court of record for the recovery of debts not exceeding £20, arising within the borough or its liberty, to be held every Thursday before the sovereign, but it has long since fallen into disuse. The manor court, held every third Thursday before the seneschal (who is appointed by the Marquess of Donegal, as lord of the manor of Belfast, within which the borough is situated), has jurisdiction over the entire parish, and over the townland of Ballynafeigh, in the county of Down, to the amount of £20 present currency, by process of attachment or arrest: the seneschal also proceeds by civil bill under the manor court acts: the prison of the court was abolished in 1828, and defaulters are now sent to the county gaol. Courts leet for the manor are also held by the seneschal; at that held in May, constables, applotters, and appraisers are appointed for the ensuing year. The sovereign holds petty sessions every Monday and Wednesday at the sessions-house, at which county magistrates may also attend. The stipendiary police magistrate, appointed in 1816, holds a court of petty session at the sessions-house every Thursday, at which other justices attend; a magistrate's court at the police-office every Tuesday and Saturday, where he disposes of cases respecting servants' wages, and other matters not requiring the attendance of two justices; and also sits daily at the office of the nightly watch establishment. The county quarter sessions are held in this town, in conjunction with other places, four times in the year; and the assistant barrister then determines causes by civil bill under his statutable jurisdiction, for the division of Belfast. The house of correction, adjoining the quarter sessions court-house, is a good building of brick, erected in 1817, but is not sufficiently

adapted for the classification of prisoners, who are chiefly employed in breaking stones for the streets of the town: it contains good schools, for both sexes, to which two hours in the day are devoted. Commissioners of police were appointed by an act of parliament passed in 1800, and amended in 1816, under which a police tax, amounting on an average of five years, ending with 1835, to £9000 per annum, is levied for the maintenance of patrols by night and by day, and for lighting, cleansing, and paving the town and precincts.

St Anne's parish church, Donegall Street, Belfast. Drawn by Horatio Nelson and engraved by F. G. Bruce. From The Dublin Penny Journal, *vol. 1, 1832 (supplement).*

The parish, according to the Ordnance survey, contains 19,559 statute acres, and was anciently called Shankill, but no church having existed at the latter place for more than two centuries, it is now generally designated the parish of Belfast. The living is a vicarage, in the diocese of Connor, and province of Armagh, and in the patronage of the Marquess of Donegal, to whom the impropriate rectory belongs: the entire parish is under the tithe composition act, and, with the exception of a portion, called the Upper Falls, pays £950 per annum, of which £600 belongs to the lay impropriator, and the remainder to the vicar, who has also a glebe-house near the church, and 20 acres of land. The parochial church, dedicated to St. Anne, was erected in 1778, at the expense of the late Marquess of Donegal: it consists of a nave and chancel, with a lofty Ionic tower surmounted by a Corinthian cupola covered with copper, forming an interesting and conspicuous object in character to the rest of the building, has been replaced by one of loftier elevation. About 1830 the late Board of First Fruits gave £666 for the repair, and the Ecclesiastical Commissioners have recently granted £375 for the improvement, of the church. *St. George's* church, or chapel of ease, was erected in 1812, on the site of a former edifice, called the corporation church, which had been built on the ruins of the ancient castle : it is a splendid structure, consisting of a nave and chancel, with a magnificent and highly enriched portico of six noble columns and four fluted pilasters, supporting a cornice and pediment, in the tympanum of which are the arms of the united sees of Down and Connor, and of the town, in alto relievo ; this splendid specimen of Corinthian architecture was removed from the front of a palace built by the late Earl of Bristol, when Bishop of Derry, on the shore of Lough Beg, the materials for which were quarried from the Derry mountains, and worked by Irish artists, and after that noble prelate's decease purchased, on the demolition of the palace, by Dr. Alexander, then Bishop of Down and Connor, and now of Meath, and by him presented to this church : the Ecclesiastical Commissioners have recently granted £123. 6. 7. for the repair of the building. The living is a perpetual curacy, in the patronage of the Vicar, and was endowed by the late Board of First Fruits with £3000, laid out in the purchase of the tithes of Naas, in the county of Kildare, producing under the composition act £126 per ann., and further endowed by the vicar with a portion of the tithes of the Upper Falls, now producing to the curate, under the same act, £50 per annum. *Christchurch*, containing 1000 free sittings, and situated near the Royal Institution, was erected by the late Board of First Fruits, aided by subscription, and was opened for divine service in 1833 : the living is a perpetual curacy, endowed with £50 per ann. by the Board, together with the rents of the pews, and in the patronage of the Vicar. It is also in contemplation to erect a church, or chapel, in the townland of Upper Malone, in this parish, about three miles south of the town.

Belfast is the seat of the R. C. see of Down and Connor, and the residence of the Bishop ; there are two spacious chapels in the town, one of which, erected in 1811, and considered as the cathedral, is an elegant edifice, in the later style of English architecture : there are also other chapels at Ballymacarrett, Hollywood,

St Patrick's chapel, Donegall Street, Belfast. Engraved by John Thomson. From George Benn, History of Belfast *(Belfast, 1823)*

Meeting house, Fisherwick Place, Belfast. From The Dublin Penny Journal, *vol. 1, 1832 (supplement).*

Green Castle, and Ballyclare, all in the R. C. parish of Belfast. There are seven places of worship for Presbyterians, of which that for the third congregation (so called from the order of its formation), built in 1831 at an expense of £10,000. by Mr. Millar, a native and resident architect, is perhaps the most elegant edifice of its kind in the three kingdoms. The front is enriched with a stately Grecian-Doric portico of ten lofty columns resting on a basement of twenty steps, and surmounted by a beautiful attic balustrade, composed of a series of pedestals and light pierced work, having a novel and pleasing effect ; the other portions of the building are noble and elegant in design, and beautiful in detail, especially the grand staircase leading to the gallery, from which may best be observed that agreeable harmony of design and unity of effect which are strikingly characteristic of this chaste and beautiful edifice. The meeting-house for the fifth congregation, in Fisherwick-place, erected in 1827 at an expense of £7000 ; and that for the sixth, in May-street, built in 1829 at an expense of £9000, are also spacious and elegant structures. There are three places of worship for the Seceders (sometimes called Burghers or Antiburghers), two for Covenanters or Reformed Presbyterians, two each for Primitive and Wesleyan Methodists, and one each for General Baptists, the Society of Friends, and Independents. Five of the Presbyterian meeting-houses are in connection with the Synod of Ulster, namely, those of the third, fourth, fifth, sixth, and seventh congregations ; the fifth and sixth are of the first class and the fourth and seventh of the second class. Two are in connection with the Presbytery of Antrim, namely, those of the first and second congregations, the first being a collegiate charge, and each of the first class ; and two more in connection with the Seceding Synod are of the first class.

The "Royal Belfast Academical Institution," which reflects so much honour on its founders, was projected in 1807 ; and, within a few weeks from the first promulgation of the design, subscriptions to the amount of £16,000 were raised for carrying it into effect : this sum was further increased by subscriptions from other parts of Ireland, and from England ; and, under the patronage of the Marquess of Hastings, and by the unwearied exertions of several gentlemen, nearly £5000 was subscribed in India : making the total amount £25,000. In 1810, the patrons and principal subscribers were by act of parliament incorporated a body politic, to consist of the Lord-Primate, the Marquess of Donegal, the Bishop of

The Incorporated Poor House, Clifton Street, Belfast. From Twenty one views in Belfast *(Dublin 1836).*

The Royal Belfast Academical Institution, College Square, Belfast. Engraved by R. Clayton. From The Dublin Penny Journal, *vol. 1, 1832 (supplement).*

Down and Connor, the Bishop of Dromore, and more than 70 of the principal subscribers, including all who should subscribe and pay 20 guineas, with power to elect a president, vice-presidents, treasurer, secretary, managers, visitors, and auditors, of whom 21 should be competent to form a board, to transact all business relative to the institution, with license to take lands not exceeding £2500 per annum, and other privileges. The buildings were completed at an expense, including furniture and apparatus, of £28,954. 3. 8., leaving no provision for the endowment of professorships; for which object the managers applied to government, and in the year 1814 received from parliament a grant of £1500, which was continued during the years 1815 and 1816; after which it ceased till 1824, when it was renewed on the recommendation of the Commissioners of Education, and in the year 1834 was increased to £3500; of which sum £2000 was for additional buildings, and £1500 for general expenditure. The institution comprehends a collegiate and a school department, the former under the direction of seven professors of natural philosophy, moral philosophy, logic and the belles lettres, mathematics, Latin and Greek, Hebrew, and anatomy, respectively; there are also two professors of divinity, one appointed by the general Synod of Ulster, and the other by the Seceding Presbyterian Synod of Ireland. The professors were, in 1818, constituted a board of faculty for superintending the courses of instruction and discipline observed in the institution, as were also the masters of the school department for that branch of it. The collegiate department is conducted on a plan similar, in most respects, to that of the university of Glasgow; the session commences in November and ends in May, when public examinations take place; the mathematical class is generally very numerous, and is considered equal to any in the United Kingdom; the classical course is also extensive; the moral philosophy class has no prescribed course of reading, but lectures are given and examinations are held; the course of anatomy is pursued rather as a branch of general education than as a medical study, though admirably calculated as a first course for medical students, for whom it is in contemplation to establish a distinct class. The school department comprises the mercantile, English, classical, mathematical, Italian, French, and drawing schools, each superintended by a separate master. There are at present about 200 students in the collegiate, and 210 pupils in the school, department of the institution, to which is attached a good library, a museum, and a valuable philosophical apparatus. Nearly all the candidates for the Presbyterian ministry in Ireland are educated here; and the Synod of Ulster, and the Seceding Synod of Ireland, by whom the institution is cordially patronised, consider the general certificate of the faculty equivalent to the degree of M. A. in any of the Scottish universities, or to that of B. A. in Trinity College, Dublin, or either of the English universities: the total receipts of this establishment, for 1835, were £3646. 8. 5., and the expenditure was £3735. 19. 5. The number of children educated in the various charity and other free schools, excepting the Sunday schools, is about 2850, of whom 1480 are boys and 1370 girls; one on the Lancasterian plan was formerly a Sunday school, and was converted into a day school in the year 1811, when a spacious school-house of brick, with a residence for the master, was built at an expense of £2000, raised by lottery and by local sub-

scriptions; the school in Brown-street was established in the year 1812, under the patronage of the Marquess of Donegal, and a large and handsome brick building, with houses for the master and mistress adjoining, was erected by subscription, at an expense of £1500; the school in Donegal-street, which was the first in the North of Ireland, that placed itself in connection with the National Board, was founded in 1829, under the patronage of the Right Rev. Dr. Crolley, R. C. Bishop of Down and Connor, and two large school-houses were built adjoining the R. C. cathedral; and in the townland of Malone the late Marquess of Donegal, in 1765, built a very large school-house on the demesne of Willmount, and endowed it with the rent of an adjoining farm, now let for £40 per annum, which appears to have been originally a charter school, but is now open to all children of the neighbourhood, of whom those attending it are educated gratuitously, and supplied with books. The number of private schools is 74, in which are 3630 boys and 2820 girls.

The Incorporated Poor-house, for the reception of the aged and infirm poor, and the support of their children during infancy, was built at an expense of £7000, raised by a lottery and by public subscription, on an elevated site at the upper end of Donegal-street, granted in 1771 by the Marquess of Donegal; and the founders of this humane institution were incorporated by act of parliament in 1774, under the title of "the President and Assistants of the Belfast Charitable Society." The funds, which from the improvement in property are likely to increase, at present exceed £2500 per annum, arising from an annuity of £750 paid by the commissioners

scriptions; the school in Brown-street was established in the year 1812, under the patronage of the Marquess of Donegal, and a large and handsome brick building, with houses for the master and mistress adjoining, was erected by subscription, at an expense of £1500; the school in Donegal-street, which was the first in the North of Ireland, that placed itself in connection with the National Board, was founded in 1829, under the patronage of the Right Rev. Dr. Crolley, R. C. Bishop of Down and Connor, and two large school-houses were built adjoining the R. C. cathedral; and in the townland of Malone the late Marquess of Donegal, in 1765, built a very large school-house on the demesne of Willmount, and endowed it with the rent of an adjoining farm, now let for £40 per annum, which appears to have been originally a charter school, but is now open to all children of the neighbourhood, of whom those attending it are educated gratuitously, and supplied with books. The number of private schools is 74, in which are 3630 boys and 2820 girls.

The Incorporated Poor-house, for the reception of the aged and infirm poor, and the support of their children during infancy, was built at an expense of £7000, raised by a lottery and by public subscription, on an elevated site at the upper end of Donegal-street, granted in 1771 by the Marquess of Donegal; and the founders of this humane institution were incorporated by act of parliament in 1774, under the title of "the President and Assistants of the Belfast Charitable Society." The funds, which from the improvement in property are likely to increase, at present exceed £2500 per annum, arising from an annuity of £750 paid by the commissioners making up any deficiency in their earnings by donations of food and clothing; it assists poor housekeepers, relieves strangers and forwards them to their destination, supplies deserving mendicants with food and punishes the refractory, accommodates industrious families with small loans or occasional grants, and has diffused great benefit over this populous town, in which it has entirely abolished mendicity. The Fever Hospital was established in 1817, and a dispensary, instituted in 1792, has been incorporated with it : the buildings, situated in Frederick-street, are handsome and commodious, with a spacious area in front, and are adapted to the reception of 226 patients ; it is supported by donations, bequests, and subscriptions, also by fines levied by magistrates and grand jury presentments, of which the last alone amount to about £400 per annum, and its annual income is about £1000 : it is open to patients not only of the town, but from the county at large, of whom a great number are annually relieved. The Lying-in Hospital was originally established in Donegal-street, in 1794, but in 1830 removed to a more spacious and handsome building erected for it on the new road ; it is liberally supported by subscription. The Belfast District Lunatic Asylum, for the reception of pauper patients from the counties of Antrim and Down, and from the county of the town of Carrickfergus, was erected on an eminence one mile from the town, near the Falls road, in 1829, at an expense, including furniture and other contingencies, of £25,319. 13., defrayed by Government under an act of the 1st and 2nd of Geo. IV. : the buildings, which are handsome, were originally adapted for 104 patients, and consist of a centre comprising the house of the governor and the committee-rooms, and two wings, in which are eight corridors containing each thirteen cells for patients, and two others of smaller size containing six cells each, for those of more violent derangement ; each corridor has a day-room for the patients, and one also for the keeper : the grounds surrounding the house comprise an area of more than 21 acres, to which the patients have free access, and the whole is enclosed with a stone wall fourteen feet high, with a porter's lodge at the entrance : the males are employed in weaving linen and cotton, gardening, and cultivating the land ; and the females in spinning, knitting, and domestic occupations. The management of the asylum is vested in a committee appointed by the general board in Dublin ; the medical department is superintended by a physician, governor, and matron, assisted by 26 keepers and others : the annual expenditure, about £2000, is advanced by Government, but repaid by the grand juries of the respective counties. Many extraordinary cures have been effected, and upon an average nearly one-half of the patients have been restored to sanity by the skilful and humane system of treatment introduced and successfully practised by the governor. A savings' bank was established in 1816, for which a handsome edifice was erected in 1830, at an expense of £1400, raised from a fund which had accumulated from the gratuitous superintendence of the committee for the fourteen years preceding ; the amount of deposits at present is nearly £90,000. There are also several minor establishments for the benefit of the poor, among which may be noticed the female penitentiary ; the society for the relief of the destitute sick, established in 1826; the society for clothing the poor, in 1827 ; the society for discountenancing vice and promoting the Christian religion, also in 1827 ; the association for the protection of the rights of conscience, in 1830 ; the society for the religious improvement of the poor, also in 1830 ; a Bible society, tract societies, and a library of religious books for the use of the poor.

There are no remains of antiquity in the town, though some are scattered over the parish : near Stranmillis, on the Lagan, was an ancient chapel; called *Capella de Kilpatrick*; on the summit of a hill in Upper Malone was the *Capella de Crookmuck*; near Callender's Fort, on the Falls road, about two miles from the town, was that of *Cranock*, of which traces of the foundations and a large cemetery are still remaining ; and on the same road, the chapel of *Kilwee*, where numerous elegantly carved crosses and other sepulchral monuments have been found. About three miles on the Carrickfergus road is a small fragment of an ancient fortress, called Greencastle ; in Upper Malone was an extensive fort called Castle Cam, or Freeston Castle, on the site of which the elegant mansion of Malone House has been erected ; at a small distance on the left of the road to Shaw's-bridge are seen the foundations of a third fort ; in the grounds of Malone, near Lismoine, are the remains of a fourth ; and in the R. C. burial-ground at Friar's Bush are the remains of a fifth. Among the most curious relics of antiquity are the caves in various places formed in the earth and in the hard limestone rock ; of the former, three were discovered in 1792 at Wolf Hill, the largest of which is eight yards long and one yard wide, with four small chambers diverging from it ; on the side of a small hill in the townland of Ballymargy is one of larger dimensions, and in a more perfect state, with two entrances ; and near Hannahstown is one still larger, which since 1798 has been closed, having at that time been a place of concealment for arms. Three large caves, which give name to the mountain called Cave Hill, are all formed in the perpendicular face of an immense range of basaltic rock ; the lowest is 21 feet long, 18 wide, and from 7 to 10 feet in height ; above this is another, 10 feet long, 7 wide, and 6 in height ; and above that is a third, said to be divided into two unequal parts, each of which is more extensive than the largest of the other caves ; but the ascent is so dangerous that few venture to visit it. The large ramparts of earth, called raths, or forts, are also numerous : of these the most extensive is Mac Art's fort, on the summit of Cave hill, protected on one side by a precipice, and on the others by a single ditch of great depth and a vallum of large dimensions ; the enclosed area is nearly level, and, from the height of the mountain, which is 1140 feet, commands a view of vast extent, variety, and beauty, including the Isle of Man, the Shores and mountains of Scotland, and a large portion of the counties of Antrim, Down, Armagh, Derry, and Donegal. Near the base of Squires hill are many smaller raths, and two of large dimensions almost at the summit of the Black mountain ; and near the shore, at Fort William, is an encampment, 70 feet square, surrounded by a deep fosse and defended by a bastion at each angle, and said to have been thrown up by King William in 1690 ; near it is another intrenchment of ruder construction. There are two large cairns on the Black mountain, in one of which, in 1829, was found a large urn filled with calcined human bones, a spear head, and two ornaments of brass ; there is also a cairn on Cave hill, and one on Squires hill. Great numbers of stone and flint hatchets, and arrow heads of flint, have been discovered ; and brazen celts and querns, or hand mill-stones, are occasionally found.

Among the gentlemen's seats in the parish the most

The White Linen Hall, Donegall Square, Belfast. Drawn by Horatio Nelson and engraved by R. Clayton. From The Dublin Penny Journal, *vol. 1, 1832 (supplement).*

conspicuous for their elegance are Ardoyne, the residence of M. Andrews, Esq.; Ballydrain, of H. Montgomery, Esq.; Ballysillen, of J. F. Ferguson, Esq.; Beech Park, of Arbuthnot Emerson, Esq.; Beech Mount, of Lewis Reford, Esq.; Brookfield, of T. Tripp, Esq.; Cromac, of T. Garret, Esq.; Duncairn, of A. J. Macrorey, Esq.; the Falls, of J. Sinclaire, Esq.; Fortfield, of W. Johnson, Esq.; Fort-William, of G. Langtry, Esq.; Glenbank of T. Mackay, Esq.; Glennalena, of W. Orr, Esq.; Glenville, of Mrs. McCance; the Grove, of W. Simms, Esq.; Jennymount, of R. Thomson, Esq.; Larkfield, of Henderson Black, Esq.; Ligoneil, of A. Stewart, Esq.; Lismoine, of R. Callwell, Esq.; the Lodge, of J. Emerson Tennent, Esq., M.P. for Belfast; Low-Wood, of J. Thomson, Esq.; Malone House, of W. Wallace Legge, Esq.; Mount Collier, of A. Mulholland, Esq.; Mount Vernon, of Hill Hamilton, Esq.; New Forge, of J. Ferguson, Esq.; Park-Mount, of J. McNeile, Esq.; Old Park, of H. Lyons, Esq.; Sea-view, of J. Boomer, Esq.; Springfield, of J. Stevenson, Esq.; Strandmillis, of G. Black, Esq.; Suffolk, of W. McCance, Esq,; Wheatfield, of J. Blair, Esq.; Willmount, of J. Stewart, Esq.; Wolf Hill, of Mrs. Thompson; Woodburn, of M. Charley, Esq.; Finaghy, of J. Charley, Esq.; and Strigoniel, of J. Steen, jun., Esq. The mineral productions are coal, iron, manganese, marble, limestone, freestone, gypsum, and fullers' earth, of which only the limestone is worked; the coal seams are seen in the Collin and Dunmurry water, and under the lands of Willmount, near which place also, and at New Forge, is the iron; the manganese, at the foot of the Black mountain, near which is a fine stratum of grey marble; and the gypsum, in the Collin and Forth water. Among the eminent natives of this place may be noticed, Dr. Black, the celebrated chymist; the Rev. T. Romney Robinson, author of an able mathematical work, and principal astronomer in the observatory at Armagh; J. Templeton, Esq., who left in manuscript the Botany and Natural History of Ireland, now in preparation for the press by his son; and J. Emerson Tennent, Esq., author of the History of Modern Greece, &c. Among the distinguished persons who have resided here may be mentioned the late Dr. R. Tennent, the philanthropist; Dr. Abernethy, author of the Attributes; Edward Bunting, a celebrated professor of music and collector of the ancient melodies of Ireland; Dr. J. L. Drummond, author of various scientific treatises and botanical works; Dr. Bruce, author of a life of Homer and other works; and Dr. W. H. Drummond, author of various poetical, religious, and political works. Belfast gives the titles of Earl and Baron to the ancient family of Chichester, Marquesses of Donegal.

BILLY, a parish, partly in the barony of CAREY, but chiefly in that of LOWER DUNLUCE, county of ANTRIM, and province of ULSTER; containing, with the post-town of Bushmills, 5845 inhabitants. This parish is bounded on the west by the river Bush, and on the south-east by the sea; it is also intersected for nearly three miles by the road from Ballymoney, through Bushmills, to the Giants' Causeway, which is within its limits. Including eight townlands which now form part of the parish of Dunseverick, it comprises, according to the Ordnance survey, 17,329¾ statute acres, of which 16,860 are applotted under the tithe act, and valued at £8139 per annum. The land is generally in a good state of cultivation; the system of agriculture is considerably advanced, and is still improving; there is very little waste land, except moss and bog, which together form nearly one-third of the surface. Whinstone abounds, and is quarried for building and for the roads; limestone is found in great quantity and occasionally burned for manure, and wood-coal is obtained near the Causeway. Among the principal seats are Bushmills House, the residence of Sir F. W. Macnaghten, Bart.; Ballylough, of W. Trail, Esq.; Ballydivity, of J. Stewart Moore, Esq.; Black Rock House, the property of Miss Wray, and now in the occupation of Hugh Lecky, Esq.; and Bentfield, formerly the residence of Col. Wray, but at present uninhabited. There are some weirs on the river Bush, near its influx into the sea, for taking salmon, of which great quantities are sent to Liverpool and London. A market on Tuesday, and five fairs are held at Bushmills (which see); and on the day after Dervock fair, which is generally on Aug. 12th (except that day falls on the Saturday or Sunday, on which occasions it is held on the Monday following), a pleasure fair, called the Causeway fair, is held at the Rock Head, above the Giants' Causeway, and is numerously attended by persons for many miles round, for whose accommodation tents are pitched. This parish was formerly the head of a union, which comprised also the parishes of Armoy, Ballyclug, Donegore, and Kilbride, together forming the corps of the archdeaconry of Connor; but by the act of the 5th of Geo. IV., obtained by Dr. Mant, the union has been dissolved, the parishes disappropriated from the archdeaconry, and the rectorial tithes annexed to their respective vicarages, with the exception only of this parish, of which the rectory and vicarage alone now constitute the corps of the archdeaconry, with the cure of souls, the former archdeacons having no cure of souls: it is in the diocese of Connor, and patronage of the Bishop. The late Archdeacon Trail, then rector of this parish, in 1830, separated nine townlands from it, giving the tithes of four; and his brother, the Rev. Robt. Trail, rector of Ballintoy, seven townlands from that parish, giving the tithes of three, for the formation and endowment of the perpetual curacy of Dunseverick, the patronage of which is vested alternately in the respective incumbents: the new church is a very neat building in a central situation. The tithes of the parish amount to £489. 4. 7½., of which £37. 9. 3. is paid to the perpetual curate, and the remainder to the archdeacon. The church, a plain substantial building, was erected on the site of a former structure, by aid of a gift of £800 and a loan of £500, in 1815, from the late Board of First Fruits. The glebe-house was built in 1810, by the Rev. T. Babington, vicar, aided by a gift of £350 and a loan of £450 from the same Board. In the R. C. divi-sions it forms part of the union or district of Coleraine. There are two meeting houses for Presbyterians in connection with the Synod of Ulster, one of which is of the third class, and there are places of worship for Seceders, Covenanters, and Wesleyan Methodists. At Eagry is a school under the trustees of Erasmus Smith's charity, for which a good school-house has been erected, with a residence for the master, who has two acres of land; a school is held in a house hired for that purpose at Bushmills, and is supported by subscription; there is a parochial school for girls, for which a house was built, in 1832, by William Trail, Esq.; also schools at Moycraig, Carnbore, Straidbilly, and Dromiarran, and another is held in the Methodist meeting-house at Castle-Cat, which was endowed with £20 by the late Dr. Adam Clarke. The Rev. Archdeacon Trail, in 1831, bequeathed £50 for the use of the poor of the parish, which has been invested in Government securities, and the interest is annually distributed by his son, W. Trail, Esq. There are some remains of the ancient castle of Ballylough, which was of much importance; the lake on which it was situated has been drained, and is now under cultivation.

The GIANTS' CAUSEWAY, probably the most extensive and curious assemblage of basaltic columns in the world, is situated between Port-na-Grange and Port Noffer, in N. Lat. 55° 20′ and W. Lon. 6° 50′; and derives its name from a popular tradition that it was erected by giants, as the commencement of a causeway across the ocean to Scotland. This very interesting natural curiosity forms part of a large promontory, of which Bengore Head, about a mile distant, is the most northern point in Ireland. The only access to it by land is down a winding path, cut at the expense of the late Earl of Bristol, while Bishop of Derry, on the western side of a verdant headland called Aird Snout, to two detached hills called the Stookans, whence the first view of this stupendous work of nature is obtained. This view is one of the most magnificent imaginable, embracing an immense bay broken with capes and headlands, rising abruptly to the height of 400 feet above the level of the sea, and consisting of lofty colonnades of the most symmetrically-formed basaltic pillars, inserted in the cliffs like artificial supporters, standing in groups like gigantic honeycombs, or scattered in pleasing disorder like the ruins of a city of temples and palaces. From the Stookans the road leads to the base of the causeway, which extends in a northerly direction from the promontory into the sea. This splendid natural pier is somewhat triangular in form; the base beneath the cliff being 135, the eastern side 220, and the western 300, yards long; while the breadth in the centre is about 60. The view of the causeway from the footpath suggests the idea of an immense unfinished embankment, forming an inclined plane, in some places rising by successive steps, in others presenting a nearly level pavement, formed by the tops of the closely united columns, with some chasms exhibiting the admirable arrangement of this wonderful structure. The causeway is divided into three unequal parts. The little, or western, causeway is 386 feet long, but only 16 high, and is separated from the central compartment by an enormous whin dyke, extending from the cliff to the sea. The middle section, which is the shortest, contains a magnificent group of lofty pillars, called "the honeycomb," and is also bounded on the east by a whin dyke. Beyond this is the grand causeway, which is 706 feet long by 109 wide in the middle: in that part of this compartment which is called "the

The Giant's Causeway. Drawn by T. M. Baynes and engraved by W. Le Petit. From G. N. Wright, Ireland illustrated *(London, 1831).*

loom " it attains an elevation of 34 feet, from which it diminishes in height gradually as it approaches the sea, into which it enters for some distance beyond low water mark. In the western and central compartments all the columns are perpendicular, but in the grand causeway they are vertical towards the east, inclining eastward as they approach the sea, and westward near the base of the cliff. The three divisions of the causeway comprise 37,426 distinct and perfect columns, besides many that are broken and scattered about in its vicinity. The columns consist of prisms of equal dimensions through their whole height, which ranges from 15 to 36 feet, with diameters of from 15 to 28 inches, and varying in their number of sides from 3 to 9, although the greater number are pentagons and hexagons. Each of the pillars is perfectly distinct, and almost invariably differs in size, number of sides, and points of articulation from the adjacent columns, to which, however, it is so close that not even water can pass between them. Almost every column is composed of several pieces, the joints of which are articulated with the greatest exactness, and in a strictly horizontal direction. Generally the upper part of the section is concave and the lower convex, but this arrangement is sometimes reversed. The cavity or socket is perfectly circular, from two to four inches deep, and in a few instances its rim is divided, covers two or three articulations, and terminates in sharp points. In a few of the columns no joints are visible; in some, three, four, or more may be traced; and, in "the loom," columns are found which are divisible into as many as 38 pieces. The basalt of which these columns is composed is of a very dark colour, approaching to black; its weight is three times as great as that of water; and of 100 of its constituent parts,

50 are silicious earth, 25 iron, 15 argillaceous earth, and 10 calcareous earth and magnesia. About 300 yards east of the causeway is the Giants' Organ, about 120 feet long, consisting of 60 columns, of which those in the centre are 40 feet high, but those on the sides are lower. At the eastern extremity of Port Noffer are four lofty and massive basaltic columns, rising to the height of 315 feet; they are hexagonal and jointed, and from their height and isolated position are called the Chimney Tops. Near these is the Theatre, consisting of three distinct colonnades, the successive tiers of which are separated by horizontal strata of amorphous basalt, red and grey ochre, and fossil coal, the alternations of which with the columnar basalt produce a very extraordinary and pleasing appearance. A little eastward of Port-na-Spagna is a perpendicular cliff, 326 feet high, composed of alternate layers of columnar and horizontal basalt, arranged with surprising regularity; but the most picturesque cliff is Pleaskin, which rises from the sea in a gentle acclivity for more than 300 feet, and then ascends perpendicularly 70 feet more to its summit. This beautiful headland is 382 feet in height, and strikingly exhibits the geological formation of this district, as it consists of numerous clearly distinguishable strata, which rise above each other in the following order; at the base is a bright red ochreous rock, on which are placed tabular basalt, grey ochreous rock, amorphous basalt, clear red basalt, irregular basalt with cracks, iron ore, imperfectly formed basaltic pillars, argillaceous rock, fossil coal, and the lower range of basaltic columns, which is 45 feet high. Imposed on this colonnade are grey rock containing nodules of iron, slightly columnar basalt, grey ochreous rock, amorphous basalt, and then the upper range of basaltic pillars,

43

which forms a magnificent colonnade 64 feet high, and has broken basalt for a superstratum, above which is vegetable mould covered with green sod. This splendid headland, which is unrivalled for beauty of arrangement and variety of colouring, is seen to most advantage from the sea, from which also some of the grandest views of the causeway and its adjacent scenery are obtained. Fossil wood, as black and compact as coal, and fossil oysters and muscles are found in the limestone rock that forms the substratum of the causeway and its neighbouring promontories; and large opals, chalcedony, agates, &c., are collected here. Specimens of these fossils and minerals, and a wooden model of the causeway, are in the museum of Trinity College, Dublin.

BROUGHSHANE, a market and post-town, in the parish of RACAVAN, barony of LOWER ANTRIM, county of ANTRIM, and province of ULSTER, 28¾ miles (N. N. W.) from Belfast, and 109 miles (N.) from Dublin; containing 828 inhabitants. This town is pleasantly situated on the river Braid, at the termination of the mail coach road from Ballymena, to which it has a sub-post-office, and consists of one long street, containing about 180 houses indifferently built. In the neighbourhood are several gentlemen's seats; and at no great distance is Tullymore Lodge, finely situated on a stream tributary to the Braid. The market is on Tuesday, and is principally for butter and pork: fairs are held on June 17th and Sept. 3rd. A constabulary police force has been stationed here; and the manorial court of Buckna is held here every month, for the recovery of debts amounting to £20. The church of the union of Skerry, or the Braid, a neat edifice with a spire, is situated in the town; in which are also a place of worship for Presbyterians in connection with the Synod of Ulster, and a dispensary. At Dumfare, in the vicinity, is a large mount of very imposing aspect.—See RACAVAN.

BUSHMILLS, a market and post-town, in that part of the parish of BILLY which is in the barony of CAREY, county of ANTRIM, and province of ULSTER, 6¼ miles (N. E. by N.) from Coleraine, and 125½ (N.) from Dublin; containing 108 houses and 507 inhabitants. This place is pleasantly situated near the mouth of the river Bush, from which it derives its name: it is neatly built, and is the general place of resort for parties visiting the Giant's Causeway, about two miles distant, for whose accommodation a large and handsome hotel has been erected by Sir F. W. Macnaghten, Bart., who, in 1827, established a weekly market here. A distillery is carried on, and is much celebrated for the quality of its whiskey, of which about 12,000 gallons are annually made and principally sent to England, Scotland, the West Indies, and America. There is a manufactory of spades, shovels, scythes, and sickles upon the river Bush; extensive paper-mills have been erected by F. D. Ward, Esq., for the supply of the home and Scottish markets, and near them are mills for flour and for dressing flax. The market is on Tuesday, and is well supplied with grain, linen yarn, pork, and provisions of all kinds; and fairs are held on Jan. 28th, March 28th, June 28th, July 21st, Oct. 21st, and Dec. 12th. Here is a constabulary police station; and the petty sessions for the district are held every fortnight. The court-house, a large and handsome building, recently erected by Sir F. W. Macnaghten, contains also apartments for the police, and some cells for the confinement of prisoners. The parish church of Dunluce is situated

in the town; and there are also a place of worship for Presbyterians in connection with the Synod of Ulster, and one for Methodists. A school has been established by the trustees of Erasmus Smith's charity, for the instruction of the children of parishioners, the master of which has a good house and two acres of land; there are also several schools in various parts of the parish. In the immediate neighbourhood is Bushmills House, the seat of Sir F. W. Macnaghten, Bart., who has made numerous improvements on his estate: the mansion is at present being rebuilt in a very splendid style, and with the grounds will form an interesting ornament to the place. In the bed of the river, near the bridge, are some small but beautiful basaltic columns fantastically curved.

C

CAMLIN, or CRUMLIN, a parish, in the barony of UPPER MASSAREENE, county of ANTRIM, and province of ULSTER; containing, with the post-town of Crumlin, 1274 inhabitants. This parish is situated on Lough Neagh, by which it is bounded on the west, and on the road from Antrim to Lurgan; it comprises, according to the Ordnance survey, 6417¼ statute acres, of which 5455 are applotted under the tithe act, and 708¼ form part of the lake. About three-fourths of the parish are good arable land, and the remainder is pasture. The system of agriculture is greatly improved, and the whole of the parish is in an excellent state of cultivation, and is well fenced, drained, and planted: wheat, which was scarcely raised in the district, has, since the establishment of large flour-mills at Crumlin, been extensively cultivated, and now forms the principal feature in its agriculture. Limestone is extensively quarried for agricultural and other purposes. The principal seats are Thistleborough, that of James Whittle, Esq.; Gobrana, of J. Whitla, Esq.; and Cherry Valley, of C. W. Armstrong, Esq. Independently of agricultural pursuits, several hundreds of the population are employed in weaving linens and cottons for the manufacturers of Belfast and its neighbourhood; here are also a flax and a flour-mill. Fairs are held monthly for cattle and pigs, and of late very valuable horses have been sold. It is a vicarage, in the diocese of Connor, and is part of the union of Glenavy; the rectory is impropriate in the Marquess of Hertford. The tithes amount to £195, of which £43. 5. is payable to the impropriator, and £151. 15. to the incumbent. The church is a fine ruin; it was destroyed by the army of Jas. II., who had its depôt here in 1689: in the north and south walls are series of sepulchral arches continued the entire length of the building, and nearly in a perfect state. In the R. C. divisions also it forms part of the union or district of Glenavy. There is a place of worship for Presbyterians in connection with the Remonstrant Synod, of the second class. The parochial school is supported by the vicar; and a school is supported by the Hon. Col. Pakenham, who erected for it a large and handsome school-house, and occasionally provides clothing for the scholars. In these schools are about 90 boys and 60 girls; and there are also three pay schools, in which are about 60 boys and 50 girls, and three Sunday schools. Dr. William Crawford, author of " Remarks on Chesterfield's Letters," " History of Ireland," and other works; and Adam Crawford, Esq., M.D., author of an " Experimental Essay on Animal Heat," and compiler of the transactions of the Royal Society, were natives of Crumlin, *which see.*

CARMAVY, a grange, in the parish of KILLEAD, barony of LOWER MASSAREENE, county of ANTRIM, and province of ULSTER, 6 miles (S. E.) from Antrim; the population is returned with the parish. This grange is situated upon the road from Belfast to Antrim: and comprises, according to the Ordnance survey, 789¼ statute acres.

CARNCASTLE, or CASTLE-CAIRN, a parish, in the barony of UPPER GLENARM, county of ANTRIM, and province of ULSTER, 3 miles (N. W. by N.) from Larne; containing 2167 inhabitants. This parish is situated on the shore of the North channel, which forms its eastern boundary, and upon the road from Larne to Glenarm, and the royal military road from Belfast to the Giant's Causeway; it contains, according to the Ordnance survey, 9725 statute acres, and is in an excellent state of cultivation. The soil is very fertile, producing excellent crops: there are only 15 acres of bog. Basalt is quarried for building and repairing the roads; limestone is abundant, and coal is known to exist in great quantities. At Ballygally is a coast-guard station, which is one of eight that are included in the district of Carrickfergus. About five miles from the coast are the Hulin or Maiden rocks, two of which are always visible above water. On these lighthouses have been built by the corporation for the improvement of the port of Dublin, which are called the North and South Maiden Rock Lights, and are 1920 feet apart. The northern light is 84 feet above high water level, and the southern, 94 feet; both are fixed and bright lights.

The living is a rectory and perpetual curacy, in the diocese of Connor, of which the rectory was united, by charter of the 7th of Jas. I., to the rectories of Kilwaughter, Ballycor, Rashee, and Derrykeighan, together constituting the corps of the prebend of Carncastle in the cathedral church of St. Saviour, Connor, and in the patronage of the Bishop; the perpetual curacy is in the gift of the rector. The tithes of the parish amount to £174. 4. 6., and the gross value of the tithes and glebe of the union is £751. 5. 4. per annum, of which £55 is paid by the prebendary to the perpetual curate, whose stipend is augmented to £96 per ann. out of Primate Boulter's fund. The church, a small plain edifice with a lofty spire, was built on the site of a former church, by aid of a loan of £350, granted in 1815 by the late Board of First Fruits; and a house was purchased for a glebe-house with a gift of £450, and a loan of £50, from the same Board: the glebe comprises five acres. In the R. C. divisions this parish forms part of the union or district of Larne and Carrickfergus; the chapel is a small building. There are two places of worship for Presbyterians, one connected with the Synod of Ulster, of the third class; the other connected with the Remonstrant Synod, of the second class. Near the church is the parochial school, endowed with £3 per annum by the late Mr. Wilson; a school of 43 boys and 9 girls is in connection with the National Board; and there are a private school of 12 boys and 25 girls, and two Sunday schools. On an insulated rock in the sea are the remains of Ballygally or Cairn castle, from which the parish takes its name. There are also some remains of the ancient manor-house, built in 1625, in

the Elizabethan style; and of an old church. In the parish are a curious perforation in a mass of basalt, called the Black Cave, and a very pure vein of feldspar, capable of being worked to advantage.

CARNLOUGH, or CARNALLOCK, a maritime village, in the parish of ARDCLINIS, barony of LOWER GLENARM, county of ANTRIM, and province of ULSTER, 2¾ miles (N. by W.) from Glenarm; containing 213 inhabitants. This place, originally a small fishing village, is pleasantly and advantageously situated between the bays of Cushendall and Glenarm, and from the fineness of its strand is much frequented during the summer months for sea-bathing. It consists of 47 houses, and many elegant villas and sea-bathing lodges have been erected in the valley of Glencule, forming an interesting and highly ornamental feature in that secluded vale. The surrounding scenery possesses great natural beauty, and in some parts assumes a character of majestic grandeur. A very extensive deer park, forming part of the demesne of Glenarm castle, and some richly wooded tracts and thriving plantations add greatly to its beauty. The bay of Carnlough is small but very commodious; and a quay for shipping, erected at an expense of £1200 by the late P. Gibbons, Esq., will contribute greatly to promote the prosperity of the place.—See ARDCLINIS.

CARNMONEY, a parish, in the barony of LOWER BELFAST, county of ANTRIM, and province of ULSTER, 3 miles (N. by E.) from Belfast; containing 5423 inhabitants. This place was anciently called *Coole*, and according to tradition there was a town of that name of considerable extent near the present church, on the decay of which the parish took its modern name from an adjoining hill with a large cairn on its summit. It is situated on Carrickfergus bay, and on the road from Belfast to Londonderry; and, according to the Ordnance survey, comprises 8937¼ statute acres, of which about 230 are too mountainous to be cultivated, and the remainder is arable or pasture land, excepting about 70 acres of bog. The land is generally in a high state of cultivation, especially near the shore, where several gentlemen, who are practical agriculturists, till their own estates, and their improved methods are almost generally followed by the farmers. Great quantities of limestone are raised in the parish, and are shipped to Scotland and other places. The village of Whitehouse (*which see*) has considerable manufactures: there are a cotton and flax-spinning manufactory, and extensive works for printing cloths, which are made here exclusively for the Manchester market; and at White Abbey also is a cotton and flax-spinning manufactory. These establishments together employ about 670 persons. The scenery is embellished with several gentlemen's seats, the principal of which are Merville, the residence of J. Rowan, Esq.; Macedon, of J. Cunningham, Esq.; White Abbey, of — Getty, Esq.; Claremont, of Mrs. Clewlow; Abbey Lands, of H. M'Calmont, Esq.; Whitehouse, of — Shaw, Esq.; and the glebe-house, of the Rev. S. Smythe, the vicar.

The living is a vicarage, in the diocese of Connor, united, it is supposed in 1614, to the vicarage of Ballylinney and the rectory of Ballymartin, together constituting the union of Carmoney, in the patronage of the Marquess of Donegal, in whom the rectory is impropriate. The vicarial tithes amount to £210; and according to the report of the Ecclesiastical Commissioners, the gross value of the union, including tithes and glebe, is

£575 per annum. The rectorial tithes were placed under composition in 1835. The church, a modern and spacious edifice in good repair, is built on an eminence near the site of a former church, and is intended for the three parishes of the union. The glebe-house is a handsome building, erected by aid of a gift of £300 and a loan of £500 from the late Board of First Fruits, in 1814: the glebe comprises 80 statute acres, valued at £115 per annum. In the R. C. divisions the parish forms part of the union or district of Belfast. There are two meeting-houses for Presbyterians in connection with the Synod of Ulster, of the first and second classes: charitable bequests to the amount of £260 have been left, the interest of which is divided annually among poor Presbyterians. There are also places of worship for Covenanters, or members of the Reformed Synod, and Independents. Near the church is the parochial school, principally supported by the vicar. A very large school-house was built at Whitehouse by the Messrs. Grimshaw, and the school is now in connection with the National Board; one has also been built and is supported by the proprietors of the White Abbey cotton works; the Presbyterians have built and support a school at Ballyduff; and there is also a school at Ballycraigy, built and supported by Francis Turnley, Esq. About 400 children receive education in these schools, and about 200 more in private schools. About a mile north from the church, near the shore, are the picturesque ruins of a large religious house, called White Abbey, from which the townland takes its name, and which was probably the original establishment that was removed to Woodburn: the principal remains are an elegant chapel, in the later Norman or early English style. On the verge of the parish, near Carrickfergus, are the remains of another religious house, called Monkstown, adjoining which is an ancient cemetery, where, according to tradition, Fergus, King of Scotland, who was shipwrecked in the adjacent bay, was interred.

Arms.

CARRICKFERGUS, a sea-port, borough, market- and post-town, and parish, and a county of itself, locally in the county of ANTRIM, of which it was the ancient capital and is still the county town, 88 miles (N.) from Dublin; containing 8706 inhabitants. This place, which is of great antiquity, is by some writers identified with the ancient *Dun-Sobarky* or *Dun-Sobairchia*, according to Dr. Charles O'Conor from a prince named Sobairchius, who made it his residence; but the correctness of this supposition is doubted by others. It is thought to have derived its present name, signifying. "The Rock of Fergus," early in the 4th century, from Fergus Mac Erch, a chieftain of Dalaradia, who established the first Irish settlement on the opposite coast of Caledonia. An ancient triad quoted by Dr. O'Conor records that St. Patrick blessed a tower or strong hold of the Dalaradians, in which was a well of miraculous efficacy, called *Tipra Phadruic*, "The well of St. Patrick." It is uncertain at what period the castle was originally erected; the present structure, from the style of its architecture, was evidently built soon after the arrival of the English. John, Earl of Morton and Lord of Ireland, was here in the lifetime of his father, Hen. II. (from whom John De Courcy received the

grant of all the lands he might conquer in Ulster); and his despatch to the king, dated at Carrickfergus, in which he mentions his having taken the castle, is still extant among the MSS. in the library of Trinity College, Dublin, and is written in Latin. This castle, with subsequent additions, is still remaining, and is justly considered one of the noblest fortresses of that time now existing in Ireland. De Courcy having fallen into disgrace with the succeeding English monarchs, his castles and possessions in this county fell into the hands of the De Lacy family, who, becoming tyrannical and oppressive, incurred the anger of King John. During the contentions which arose among the English settlers, after they had established themselves in the country, this place suffered so much that Hugh de Lacy the younger, who, on the restoration of his family to the royal favour, repaired the town and strengthened it by the introduction of new settlers, has even been regarded as its founder. In 1234 Carrickfergus is mentioned as one of the haven towns of Ulster; but from that period till shortly after the commencement of the 14th century, little of its history is known. The De Lacys, again becoming obnoxious to the English monarch, and the Lord-Justice Mortimer being sent against them with a considerable force, they made their escape into Scotland, and invited Edward Bruce, the brother of the Scottish monarch, to invade the country, and become their king. Accordingly, in 1315, Bruce embarked 6000 men at Ayr, and, accompanied by the De Lacys and several of the Scottish nobility, landed at Wolderfirth, now Olderfleet, where, being joined by numbers of the Irish chieftains, he routed Richard de Burgo, now Earl of Ulster, who had been sent against him; and having slain several of the English nobles and taken many of them prisoners, advanced to lay siege to the castle of this place. During the siege, Thomas, Lord Mandeville, who commanded the garrison, made a sally on the assailants, whom he repulsed at the first onset; but, being recognised by the richness of his armour, he was felled to the ground by the blow of a battle-axe and instantly killed. The garrison, disheartened by the loss of their commander, agreed to surrender the castle within a limited time, and on the appointed day, 30 of the Scottish forces advancing to take possession, were seized as prisoners, the garrison declaring that they would defend the place to the last; but for want of provisions they were soon obliged to surrender. Bruce, having secured Carrickfergus, advanced to Dublin, and arrived at Castleknock, within four miles of the city; but finding the citizens prepared for his reception, he entered the county of Kildare, and advanced towards Limerick, laying waste the country with fire and sword; on his retreating towards the north, he was attacked near Dundalk by Sir John Bermingham, who defeated the Scottish forces and killed their leader. King Robert Bruce arrived soon after with a strong reinforcement, but on learning the fate of his brother, returned to his own dominions, and thus terminated an enterprise which had thrown the country into a state of unprecedented desolation.

After the evacuation of the country by the Scots, Carrickfergus again reverted to its former possessors; but the desultory warfare carried on at intervals for successive ages in the north of Ireland, during which its strength and situation rendered it the centre of operations, subjected it to many severe calamities. In 1333, William, Earl of Ulster, was assassinated here by his own servants; and his countess, with her infant daughter, fleeing into England, the O'Nials, the original

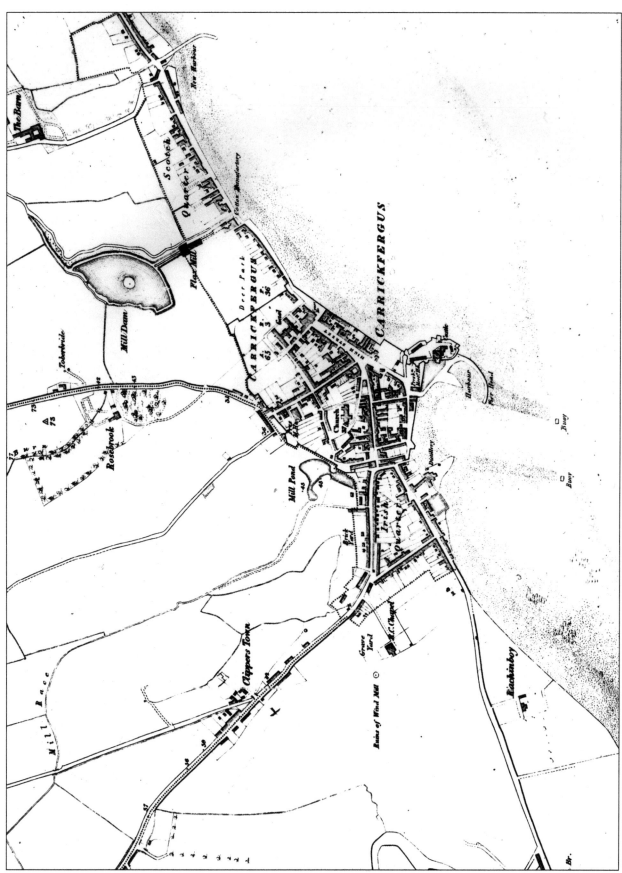

Carrickfergus. Part of 6 inch O.S. map of Co. Antrim, sheet 52, published 1834 (reproduced at 140%).

47

Carrickfergus Castle. Drawn by T. M. Baynes and engraved by W. Miller. From G. N. Wright, Ireland illustrated *(London, 1831).*

lords of the soil, immediately succeeded in expelling the English settlers, and for a time retained possession of the place. In 1386 the town was burned by the Scots; and in 1400 it was again destroyed by the combined forces of the Scots and Irish. In 1481 a commission was granted to the mayor and others, to enter into a league with the Earl of Ross, Lord of the Isles, who had usurped the sovereignty of the Hebrides from the Scottish crown. In 1497 the town and neighbourhood were visited by famine; and in 1504 it was resolved that none but an Englishman should be entrusted with the custody of its castle, or with that of Green Castle, in the county of Down. The town continued for many years to be a strong hold of the English, and even when the English Government was so reduced as to be scarcely able to maintain a standing army of 140 horse within the English pale, the castle still remained in their possession. In 1573 the corporation addressed a remonstrance to the Lord-Deputy Fitzwilliam, representing that one-third of the town was then in ruins; and, in the summer of the same year, it was still further desolated by fire. In this state it remained for many years, though the Earl of Essex landed here with his train, on taking possession of the government of Ulster, to which he had been appointed; and though Sir Henry Sidney, the succeeding lord-deputy, gave the English council a forcible representation of its deplorable condition, in the account of his northern expedition, two years afterwards. The particular events by which it was reduced to this state of desolation are detailed in a "Discourse of Knockfergus," preserved among the Cottonian manuscripts in the British Museum, in which its calamities are ascribed to an early quarrel with Bryan Balloughe, chieftain of the adjoining territory of Claneboy, whose

son and successor continued to harass the inhabitants till they were compelled to purchase peace by consenting to pay an annual tribute; to the repeated devastating incursions of the Scots; to the continued depredations of the O'Nials and Mac Donnels, and to various other causes. The Lord-Deputy, Sir Henry Sidney, made great efforts for the improvement and security of the town, but so greatly were the resources of the townsmen reduced that, in 1581, Lord Grey, then deputy, found it necessary to issue an express edict prohibiting them from paying to the Irish lord of the country the tribute hitherto paid to the successors of Bryan Balloughe, and called, in that document, "Breyne Balaf's Eric."

The extensive privileges enjoyed by the inhabitants of this place, and the protection afforded by new fortifications, soon caused an increase in its population and importance. On the breaking out of the war in 1641, Sir Henry Mac Neill was to have surprised the town, but was defeated by the vigilance of Col. Arthur Chichester, the governor; and it now became one of the principal places of refuge for the Protestants of the neighbouring counties. In 1642, the town and castle were, according to agreement, delivered up to General Monroe, who, having landed with 2500 Scottish auxiliaries, to carry on the war against the Irish, made this place his head-quarters till 1648, when he was taken by surprise in the castle, and sent prisoner to England by General Monk, who was, by the parliament, appointed governor in his place, and rewarded with a gratuity of £500; and in the year following, the castle, which had been surrendered to the Earl of Inchiquin, was reduced for Cromwell by Sir Charles Coote. In 1666, the garrison mutinied, seized the castle and the town, and acted with such desperate resolution that the Government, alarmed at their excesses, sent the Earl of Arran, son of the Duke of Ormonde, by sea, to reduce them; and the latter nobleman marching also against them with the few forces on whose fidelity he could rely, the mutineers, after some resistance, surrendered; 110 of them were tried by a court martial, of whom nine were executed, and the companies to which they belonged were disbanded. In the early part of 1689, an attempt was made by the Protestant inhabitants of the neighbourhood to take this fortress, which was then held by the troops of James II., but without success; in the course of the year, however, Schomberg, William's general, invested it with a large force, and the garrison, after having exhausted all their ammunition, surrendered. In 1690 William III. landed here to take the command of his army; and from this time the town was undistinguished by any historical event till the year 1760, when it was attacked by the French, under the command of Thurot. The gates were quickly closed, and though General Flobert, who led the assault, was wounded, the garrison, consisting only of one hundred men, was soon obliged to capitulate for want of ammunition. The country people, however, supported by reinforcements from the interior, rose on all sides to repel the assailants; and on the approach of an English squadron, which had been despatched on the first intelligence of the projected invasion, the French, after supplying themselves with provisions and water, hastily re-embarked, taking with them three of the principal inhabitants, who were afterwards found on board the commander's ship, when she struck to the English off the Isle of Man. In 1778, the celebrated Paul Jones appeared off the town, but did not land, contenting himself with the capture of an armed vessel that had been sent to attack him. In 1785, His present Majesty, when lieutenant on board the ship of Commodore Gower, arrived in the bay; on which occasion the Carrickfergus volunteers solicited the honour of forming a body guard for his Royal Highness, which was courteously declined.

The town is situated on the north-western shore of Carrickfergus bay, or Belfast Lough, along which it extends for nearly a mile, comprising three portions, the town within the walls, and two suburbs, called respectively the Irish and the Scottish quarters; the former situated to the west, along the road leading to Belfast; and the latter to the north-east, along the road to Larne and Island Magee, and inhabited by the descendants of a colony of fishermen from Argyle and Galloway, who took refuge here from the persecutions of 1665. The town within the walls was formerly entered by four gates, of which only the remains of the North or Spittal gate now exist; of the walls there is yet a considerable portion on the north and west sides in a very perfect state. The town contains about 800 houses, built chiefly of stone and roofed with slate; several of superior character have been built within the last forty years, during which period considerable improvements have taken place. The castle, which is in good preservation, and during the disturbances of 1798 was used as a state prison, is situated on a rock projecting boldly into the sea, by which it is surrounded on three sides at high water; this rock is 30 feet in height at its southern extremity, and declines considerably towards the land; the outer walls of the castle are adapted to the irregularities of its surface; and the entrance is defended by two semicircular towers, with a portcullis and machicolation above. In the interior are barracks for the

reception of two companies of foot and a few artillerymen. The keep is a square tower 90 feet high, the lower part of which is bomb-proof, and is used as a magazine: in the third story is an apartment 40 feet long, 38 feet wide, and 26 feet high, called Fergus's dining-room. The well in this tower, anciently celebrated for its miraculous efficacy, is now nearly filled up; a quantity of old iron was taken out of it many years since, from which it may have derived its medicinal properties. The castle was formerly governed by a constable, who had very extensive powers; the present establishment consists only of a governor and a mastergunner. Musical societies formerly existed and occasional assemblies were held in the town, but the only source of public amusement at present is a sporting club. Though formerly celebrated for its trade and commerce, this place has never been distinguished for the extent of its manufactures: the linen manufacture, which was the staple, has, within the last fifty years, been superseded by that of cotton, for which there are at present two spinning factories; and many persons are engaged in weaving checks, ginghams, and other cotton goods for the manufacturers of Belfast and Glasgow. There are also two mills for spinning linen yarn, and an extensive distillery, producing annually about 90,000 gallons of whiskey, with mills, malt-kilns, and other conveniences on an improved system; the tanning of leather, which was introduced here at an early period, is still carried on to a great extent. The vicinity affords numerous advantageous sites for the establishment of manufactories: a considerable water power is supplied by the Woodburn and Sulla-tober rivers, and by the water of Lough Morne; there are 1070 feet of waterfalls, calculated at 676-horse power, of which by far the greater part is unoccupied.

The fishery in the bay constitutes the chief employment of the poorer inhabitants of the suburbs, and the boats fitted out from the two quarters differ in their construction and the mode of working them: those from the Irish quarter, of which there are about seven or eight, with four men each, are smack-rigged and work by trawling or dredging; the fish generally taken is plaice, but skate, sole, and lythe or pollock are occasionally caught, and lobsters and oysters of very large size and good flavour are also dredged. The boats from the Scottish quarter are small and without decks, of not more than two or three tons' burden, rigged with a fore and main lug sail, and are occasionally worked with oars to the number of six in winter and four in summer: in the latter season from 16 to 20 boats, carrying four or six persons each, are generally employed, and both lines and nets are used; but in the former, when lines are principally used, the number of hands is increased to nine or ten: the fish chiefly taken by these boats are cod, ling, hake, lythe, and herring; lobsters are also caught and kept in traps or baskets. The town derives also an accession of trade from its being frequented as a bathing-place during summer, and from the assizes, sessions, and parliamentary elections for the county of Antrim being held in it. From the privilege of importing merchandise at lower duties than were paid throughout the rest of the country, its commerce was formerly very extensive, and its returns were greater than those of any other port in Ireland; but this privilege was sold to the crown in 1637, and the trade was immediately transferred to Belfast, to which place even the produce of its cotton manufacture is sent for exportation. It is now a member of the port of Belfast, under which head the registry of its vessels and the duties paid at the custom-house are included. The trade consists principally of the importation of coal and the exportation of cattle and occasionally of grain.

The harbour is situated in latitude 54° 42′ 45″ (N.), and longitude 5° 47′ (W.), 9½ miles (N. W. by W.) from the Copeland islands' lighthouse. It is formed by a pier extending from the old castle, in a western direction, to a distance of 460 feet, and within about 400 feet of low water mark at spring tides; at high water it affords only a depth of from six to nine feet, so that vessels of more than 100 tons cannot approach the quay; it is also subject to the accumulation of mud and sand. A handsome pier was erected for the use of the fishermen, in 1834, at an expense of £2600, defrayed by a grant from Government and by local subscriptions. The port is sheltered by land from the prevailing south and west winds; and though winds from the other points produce a certain degree of swell in the offing, yet, from the situation of the Copeland islands and Kilroot point, it is so protected as not to be open seaward more than 2½ points of the compass. But the imperfections of the harbour greatly restrict the trade of the port: a plan and report were drawn up by Sir John Rennie for constructing a new harbour outside the present, so as to insure a depth of 15 feet at low water of spring tides, the estimate for which, including the construction of works for protecting it against the accumulation of sand, and for the requisite accommodation of the shipping, was £55,150; these improvements, from a variety of causes, would render the port one of the most thriving and convenient in the North of Ireland, and a useful auxiliary to the flourishing town of Belfast. A new road leading to Doagh, Templepatrick, and Antrim is in progress, which, when completed, will afford the means of a direct conveyance of grain from an extensive tract to this port, and open a market for the consumption of coal, groceries, and other commodities imported. The market is on Saturday; and fairs are held on May 12th and Nov. 1st. The market-house, built by subscription in 1755, is also used for the meetings of the "Assembly," or aldermen and burgesses of the corporation.

The incorporation of the town as a county of itself is ascribed by tradition to King John; the shrievalty was held jointly with that of the county of Antrim. But although it existed as a separate county long prior to the time of Elizabeth, the charter of the 11th of her reign is the earliest on record containing such incorporation. Its boundaries are described in this charter and in one of the 7th of Jas. I., with a reservation of the castle and its precincts, together with the ancient liberties and royalties appertaining to it, and of sites for a sessions-house and prison for the county of Antrim; but the latter charter excluded from the county of the town certain lands which had been granted and confirmed to the corporation by charter of the 44th of Elizabeth. The franchise now acknowledged is stated to differ from both, and to be in conformity with a riding of the franchises made by the corporation in 1785. In 1810 it was decided, on an issue tried at the assizes, that the lands of Straid and Little Ballymena, described by the charter of Elizabeth as being within the boundary, but not within that marked out by the charter of James, though still belonging to the corporation, are not within the franchise. This is probably a borough by prescription: the earliest notice of the existence of a corporation is in the record of a commission dated 1274, in which year the Scots landed on the neighbouring coast to assist the O'Neills against the English. Hen. IV., in 1402, on the petition of the mayor and three burgesses released them, for one year, from the payment of the annual rent of 100s. for the customs, to aid them in rebuilding the town, which had been burned by his enemies. Queen Elizabeth, in the 11th of her reign (1569), on a representation of the inhabitants that they had lost their letters patent in the disturbances and persecutions of rebels and enemies, by which they were deprived of the enjoyment of their franchises, granted a charter of incorporation conferring on them, besides several special immunities, all such other privileges and jurisdictions as the corporation of Drogheda possessed; and ordaining that they should hold the borough of the king, as of his castle of Knockfergus, at an annual rent of 10s., payable half-yearly, until the fortifications should be repaired and a grant of lands made, and then at a rent of £40 per annum. The grant of lands was conferred by charter of the 44th of Elizabeth, founded on an inquisition issued to ascertain the quantity which had previously belonged to the corporation. James I., in addition to the charter of the 7th of his reign, before noticed, granted others in the 10th and 20th, the former of which is now the governing charter, and the latter created fourteen persons and their successors a corporation, by the style of the "Mayor, Constables, and Society of the Merchants of the Staple." In the "new rules" of the 25th of Chas. II., for regulating corporations in Ireland, it was ordained that the appointment of the mayor, recorder, sheriffs, and town-clerk should be subject to the approbation of the lord-lieutenant and privy council.

The corporation, under the style of "the Mayor, Sheriffs, Burgesses, and Commonalty of the Town of Carrickfergus," consists of the mayor (who is an alderman), 16 other aldermen, two sheriffs (who are burgesses), 22 other burgesses, and an indefinite number of freemen, assisted by a recorder and town-clerk (who is also clerk of the peace), two coroners, three town-serjeants, a water-bailiff, sword-bearer, and other officers. The charter of the 10th of Jas. I. granted a guild merchant within the town, and ordained that all the merchants should be a corporation, by the name of the "Two Masters and Fellows of the Guild Merchant of the Town of Knockfergus," the masters to be elected annually from and by the merchants of the guild, on the Monday after the feast of St. Michael, with power to make by-laws and impose fines. The guilds now remaining are those of the Hammermen, Weavers, Carters, Taylors and Glovers, Butchers, Trawlers and Dredgers, Hookers, and Shoemakers or Cordwainers, incorporated at different periods; but their restrictive privileges in trade have been abandoned as impolitic or useless, and they are now kept up only in form. The mayor is elected annually from among the aldermen, at an assembly of the corporation at large, on the 24th of June, and by the charter must be sworn before the constable of the castle, or, in his absence, before the vice-constable, and in the presence of the mayor for the preceding year, on Michaelmasday; he has power, with the assent of a majority of the aldermen, to depute one of that body to be vice-mayor in his absence. The aldermen, who may be from 8 to 16 in number, are chosen, on vacancies occurring, from the 24 burgesses by the remaining aldermen, and are removable for misbehaviour by a majority of the body.

The sheriffs are eligible from the free burgesses by the mayor, sheriffs, burgesses, and commonalty, annually on the 24th of June : they are sworn on the feast of St. Michael before the mayor and burgesses, and are removable for cause. The burgesses, who are not mentioned by any of the charters as a definite class in the corporation, and were formerly unlimited in number, have been restricted to 24, and, according to practice, are elected in an assembly of the mayor, sheriffs, and remaining burgesses, neither freedom nor residence being requisite as a qualification, and are supposed, like the aldermen, to hold during good behaviour. The freemen are admissible, in courts of the whole corporation held by the mayor, by the right of birth extending to all the sons of freemen, also by marriage, apprenticeship to a freeman within the county of the town, and by gift of the corporation : among other privileges granted by charter to the freemen, of which most have been long disused, it was ordained that no person should be attached or arrested in the house of a freeman, except for treason or felony. The recorder is eligible by the mayor, sheriffs, burgesses, and commonalty, to hold his office either for life, for a term of years, or at the will of the corporation, as may be deemed expedient, but is usually elected for life : he may, with the consent of the mayor and a majority of the aldermen, appoint a deputy to execute the office. The town-clerk is eligible by the whole body, and holds his office during pleasure ; and the coroners, by the charter, are eligible by the mayor, sheriffs, burgesses, and commonalty, from the inhabitants, annually on the same day with the mayor and sheriffs, or any other deemed more expedient, and are removable for cause ; but in practice it is considered that they ought to be elected from the freemen, and they appear to hold office for life or good behaviour. A treasurer, who was formerly the mayor for the time being, is now appointed by the assembly, and is usually an alderman. The "assembly" is composed of the mayor, aldermen, sheriffs, and burgesses, who manage all the affairs of the corporation ; they assume the power of making by-laws, and of demising the property of the corporation. The charters of Elizabeth and James confirmed to this borough the right of sending two representatives to the Irish parliament, which it continued to exercise till the Union, since which period it has returned one to the Imperial parliament. The elective franchise was vested in the mayor, aldermen, burgesses, and freemen of the town, and in the freeholders to the amount of 40s. per annum and upwards in the county of the town, amounting, in Jan., 1832, to about 850 ; but by the act of the 2nd of Wm. IV., cap. 88, the non-resident freemen, except within seven miles, have been disfranchised, and the privilege has been extended to the £10 householders and the £20 and £10 leaseholders for the respective terms of 14 and 20 years ; by this act the 40s. freeholders retain the franchise for life only. The number of voters registered at the close of 1835 was about 1200 : the sheriffs are the returning officers.

The mayor (as also his deputy or vice-mayor) is a justice of the peace within the town, and is further (without mention of the vice-mayor) constituted a justice of the peace throughout the county of the town, being empowered, with the recorder, to hold courts of session and gaol delivery : he is admiral of the liberties, which extend northward to Fair Head and southward to Beerlooms, about 40 miles in each direction, with the exception only of Bangor and the Pool of Garmoyle ; and may

issue attachments against ships and cargoes, or against persons on board, for the recovery of debts wherever contracted : he is also a magistrate for the county of Antrim, and he or his deputy is judge of the Tholsel court ; he is appointed *custos rotulorum* of the county of the town, and is escheator, master of the assays, and clerk of the market ; and the charter empowers him to grant licences for ships coming to the port, upon entering, to buy or forestall merchandise, and also for the salting of hides, fish, &c. The recorder is a justice of the peace within the county and county of the town ; he is the assessor of the mayor in the Tholsel court, and he or his deputy is judge of the court leet and view of frank-pledge to be held in the town twice a year, within a month after Easter and Michaelmas. In 1828, on the petition of the inhabitants, two additional justices were appointed by the lord-lieutenant, under the powers of the act of the 7th of Geo. IV., cap. 61. The corporation has not any exclusive jurisdiction over matters arising within the borough, except that which results from its forming a county of itself : the courts are those of assize and quarter and petty sessions, also a Tholsel court, a sheriffs' or county court, a court leet with view of frankpledge, and a court of pie-poudre. The assizes for the county of the town are held at the usual periods before the mayor, with whom the other judges of assize are associated in commission ; since 1817 they have been held in the county of Antrim court-house, under the act of the 28th of Geo. III., cap. 38, confirmed by several succeeding statutes. The quarter sessions are held before the mayor, recorder, and the two additional justices, in the market-house, which has been appropriated for that purpose since the building called the Tholsel was taken down : the court has jurisdiction over all felonies and minor offences committed within the county of the town, with power to inflict capital punishment, which, however, is not exercised, offences of a more serious kind being referred to the judges of assize. The Tholsel court, which is a court of record, having jurisdiction over the county of the town to an unlimited amount of pleas in personal actions, is by the charter to be held every Monday and Friday, but is now held on the former day ; and is empowered to proceed by summons, attachment (which is the usual form), *distringas*, or any other process, on affidavit before the mayor, whose presence is only deemed necessary in the event of a trial, which seldom takes place. Petty sessions are held once a week, usually before the two additional justices. The assistant barrister for the county of Antrim holds his courts here for trying causes by civil bill ; and the assizes and two of the quarter sessions for the county of Antrim are held here. The local police consists of three constables, appointed and paid by the grand jury of assize, and of twelve unpaid constables appointed at the court leet.

The charter granted one-third part of the customs' dues of the port to the corporation, who enjoyed considerable advantages under this privilege, which, in the year 1637, they surrendered to the Crown in consideration of a sum of £3000, to be paid to trustees and invested in land, but from its non-investment the town has been deprived of all benefit accruing from this grant. The charter of the 10th of Jas. I. also granted the right of fishery in the river and a ferry over it, with various fines, waifs, wrecks of the sea, forfeitures, &c., arising within their liberties, from which they derive no

Town of Carrickfergus. Engraved by C.E. Bruce. From The Dublin Penny Journal, *vol. 3, 1834.*

advantage at present. Their revenue arises exclusively from rents reserved out of their property in lands, amounting to about £359 late currency. The corporation court-house and gaol were at "Castle Worraigh" previously to 1776, in which year the county of Antrim grand jury exchanged their gaol and court-house in the vicinity of the castle of Carrickfergus for "Castle Worraigh," on the site of which part of the present court-house for that county was built, and the corporation continued to use the old gaol of the county of Antrim until 1827, when prisoners under criminal charges were removed from it to the new gaol; and after the passing of an act for regulating prisons, the old Tholsel having become ruinous, a new arrangement was entered into between the respective grand juries of Carrickfergus and Antrim, by which the former pay, in lieu of all charges, "£13 for every 365 days of a prisoner confined in the county of Antrim gaol." The court-house for the county of Antrim is a neat building, fronted with hewn stone, situated at the east end of the main street; and adjoining it, on the north side, is the gaol, which, though capable of containing 340 prisoners, is but ill adapted for their classification or for the preservation of strict discipline.

The county of the town extends about five statute miles along the shore, and its mean length and breadth are nearly equal; it contains, according to the Ordnance survey, 16,700*a.* 1*r.* 34*p.*, including Lough Morne, which comprises 89*a.* 3*r.* 22*p.* The amount of Grand Jury pre-

sentments, for 1835, was £839.5.7½., of which £186.8.9. was for repairing the roads, bridges, &c.; £386.10.3. for public establishments, charities, officers' salaries, &c.; and £266. 6. 7½. for the repayment of a loan advanced by Government. Lough Morne, or More, about three miles north of the town, is said to be the largest in Ireland at the same elevation, which is 556 feet above the level of the sea; it has a powerful spring near the centre, and is well stored with eels and pike. The principal streams, all of which take a nearly direct course into the bay, are the Woodburn, which is formed by the union of two rivulets about two miles above the town (on each of which is a picturesque cascade), and supplies two large cotton mills, a flour and corn-mill, and a large mill for spinning linen yarn near the town; the Orland Water, which descends from Lough Morne, and falls into the bay at the eastern suburb of the town; the Sulla-Tober, which falls into the bay near the same place; the Copeland Water, which forms the eastern boundary of the county; the Silver Stream, which bounds it on the south-west; and the Red River: in all of these are found black and white trout, eels, and stickleback. The surface is studded with the villages of Eden or Edengrenny, Clipperstown, Woodburn, and Bonnybefore; with several hamlets, numerous gentlemen's seats scattered along the shore, and surrounded with ornamental plantations; and several farm-houses of comfortable appearance interspersed throughout. The principal gentlemen's seats are Thornfield, the residence of P. Kirk, Esq., M. P.;

Oakfield, of W. D. D. Wilson, Esq.; St. Catherine's, of Col. Walsh; Glen Park, of Capt. Skinner; Barn Cottage, of J. Cowan, Esq.; Prospect, of — Vance, Esq.; Woodford, of the Rev. J. Gwynn; Sea Park, of the Rev. J. Chaine; and Scout Bush, of Edw. Bruce, Esq.

The parish is co-extensive with the county of the town; the living is a rectory, in the diocese of Conner, united, by charter of the 7th of Jas. I., with the rectories of Island Magee and Ralloo, the vicarage of Inver, and the grange of Moylusk or Moblusk, which union constitutes the corps of the deanery of Connor, in the patronage of the Crown: the tithes of the parish amount to £400; and the gross annual income of the deanery, tithe and glebe inclusive, is £1004. 7. The church, dedicated to St. Nicholas, is an ancient cruciform structure, with a tower, surmounted by a lofty spire; it is said to have been erected on the site of a pagan temple, and appears to have been attached to the Franciscan monastery formerly existing here; the chancel window is embellished with a representation of the baptism of Christ, in painted glass. The north aisle was the property and burial-place of the family of Chichester; having fallen into a ruinous condition, it was parted by a wall from the rest of the church, but in 1830 was given to the parishioners by the present Marquess of Donegal, the head of that family, and is now fitted up as free sittings for the poor: it contains a large mural monument, with effigies of several of the Chichesters; and round the walls were formerly armorial bearings and trophies, of which only a few fragments are remaining. The subterraneous passage under the altar, which communicated with the ancient monastery, may still be traced. The Ecclesiastical Commissioners have lately granted £141 for the repair of this church. There is no deanery-house: the glebe lands are let for £32. 7. per annum. In the R. C. divisions the parish forms part of the union or district of Larne and Carrickfergus; the chapel, in the western suburbs, was erected in 1826. There are places of worship for Presbyterians in connection with the Synod of Ulster, of the first class (a large and handsome edifice), Wesleyan Methodists, Independents, and a small congregation of Covenanters; one for Unitarians is in course of erection.

The Diocesan free grammar school, founded here by Queen Elizabeth, was discontinued about 35 years since. A free school for boys and girls is supported by a bequest of £42 per annum by the late E. D. Wilson, Esq., arising from lands in the borough, to which the rector adds £2 annually: by the testator's will, the children are required to attend every Sunday in the Established Church. There are two public schools in the town, and others at Woodburn, Duncrew, Loughmorne, and Ballylaggin. In 1811 a Sunday school was opened in the town, which for several years was the only one, and was attended by 400 children and 30 gratuitous teachers; but it has partially declined, from the institution of other schools in the town and neighbourhood, in connection with the Established Church and the several dissenting congregations. The number of children on the books of the day schools amounts to more than 400 boys and 300 girls; and in the private pay schools are about 60 boys and 40 girls. In 1761, Henry Gill, Esq., bequeathed £10 per annum each, arising from property in the borough, "to fourteen aged men decayed in their circumstances," and also houses and gardens to such of them as might not have residences: this sum, by an increase in the value of the property, has been augmented to £14 each, late Irish currency, or to

£12. 18. 6. sterling, which is annually received by fourteen aged men of whom ten have also houses. In 1782, William Adair, Esq., of Westminster, gave £2000 three per cent. stock, in trust to the Adairs, proprietors of the Ballymena estate, the interest to be distributed among the poorer freemen, of whom nineteen received annually £3. 3. each; but at present the sums distributed to each vary in proportion to the necessities of their several families; there are also several minor charitable bequests. In 1826 a mendicity association was established, which is supported by subscription; and there are societies for the distribution of clothing among the poor, and for other benevolent purposes.

The Franciscan monastery above noticed, as connected with the parish church, was founded in 1232, and became of so much importance that, in 1282, a general chapter of the whole order was convoked here: it stood within the walls of the town, and its site is at present occupied by the gaol for the county of Antrim. Immediately to the west of the town was the Premonstratensian priory of Goodburn or Woodburn, on the western bank of that stream; it was dedicated to the Holy Cross, and its foundation is attributed to a member of the family of Bisset, which quitted Scotland about the year 1242, in consequence of the murder of the Duke of Athol. Adjoining the eastern suburb was the hospital of St. Bridget, said to have been founded for the reception of lepers; the lands adjoining the site are still called the Spital parks. To the north of the town a well, now called Bride-well, marks the site of another hospital dedicated to St. Bridget. Several silver coins, of the reign of Hen. II., have been found about the castle. There are numerous barrows or tumuli scattered over the face of the county of the town, of which some have been opened and found to contain rude urns, ashes, and human bones; the largest of these, which are chiefly sepulchral, is called *Duncrue*, or the "fortress of blood." At Slieve-True is a cairn, 77 yards in circumference and 20 feet high; a little towards the west of the same mountain is another, of nearly equal dimensions; and about a mile to the north-east is a third, exactly similar. In several places are artificial caves, probably intended as places of concealment. At a place called the Friars' Rock are traces of small circular buildings, supposed to have been friars' cells; and about two miles north-west of the town are the ruins of two churches, called respectively Killyan, or Anne's Church, and Carnrawsy. The mineral springs, though not very numerous, are of various qualities: one of these, in the bed of a stream in the eastern part of the town, is a nitrous purgative water; another, about a mile to the east of it, is a fine saline spring; and the waters of another, near the western bank of Lough Morne, are sulphureous and chalybeate, and were once in great repute for their efficacy. Among the distinguished persons born here may be noticed Bishop Tennison, and Richard Kane, a general in the army of Wm. III. The women of the Scottish quarter and the county adjacent commonly retain their maiden surnames after marriage.

CLOGH, or CLOUGH, a village, in the parish of DUNAGHY, barony of KILCONWAY, county of ANTRIM, and province of ULSTER, 6 miles (N. W. by N.) from Broughshane; containing 121 inhabitants. This place is situated at the junction of several roads, on the acclivity of a hill near the Ravel water, and comprises 20 houses. It is the head of the manor of Old Stone, and contains the manorial court-house, in which the court was formerly held once in three weeks; but the court leet only is now held there. The court-room is large and of good proportions; adjoining it is a jury-room, and underneath are two rooms for debtors, against whom decrees have been issued out of the manor court: it is maintained by the barony. On a high rock which overlooks the village and surrounding country to a considerable distance formerly stood a castle, of which the principal remains are part of a gateway of great strength. Within it there appears to have been a draw well, and beyond it a fosse, which divides the surface of the rock' into two equal parts: the foundations of various buildings may yet be perceived. It is stated by tradition to have belonged originally to the Mac Quillans, until taken from them by the Mac Donnells, the result of a great battle fought on the mountain of Ora or Slievenahera. At an early period a nunnery is also said to have stood on this rock. Fairs are held on Feb. 8th, April 4th, May 27th, Aug. 5th, Nov. 8th, and Dec. 9th, chiefly for the sale of cattle, and a great number of ponies are brought to them from the highlands of Scotland.—See DUNAGHY.

CONNOR, a parish, and the head of a diocese, in the barony of LOWER ANTRIM, county of ANTRIM, and province of ULSTER, 4 miles (S. S. E.) from Ballymena; containing 8682 inhabitants, of which number, 289 are in the village. A religious establishment was founded here at an early period, of which little beyond the names of some of its abbots is now known. It was made the head of the diocese of Connor, and the first bishop was Ængus Macnisius, commonly called St. Macnise, who died soon after the commencement of the sixth century: he is said to have been a disciple of St. Olcan, who was one of St. Patrick's pupils. Connor appears anciently to have been called *Dailnaraigh*, from its cathedral being in the territory of Dalaradia. In 1124, Malachy O'Morgair was consecrated bishop. At this time, according to St. Bernard, the inhabitants of the diocese were very uncivilised; but by a few years' residence among them, St. Malachy wrought as great a change in their morals as was effected by St. Patrick in the fifth century. By the solicitations of John, Bishop of Connor, Pope Eugene IV. was prevailed upon, in 1442, to unite the bishopricks of Down and Connor, the former being then vacant by the deprivation of John Cely. This union had been approved by letters patent of Hen. IV., in 1438, when the bishops of the two sees were desirous that the survivor should have both; but when it was effected the union was strongly opposed by John Prene, Archbishop of Armagh, who wished the pope to appoint William Bassett, a Benedictine monk, to the bishoprick of Down. The union has, however, continued without interruption since that period, and the subsequent history of the diocese of Connor is included in that of Down and Connor. By the Church Temporalities Act (3rd of Wm. IV.) the see of Dromore is to be united with Down and Connor, on the death or translation of either of the bishops; and the title of the united sees is to be the Bishoprick of Down, Connor, and Dromore.

The diocese is one of the ten which constitute the ecclesiastical province of Armagh: it comprehends parts of the counties of Down and Londonderry, and the greater part of that of Antrim, containing an estimated superficies of 395,500 acres, of which 3700 are in Down, 9400 in Londonderry, and 382,400 in Antrim. The cathedral establishment appears to have been refounded by patents of the 7th of Jas. 1. (1610), which ordained

that the church should be called the church of St. Saviour, Connor, and that the chapter should consist of a dean, archdeacon, chancellor, precentor, and treasurer, and the four prebendaries of Connor, Cairn-Castle, Rasharkin, and Kilroot. There are no canons or vicars choral, and neither the dignitaries nor prebendaries have any ecclesiastical duties to perform in respect of their offices. Chas. II., by letters patent in 1663, constituted the church of Lisburn the cathedral for the united dioceses, both the old cathedrals being then in ruins; but, in 1790, an act was passed for the restoration of Down cathedral at Downpatrick. Lisburn church, however, is still used as the cathedral for the bishoprick of Connor: there is no economy fund connected with it, but the building is in a good and sound state, and has hitherto been kept in repair by the parishioners. The extent of see lands is 6411 profitable acres, and the gross yearly income of the bishoprick, on an average of three years ending Dec. 31st, 1831, amounted to £3065. 3. 4¾. The consistorial court is the same as for that of Down, and is held at Lisburn, where the records of the united dioceses are preserved. The diocesan school, which was originally established at Carrickfergus, was removed to Ballymena in 1829, when a consolidation was made of part of the diocese of Armagh and the whole of that of Connor, under the act of the 3rd of Geo. IV.; and an acre of land was given by William Adair, Esq., on which the school-house was erected, in 1830, at an expense of £900. The master, who is allowed to receive boarders, is nominated alternately by the Archbishop of Armagh and the Bishop of Down and Connor: the emoluments, which are small, are contributed by the bishops and beneficed clergy of both dioceses. The number of parishes in the diocese is 72, exclusively of 6 without cure of souls; they are included in 47 benefices, of which, 2 are in the patronage of the Crown, 1 in that of the Lord-Primate, 21 in that of the Bishop, and 15 in lay patronage; the remainder are perpetual or district curacies, in the gift of the respective incumbents of benefices out of which they were formed. The number of churches is 57, besides eight other places of worship, and of glebe-houses, 30.

In the R. C. divisions this diocese is united as in the Established Church, forming the bishoprick of Down and Connor, in which are 21 parochial unions or districts, containing 45 chapels served by 31 clergymen, 21 of whom are parish priests, and 10 coadjutors or curates. The cathedral is an elegant edifice in the town of Belfast, and is used as one of the parochial chapels. Belfast is also the residence of the R. C. Bishop.

The village consists of about 50 houses, and contains a dispensary. Fairs are held on Feb. 1st, May 2nd, Aug. 2nd, and Oct. 28th. The parish, which is situated on the river Glenwherry, comprises, with Kells, according to the Ordnance Survey, 17,135¾ statute acres, about one third of which is arable, one-half pasture, and one-sixth bog. The living is a vicarage, in the diocese of Connor, united, with part of the rectory, by charter of the 7th of Jas. I., to the rectories of Killagan and Killyglen, and the vicarage of Solar, which constitute the union and corps of the prebend of Connor in the cathedral of St. Saviour, at Lisburn, in the patronage of the Bishop; the remainder of the rectory is impropriate in Viscount Ferrard. The tithes of the parish amount to £151, of which £86 is payable to the impropriator, and £65 to the vicar; and the gross tithes of the benefice amount to £279. 12. The glebe-house was built by a gift of £400 and a loan of £400, in 1820, from the late Board of First Fruits; the glebe comprises 40 acres, valued at £40 per annum. The church was erected by aid of a gift, in 1815, from the same Board. In the R. C. divisions this parish is united with those of Drummaul and Antrim, forming the union or district of Drummaul; there is a chapel in each. There are two places of worship for Presbyterians, the largest of which is in connection with the Synod of Ulster, and of the first class. There are national schools at Tannybrack, in which are 47 boys and 14 girls, and at Tamnaghmore, of 80 boys and 54 girls; two schools, in which are about 200 children, are partly maintained by Lord Ferrard, who subscribes £15. 15. annually; and there are several private pay schools, and some Sunday schools. In the vicinity is an artificial mount with outworks.

CRANFIELD, a parish, in the barony of UPPER TOOME, county of ANTRIM, and province of ULSTER, 1 mile (S. W. by S.) from Randalstown; containing 386 inhabitants. This parish is situated on the road from Randalstown to Toome, and on the western shore of Lough Neagh, of which, according to the Ordnance survey, it comprises 2691½ statute acres, besides 834½ acres of land in a good state of cultivation, agriculture having greatly improved; there is neither bog nor waste land: the spinning and weaving of linen cloth is carried on. It is within the jurisdiction of the manorial court of Mullaghgane, held every month at Toome. The living is a rectory, in the diocese of Down and Connor, partly impropriate in William Cranstone, Esq., of Belfast, and partly episcopally united, from time immemorial, to the vicarage of Duneane, to the church of which the Protestant inhabitants of this parish resort. The tithes amount to £35. 11. 11. The ancient parish church is now a noble pile of ruins, situated on the verge of Cranfield Point, overlooking Lough Neagh. Near them is a celebrated well, to which the peasantry resort in great numbers on June 26th, 27th, and 28th, and booths are erected for their accommodation; they perform "stations" round the ruins of the church, and drink and wash in the waters of the well, which is supposed to have been endued with healing properties by St. Olcan, who is traditionally recorded to have been buried here in earth brought from Rome; and in which are found beautiful yellow crystals, very scarce and held in high estimation. A curiously carved cross of wood, marking the limit of what is considered holy ground, stands a mile from the well.

CRUMLIN, a post-town, in the parish of CAMLIN, barony of UPPER MASSAREENE, county of ANTRIM, and province of ULSTER, 5½ miles (S.) from Antrim, and 79 (N.) from Dublin; containing 128 houses and 641 inhabitants. This town is situated on the river Camlin, of which its name is a corruption, and on the road from Lurgan to Antrim; it consists of one long wide street, from which branches one of smaller dimensions leading to the Antrim road, and has a neat and cheerful appearance. At one extremity is the beautiful cottage and highly embellished grounds of Glendarragh, the seat of Col. Heyland, through which flows the river Camlin, noted for the petrifying quality of its waters: among the many fine specimens of petrified substances which it has afforded is the entire root of a tree, of five cubic feet. Adjoining the town are the most extensive and complete flour-mills in the country; they were

originally built in 1765, by Rowley Heyland, Esq., and were the first that were erected in the north of Ireland. These mills were considered of so much importance that Government erected very extensive warehouses for storing wheat and other grain, and encouraged by every means the growth of wheat in the surrounding district. There are several other mills belonging to the same concern, but as all purchases and sales are made at this place, they all come under the denomination of the Crumlin mills. They are now the property of Messrs. Robert Macaulay and Son; the machinery, which is of very superior construction, is impelled by the water of the Camlin river, and the quantity of grain annually consumed is on the average 3000 tons of wheat and the same quantity of oats. A large portion of the flour is shipped for the Clyde, and the several ports of the north of England; and during the year 1833, 2000 tons of flour and oatmeal were sent from this establishment to Liverpool and Manchester alone. A flaxmill has been erected by the Messrs. Macaulay, and several hundred persons in the town and neighbourhood are constantly employed in weaving linens and cottons for the manufacturers of Belfast and other places. From its situation on Lough Neagh, this place derives every possible facility of communication by water with Belfast, Newry, Antrim, and other towns. Fairs are held on the first Monday in every month, for horses, cattle, and pigs; and a constabulary police force is stationed in the town. Petty sessions are held once a fortnight. There is a place of worship for Presbyterians in connection with the Synod of Ulster.—See CAMLIN.

CULFEIGHTRIN, or COOLFAYTON, a parish, in the barony of CAREY, county of ANTRIM, and province of ULSTER, ½ a mile (E.) from Ballycastle; containing 5012 inhabitants. This parish, which is also called Carey, from Castle Carey or Kerragh, which gave name to the barony, was the scene of a sanguinary conflict that took place between the forces of Mac Quellan and those of Sorley Boy Mac Donnell, who encamped on the plains of Bonamargy, on the 4th of July, 1569. This battle, by which the Mac Donnells obtained possession of the castles and estates of the Mac Quellans, is described as having continued throughout the whole vale of Glenshesk, of which every yard was fiercely contested, and nearly the entire surface strewed with the slain. The victory was at length determined in favour of the Mac Donnells, and the fate of Mac Quellan was finally decided on the mountains of Aura, on the 13th of the same month; Shane O'Dennis O'Nial fell in this battle, and his cairn or tumulus is still shewn near Cushendun. The parish, which is bounded on the north by the Atlantic ocean, comprises, according to the Ordnance survey, an area of 26,338 statute acres, including 49 acres under water. The surface is mountainous; the entire mountain of Carey, and the promontories of Fair Head, the most northern part of Ireland, and Tor Point being within the parish: the highest spot is Carnlea, which, according to the same survey, is 1253 feet above the sea. The system of agriculture is improving, but there are very large tracts of waste land, among which is the extensive mountain of Carey, covered with heath; the only profit from it is the peat or turf carried from its bogs for fuel: it is well stocked with grouse. The lower grounds are well cultivated, and the townland of Murloch, which is an inland continuation of the bold and craggy promontory of Fair Head, is extremely fertile, producing an abundance of corn and excellent pasturage. The collieries, generally known by the name of the Ballycastle mines, which were extensively worked about the middle of the last century, are in this parish, but were discontinued in 1833 : it is supposed that the mines are exhausted, the workmen, on penetrating inland from the face of the promontory, for a distance of from a quarter to half a mile, having been stopped by a whin-dyke which here crosses the country, and though experimental shafts have been sunk on the other side of the dyke, lower than the levels previously wrought, no coal has been found : it is, however, conjectured that this mineral could be found by sinking under the former levels or beneath the surface of the sea. There are fine quarries of freestone, which are extensively worked, affording employment to a considerable number of persons; also valuable mines of coal under the promontory of Fair Head, and at Murloch; the former have never been worked, and the working of the latter has been discontinued for some years. The road from Belfast to the Giants' Causeway, along the shore, formerly led over the dreary mountain of Carey, where, for nearly ten miles, not a single habitation was to be seen. The royal military road is now in course of formation, by means of which that mountain will be avoided, or its difficulty obviated, and the baronies of Carey and Glenarm will be united by a splendid viaduct thrown across the romantic valley of Glendun. Great preparations have already been made by levelling the hills and the draining of bogs and lakes; the whole line of road for 8 miles through this parish is entirely new. The scenery is boldly diversified, including the stupendous rocks of Glendun, the lakes of Cranagh, and Tor Point and Fair Head, in the crags of which eagles build their nests. Within the limits of the parish are Churchfield, the residence of T. Casement, Esq.; Cushendun House, of Edm. A. McNeill, Esq.; Cottage, of Major McAulay; Glenmona, of M. Harrison, Esq.; and a cottage residence of Gen. O'Neill. At Tor Point and Cushendun are coast-guard stations, which are two of the eight that form the district of Ballycastle.

The living is a rectory and vicarage, in the diocese of Connor, and in the patronage of the Bishop; the rectory was attached to the Chancellorship of Connor from the year 1600 till 1831, when, on the death of Dr. Trail, the late chancellor, it became a separate consolidated rectory and vicarage under Bishop Mant's act. The tithes amount to £350 : there is neither glebe-house nor glebe. The church, a neat edifice, in the later English style, was erected in 1830, on the site of the ancient structure, by a loan of £600 from the late Board of First Fruits. It is in contemplation to erect a chapel of ease at Cushendun, now a fashionable watering-place, at the eastern extremity of the parish, and seven miles distant from the mother church, which is situated at the opposite extremity. In the R. C. divisions the parish is the head of a union or district, comprising also the Grange of Innispollan, and containing two chapels; that in Culfeightrin is at Carey, near the church. An excellent school-house was built at Bonamargy, near the bridge, by Alexander McNeil, Esq.; and there is also a school at Cushendun, chiefly supported by the resident gentry of the neighbourhood. About 180 children are educated in four private schools. On the bay of Cushendun are some fine remains of Castle Carey.

CULLYBACKEY, a village, in the parish of AHOGHILL, barony of LOWER TOOME, county of ANTRIM, and province of ULSTER, 3 miles (N. W.) from Ballymena; containing 235 inhabitants. This village, which is situated on the river Maine, contains about 50 houses, including a place of worship for Presbyterians. The manufacture of linen is extensively carried on, and a fair was formerly held for its sale. Cullybackey House was formerly the residence of John Dickey, Esq., by whom, in 1778, a corps was raised, called the Cullybackey volunteers; it is now the seat of John Dickey, Esq. Iron-works are said to have formerly existed here, and vitrified substances have been found.

CUSHENDALL, or NEWTOWN-GLENNS, a post-town, in the parish of LAYDE, barony of LOWER GLENARM, county of ANTRIM, and province of ULSTER, 10 miles (N. W.) from Glenarm, and 116 miles (N.) from Dublin; containing 481 inhabitants. This place is beautifully situated within a quarter of a mile from the sea, on the Glenagan stream, which falls into Cushendall bay immediately below the town; it is also intersected by the river Dall, over which a handsome stone bridge has been erected. The surrounding country is strikingly romantic; and the coast, independently of the picturesque scenery it affords, is highly interesting to the geologist, from the diversity of its strata and the numerous caverns with which it abounds. The town, which is neatly built, contains about 90 houses, and is much frequented by persons visiting the Giants' Causeway, to which the new military road along the coast passes through it, and a handsome and commodious hotel has been built for their accommodation. The parish church of Layde, a small neat edifice at the western end of the town, was built in 1832, by a gift of £900 from the late Board of First Fruits. Cushendall bay affords good anchorage for vessels in from 3 to 9 fathoms of water. Fairs, chiefly for Raghery ponies, cattle, sheep, and provisions, are held on Feb. 14th, March 17th, May 14th, Aug. 15th, Sept. 29th, Nov. 14th, and Dec. 22nd. The market-house is a convenient building. A constabulary police station has been established here; also a coast-guard station, which is one of the eight constituting the district of Ballycastle. Petty sessions are held every alternate week; and there is a house of correction in the town. On a mount in it is a castle, which is attributed to the Danes. —See LAYDE.

CUSHENDUN, a small sea-port, partly in the parish of CULFEIGHTRIN, in the barony of CAREY, and partly in that of LAYDE, barony of LOWER GLENARM, county of ANTRIM, and province of ULSTER, 3 miles (N. N. E.) from Cushendall; the population is returned with the respective parishes. This place is situated on a small bay of that name, at the mouth of the river Dun or Glendun, and has recently been much frequented as a watering-place during the summer season. It appears to have derived its name from its situation near the mouth of the Dun, and carries on some trade in cattle and pigs with the opposite coast of Cantire, in Scotland. Here are extensive quarries of freestone. The harbour, which has been formed by the construction of a pier, partly at the expense of Government, affords good shelter to a number of small vessels, which remain here all the winter; it has good anchorage in winds blowing from the shore, and vessels of 50 tons' burden can cross the bar. There are a few small vessels from 14 to 20 tons' burden belonging to the port, and several boats are employed in the herring fishery in the bay. Here is a coast-guard station, forming one of the eight which constitute the district of Ballycastle. On the coast are some spacious caverns of singular construction.

Village of Cushendall. From The Dublin Penny Journal, *vol. 2, 1833.*

D

DERRYAGHY, or DERRIAGHY, a parish, partly in the barony of UPPER BELFAST, but chiefly in that of UPPER MASSEREENE, county of ANTRIM, and province of ULSTER, 2 miles (N.) from Lisburn; containing 5325 inhabitants. In 1648, a severe battle was fought near the church, between the royalist forces commanded by Col. Venables and Sir Charles Coote, and the Scots under Monroe, in which the latter were defeated. The parish, which is bounded on the southeast by the Lagan Canal, and situated on the road from Belfast to Dublin and Armagh, comprises, according to the Ordnance survey, 12,479¾ statute acres, of which 6857¾ are in Upper Massereene; about one-third is under tillage, and two-thirds are in pasture. The surface is in many parts mountainous; the soil in the lower part is fertile, producing excellent crops of wheat and barley in the plains, and of oats and potatoes in the mountainous districts; the system of agriculture is rapidly improving; there is a considerable tract of bog, and a large extent of uncultivated land in the mountains, which affords excellent pasturage for cattle. Coal and iron-stone abound in the parish, and attempts have been made to work mines, but the adventurers abandoned their enterprise before they had penetrated to a sufficient depth. There is an extensive limestone district, which is worked for building and for manure. The parish is rich in mineral productions, but none of the mines are worked to any extent, though the Lagan Canal affords every facility of water conveyance. The surrounding scenery is boldly varied and enlivened with several gentlemen's seats, among which are Ballymacash, the elegant mansion of E. Johnson, Esq., J. P.; Seymour Hill, of W. Charley, Esq.; Ingram Lodge, of Jonathan Richardson, Esq.; and Collin, of Walter Roberts, Esq. There are three extensive bleach-greens, the property of Messrs. Charley, Richardson, and Roberts, in which, upon the average, more than 50,000 pieces of linen, lawn, and damask of the finest quality are annually bleached and finished for the English markets. A manorial court is held here every three weeks, for the manor of Derryvolgie, for the recovery of debts under £2; and a court of record is held occasionally, for the recovery of debts and determination of pleas under £200.

The living is a vicarage, in the diocese of Connor, and in the patronage of the Lord-Primate, to whom the rectory is appropriate: the rectorial tithes, which belonged to Black Abbey in Ardes, previously to the Reformation, are now held under the Lord-Primate, on a lease which will expire in 1841, when the living, by his lordship's munificence, will become a rectory: the tithes amount to £450, of which £300 is paid to the lessee of the Lord-Primate, and £150 to the vicar. The church, which was nearly destroyed in the battle previously mentioned, was shortly after rebuilt, and was enlarged and beautified in 1813. In the R. C. divisions the parish forms the head of a union or district, comprising also a small portion of that of Belfast, or Shankill, and containing three chapels, one near the village of Milltown, the Rock chapel in the mountains, and one at Hannah's town, in the Belfast portion of the union. A parochial school was established here previously to 1750, and endowed by Mrs. Hamill with £50 for the instruction of 12 children; it has been rebuilt, and is now well attended. A school was built at Ballymacash, in 1790, by the Rev. Philip Johnson, and handsomely rebuilt in 1833, by E. Johnson, Esq., by whom it is supported: a school was also built at Stonyford by the Marquess of Hertford, and other subscribers; and there are schools at Collin and Rushy Hill, in connection with the National Board, also six pay schools. In the mountain district are the interesting ruins of Castle Robin, once the residence of Shane O'Nial, and subsequently rebuilt by Sir Robert Norton, in 1579. On the mountain of Collin is a large cairn, and there are several raths and forts scattered throughout the parish. Bishop Jeremy Taylor resided for some time at Magharalave House, now in ruins; Dr. William Smith, Bishop of Raphoe, was born at Ballymacash; Philip Skelton, author of some valuable works on divinity, was born here in 1707; and the Rev. Philip Johnson, for 61 years vicar, was also a native of this parish. He distinguished himself during the disturbances of 1798; wrote a reply to Plowden, who had made mention of him in his History of Ireland, and died in 1833.

DERRYKEIGHAN, a parish, partly in the barony of LOWER DUNLUCE, and partly in that of CAREY, county of ANTRIM, and province of ULSTER; containing, with the Grange of Drumtullagh, and post-town of Dervock, 5134 inhabitants. This parish is situated on the river Bush, and is intersected by the roads from Coleraine to Ballycastle, and from Ballymoney to the Giants' Causeway: according to the Ordnance surveys it comprises 11,396¼ statute acres. Great improvement has been made in the system of agriculture since the commencement of the present century, by the exertions of gentlemen residing on their own estates, in which they have been greatly assisted by G. Macartney, Esq., of Lisanour Castle, and J. Montgomery, Esq., of Benvarden. The bogs have been drained and partly reclaimed; the crops are excellent, and the wheat, though only cultivated since 1827, is inferior in quality and produce to none in the county; there is still some bog remaining, which produces excellent fuel, and of which part is being brought into cultivation every year. The scenery is pleasingly diversified, and enriched with the flourishing plantations with which, notwithstanding their elevated situation and proximity to the sea, the neighbouring gentlemen's seats are surrounded. Of these the principal are Ballydivity, the residence of J. Stewart Moore, Esq.; Lisconnan, of J. Allen, Esq.; Grace Hill, of H. Irwin Stuart, Esq.; and Knockmore, of Hugh Mackay, Esq. Bush Bank, the seat of Capt. Pottinger, was destroyed by an accidental fire in 1833, but is about to be rebuilt. At Mosside is a manufactory of ropes and cordage made from the bog fir, which is found in large quantities and prepared for that purpose; it affords employment to a great number of persons. The whole

of the parish is within the Bushmills district, where courts and petty sessions are held every alternate Monday. It is a rectory, in the diocese of Connor, and is part of the union and corps of the prebend of Cairncastle in the cathedral of Connor: the tithes amount to £430. The glebe-house was built in 1826, by a loan of £1107. 13. 10. from the late Board of First Fruits: the glebe comprises 28½ acres valued at £25 per annum. The Ecclesiastical Commissioners have recommended that on the next avoidance of the union this parish be severed from the rest, and constituted a separate and distinct benefice. The original church was a very small and incommodious building; but in 1831 G. Macartney, Esq., gave an Irish acre of land, which he enclosed with a stone wall, close to the town of Dervock, as a site for the erection of a new church, towards the building of which he contributed also £150; a sum was raised by subscription in the neighbourhood, and the late Board of First Fruits granted a loan of £600, and with these sums the present church was completed. It is a spacious and handsome structure, in the later English style of architecture, with a lofty square embattled tower crowned with pinnacles; being too small for the congregation it is about to be enlarged by the addition of transepts, which will give it a cruciform character. There are two places of worship for Presbyterians, one near the town of Dervock, in connection with the Synod of Ulster, of the second class; the other for Seceders, at Mosside, also of the second class. There are six public schools, one of which is aided by Mrs. Macartney; five private pay schools, and three Sunday schools. Attached to this parish are the 13 quarters called the Grange of Drumtullagh, which was probably an appendage to a monastery at some remote period. There are some large caves at Ballylusk and Idderoan, which were first discovered in 1788; and there are several large forts and tumuli at Cairncullough, Cairncarn, and other places in the parish.—See DERVOCK.

DERVOCK, a post-town, in that part of the parish of DERRYKEIGHAN which is in the barony of LOWER DUNLUCE, county of ANTRIM, and province of ULSTER, 10 miles (E. N. E.) from Coleraine; and 123 (N. by W.) from Dublin, on the turnpike road from Ballycastle to Ballymoney; containing 362 inhabitants. This is a neat and well-built town, consisting of two streets, one on each side of the river Bush, and containing about 65 houses. It belongs entirely to G. Macartney, Esq., and has been greatly improved of late years. While in the possession of the late Lord Macartney, great encouragement was afforded to the linen manufacturers to settle here. There are some extensive corn and flour-mills on the banks of the river. Fairs are held for cattle and sheep, but chiefly for horses, on Jan. 12th, Feb. 23rd, May 14th, June 22nd, Aug. 12th, and Oct. 29th. A constabulary police force has been stationed here. The parish church, a handsome structure, is situated close to the town; as is also a R. C. chapel dependent on that of Ballymoney, and the Presbyterian meeting-house of the Synod of Ulster, which is a large building. A very handsome school-house was erected by G. Macartney, Esq., in 1829, and given by that gentleman for a parochial school; attached to it is a girls' school, established in 1832, and principally supported by Mrs. Macartney. —See DERRYKEIGHAN.

DOAGH, a grange and village, in the barony of UPPER ANTRIM, county of ANTRIM, and province of ULSTER, 1½ mile (S.W.) from Ballyclare; the population of the grange is returned with the parish of Ballyeaston; the village contains 49 houses and 195 inhabitants. This place comprises, according to the Ordnance survey, 2304½ statute acres, of which 9½ are under water, 48 woodland, 140 bog and marsh, and the remainder good arable land. The village is pleasantly situated near the Six-mile-water, and adjoining it is Fisherwick Lodge, a hunting seat belonging to the Marquess of Donegal, a very handsome house surrounded with thriving plantations, which add much to the beauty of the place. The tithes amount to £191. 3. 7½., of which £127. 7. 1. is payable to the impropriator, and the remainder to the vicar.

DONEGORE, a parish, in the barony of UPPER ANTRIM, county of ANTRIM, and province of ULSTER, 3½ miles (E. by N.) from Antrim; containing 2532 inhabitants. It comprises, according to the Ordnance survey, 6650 statute acres. The living is a rectory and vicarage, in the diocese of Connor, united to that of Kilbride, and the granges of Nalteen and Doagh, forming the union of Donegore, in the patronage of the Bishop. The tithes of the parish amount to £393. 7. 10½., and of the entire benefice, to £954. 5. 9.: there is a glebe-house. The church, which is nearly in the centre of the parish, was built in 1659. Divine service is also performed every Sunday in a private house at Kilbride. There is a meeting-house for Presbyterians in connection with the Synod of Ulster, of the first class, and one in connection with the Seceding Synod, of the second class. The parochial school, in which are about 60 children, is aided by the rector; and there are three Sunday schools.

DRUMMAUL, a parish, in the barony of UPPER TOOME, county of ANTRIM, and province of ULSTER; containing, with the post-town of Randalstown (which is described under its own head), 9737 inhabitants. During the revolution of 1688, this parish was frequently the head-quarters of the Earl of Antrim's regiment, which marched hence to the attack of Londonderry; and in the disturbances of 1798, the insurgents were driven from Antrim into Randalstown, in this parish, by the king's troops. The parish is situated on the river Main, and on the northern shore of Lough Neagh; it is intersected by the road from Belfast to the eastern parts of the counties of Derry and Tyrone, and by the mail roads from Belfast to Coleraine, and from Antrim to Cookstown. It comprises, according to the Ordnance survey, 32,394 statute acres, of which 11,472 are in Lough Neagh, and 171¼ in the river Main. The land, with the exception of a few farms, is in a very indifferent state of cultivation; the system of agriculture is, however, beginning to improve; there are bogs containing about 2800 acres. The beautiful demesne of Shane's Castle, which contains nearly 2000 acres, the property of Earl O'Neill, and for many years the principal seat of his family, is situated on the margin of Lough Neagh, and the grounds and plantations extend far on both sides of the river Main: the mansion was destroyed by fire in 1816, and is now in ruins; the park, which is well stocked with deer, is ornamented with fine timber. Millmount, the seat of G. Handcock, Esq., agent to Earl O'Neill; Hollybrook and Sharoogues are also in this parish. Coal and iron-stone were formerly obtained here, and there are remains of extensive forges and smelting-furnaces at Randalstown. There are quarries of basaltic stone, from which materials are obtained in abundance both for building

and for the roads. The spinning of cotton and weaving of calico were extensively carried on at Randalstown, there are excellent sites for bleach-greens and beetling-engines at Hollybrook, and a considerable quantity of linen is woven in various parts of the parish. The living is a vicarage, in the diocese of Connor, and in the gift of the Marquess of Donegal, in whom the rectory is impropriate: the tithes amount to £996. 6. 6., of which £546. 6. 6. is payable to the impropriator, and £450 to the vicar. The church, which is at Randalstown, is a neat edifice in the ancient English style, with an octagonal spire of freestone: it was built in 1832, on the site of a church erected in 1709, and cost £1800, of which, Earl O'Neill subscribed £300, besides giving a fine-toned organ; his lordship has also built a beautiful mausoleum for his family close to the church, the family burial-place having been at Edenduff-Carrick since 1722. In the R. C. divisions the parish is the head of a union or district, called Drummaul or Randalstown, comprising the parishes of Drummaul and Antrim, and parts of Connor, Templepatrick, Donegore, and Kilbride; there are three chapels, of which that of Drummaul is a large handsome building near Randalstown. In that town there is a Presbyterian meeting-house in connection with the Synod of Ulster, and one connected with the Seceding Synod, both of the first class; and the Covenanters have a meeting-house at Craigmore. There is a parochial school at Randalstown for children of both sexes, aided by a grant from Earl O'Neill, and six other schools in the parish; also another school at Randalstown. In these schools about 330 children are educated, besides which about 440 are taught in seven private schools, and there are also eight Sunday schools. There are some remains of the ancient church at Drummaul, and the site of an old church at Edenduff-Carrick, or Shane's-Castle. Adjoining the gardens of Shane's-Castle are some very fine columnar masses of basalt, similar to those of the Giant's Causeway, but less perfect in their form and less regular in their divisions; they descend into Lough Neagh, and disappear under the water. There are chalybeate springs in various parts of the parish.

DRUMTULLAGH, a grange, in the barony of CAREY, county of ANTRIM, and province of ULSTER, on the road from Ballycastle to Coleraine; containing 1468 inhabitants. It comprises, according to the Ordnance survey, 3753½ statute acres, and is ecclesiastically regarded as forming part of the parish of Derrykeighan.

DUNAGHY, a parish, in the barony of KILCONWAY, county of ANTRIM, and province of ULSTER, 6 miles (N. W. by N.) from Broughshane; containing 3451 inhabitants. It comprises, according to the Ordnance survey, 13,743¼ statute acres, of which 12,040 are applotted under the tithe act; about one-sixth is irreclaimable mountain and bog, one-fourth rough mountain pasture, a twelfth, pasture of a better quality, and one half, arable land. Towards the east the hills attain a mountainous elevation; the highest are those of Moneyduff and Ballyboggy. A great portion of the summits of the hills towards the north is unprofitable; but nearer their base they afford good pasture to young cattle during the summer. Along the banks of the Ravel and Altakeerag are considerable tracts of low meadow land, subject to floods from the former river which pours down with great rapidity. The females are employed in spinning, and the males, in addition to their agricultural pursuits, in weaving coarse linens and calico.

The living is a rectory, in the diocese of Connor, and in the patronage of the Bishop: the tithes amount to £311. 18. 7¼. The glebe-house was built by aid of a gift of £350 and a loan of £450 from the late Board of First Fruits in 1816; the glebe comprises 25 acres. The church, a small edifice with an open belfry turret, occupies an elevated site. In the R. C. divisions the parish is the head of a union or district called Glenravel, and comprises Dunaghy and Skerry, in each of which is a chapel; the chapel for this parish, a neat edifice, is at Glenravel, near the bridge over the Ravel. There is a place of worship in the village of Clough for Presbyterians in connection with the Synod. of Ulster, of the first class. There are two public schools, in which are about 260 children, and three Sunday schools. There are several Danish forts, of which the most remarkable are, one on the hill of Dungonnell, two on Dunbought, and one nearly effaced on Carnbeg, in levelling which were found an urn, a small statue, a cross, and some silver coins. There are many sepulchral monuments in the churchyard, among which those of the Crawford and Hamilton families are the most remarkable. Corby Rock is a bold precipice forming the termination of a hill; it is covered with ivy and washed at its base by the Ravel.

DUNDERMOT, a grange, in the barony of KILCONWAY, county of ANTRIM, and province of ULSTER, on the Ravel water; containing 1069 inhabitants. It comprises, according to the Ordnance survey, 3003¾ statute acres: the tithes, which are impropriate, amount to £65. There is a meeting-house for Presbyterians of the Seceding Synod in connection with that at Ahoghill. Near the Ballymena road is a Danish fort or mound of an oval form, 60 feet by 30, the summit of which is level, and the base surrounded by a deep fosse and counterscarp: towards the bridge over the Ravel two parallel branches from the fosse enclose another area of a quadrangular form, now called "the parade."

DUNEANE, a parish, in the barony of UPPER TOOME, county of ANTRIM, and province of ULSTER, 6 miles (W. N. W.) from Randalstown, on the road from Belfast to Londonderry; containing 6812 inhabitants. This parish is bounded on the west by Lough Beg and the river Bann, and on the south by Lough Neagh, in which, at the distance of half a mile from the shore, is a group called the Three Islands, which are within its limits. It comprises, according to the Ordnance survey, 13,128 statute acres, of which 1628¼ are in Lough Neagh, 415¾ in Lough Beg, and 29½ in the river Bann. About two-thirds of the land are in a state of good cultivation, one-tenth is bog, and the remainder waste: the soil is fertile and the system of agriculture greatly improved. Basaltic stone is quarried in large quantities for building and for repairing the roads. The principal seats are Reymond Lodge, that of Earl O'Neill; Moneyglass, of J. Hill, Esq.; St. Helena, of — Reford, Esq.; and Brecart, of Capt. O'Neill. The weaving of calico and union cloths, and also of fine linen, is carried on extensively. The living is a vicarage, in the diocese of Connor, united from time immemorial to the rectory of Cranfield, and in the patronage of the Marquess of Donegal; the rectory is impropriate in W. Cranston, Esq., of Belfast. The vicarial tithes, as returned by the Ecclesiastical Commissioners in 1831, amounted to £240, and of the whole union to £270; there is neither glebe nor glebe-house. The church is a

small plain edifice, nearly in the centre of the union. The R. C. parish is co-extensive with that of the Established Church; there are chapels at Moneyglass and Cargin, the former built in 1826. There is also a place of worship for Presbyterians in connection with the Synod of Ulster, of the third class. About 840 children are taught in nine public schools, of which the parochial school is aided by donations from the vicar; and there are eight Sunday schools. There are some remains of a circular camp, called Ballydonnelly fort, similar to the Giant's Ring in the county of Down.

DUNLUCE, or DOONLISS, a parish, in the barony of LOWER DUNLUCE, county of ANTRIM, and province of ULSTER, 6 miles (N. N. E.) from Coleraine, on the road to the Giants' Causeway; containing 3605 inhabitants. This parish, which gives name to the barony, was anciently called Portramon, and distinguished as the residence of the celebrated chieftain Mac Quillan, who was lord of a castle of which the original foundation is not precisely known. Mac Quillan, who was brave, hospitable, and improvident, unwarily suffered the Scots around him to increase in strength, till at length they expelled him from all his possessions; and Sorley Boy, brother of James Mac Donnell, having obtained possession of the district called the Glynnes, made himself master also of this place. But Sir John Perrot, the English lord-deputy, assaulted the intruder, and, after a vigorous resistance, drove him from the castle, in which he placed Sir Peter Carey, whom he thought to be a man of the English pale, as governor, with a garrison of fourteen soldiers. Sir Peter, who was in reality one of the Carews of the north, brought around him some of his own country and kindred, and unknown to the deputy discharged the English soldiers; two of his garrison, however, confederating with the party of Mac Donnell, drew up fifty of them by night into the castle, and these having taken possession of the fortress by surprise, attacked and slew the governor and a few of his companions. On this event, which took place in 1585, the lord-deputy despatched to the assault of the castle an officer named Merriman, who slew the two sons of James Mac Donnell, and Alexander, the son of Sorley Boy, and so harassed the latter by driving away the vast herds of cattle which were his only wealth, that he surrendered Dunluce, and repaired to Dublin to make his submission, which was accepted; and on condition of his fidelity to the English crown, and payment of a tribute of cattle and hawks, he received a regrant of all his possessions, with the government of Dunluce castle. This family was afterwards ennobled by the title of Earl of Antrim; and in 1642, Gen. Monroe, commander of the Scottish army in Ulster, with a party of his forces, paid a friendly visit to the Earl, by whom he was hospitably received; but at the conclusion of the entertainment, Monroe gave the signal to his armed followers, who instantly made the Earl prisoner and seized the castle, and this act was followed soon afterwards by the seizure of all his possessions.

The parish, which is within a mile and a half of the Giants' Causeway, extends for a considerable distance along the coast, and, according to the Ordnance survey, comprises 9381 statute acres. The land is fertile and generally in the highest state of cultivation; the system of agriculture is in a very improved state; there is very little waste land, some excellent pasturage, and a bog of about 500 acres. Limestone abounds, and to the westward of Dunluce castle are the White Rocks lime-works,

Dunluce Castle. From The Dublin Penny Journal, *vol. 4, 1836.*

the most extensive in the North of Ireland. There are numerous quarries of basalt, and great quantities of flint are exported. Coal exists on the estate of John Montgomery, Esq., but no mines have yet been worked. The principal gentlemen's seats are Benvarden, that of J. Montgomery, Esq.; Seaport, of J. Leslie, Esq.; Bardyville, of Sir F. W. Macnaghten, Bart.; and the Cottage, of F. D. Ward, Esq.: there are also some elegant sea-bathing lodges at Ballintra. The manufacture of paper affords employment to 190 persons, who, with the aid of the most improved machinery, are engaged in making the finer kinds of paper for the English, Scotch, and home markets. A facility of conveyance for the produce of the quarries and limeworks, and for the various sorts of merchandise, is afforded by the small but commodious port of Ballintra. A fair is held annually on Nov. 12th, and petty sessions for the district every fortnight at Bushmills.

The living is a consolidated rectory and vicarage, in the diocese of Connor, and in the patronage of the Bishop: the tithes amount to £369. 4. 7. The glebe-house was built by a gift of £400 and a loan of £300 from the late Board of First Fruits, in 1812; the glebe comprises 20 acres. The church, a handsome edifice, situated at the extremity of the parish, near Bushmills,

was erected by aid of a gift of £900 and a loan of £300 from the same Board, in 1821, on the site of an ancient church, which was a ruin in 1625. In the R. C. divisions the parish forms part of the union or parochial benefice of Ballymoney; the chapel near Bushmills is a very small edifice. There is a place of worship for Presbyterians in connection with the Synod of Ulster, of the second class. About 80 children are taught in the public schools, of which the parochial school is chiefly supported by the rector, and a female school was built and endowed by Mrs. Montgomery. There are also three private schools, in which are about 160 children and four Sunday schools. A dispensary was established at Bushmills in 1830, for the parishes of Dunluce, Billy, and Dunseverick. A loan fund was established in 1828, for which purpose the late Hugh Montgomery, Esq., gave £100. The ruins of Dunluce castle are remarkable for their extent and picturesque appearance, especially when viewed from the shore immediately below; the fortified parts occupy the summit of a rock projecting into the sea, and separated from the adjacent cliffs by a deep chasm, over which is an arch forming the only entrance, defended on one side by a wall only 13 inches in thickness; there appears to have been a corresponding wall in a parallel direction with the former, which together were probably the parapets of the bridge. The domestic apartments and offices, of which the remains are extensive, were situated on the main land, and though at a distance appearing only as a massive rugged pile, upon a nearer approach display characteristics of architectural beauty. Underneath the castle is a natural cavern forming a noble apartment, the walls and roof of which are of rude basalt. Near the castle is a very large Danish camp. Splendid specimens of opal, jasper, and cornelian are found upon the shore. Dunluce gives the inferior title of Viscount to the Earls of Antrim.

DUNMURRY, a village, in that part of the parish of DRUMBEG which is in the barony of UPPER BELFAST, county of ANTRIM, and province of ULSTER, 3½ miles (N. E.) from Lisburn, on the river Glenwater and the road from Belfast to Lisburn; containing 479 inhabitants. This place, which takes its name from two Danish forts, or raths, in its immediate vicinity, was formerly the parish of Ballygosh, which soon after the Reformation was annexed to that of Drumbeg. Its ancient name has been superseded by that of the village which has been recently erected, and which is beautifully situated in a sequestered and fertile vale, and remarkably neat. Over the Glenwater are two bridges, one at the village, an ancient structure, and the other, over which the Dublin road passes, a noble pile of two arches of freestone, quarried on the spot. The surrounding hills being richly planted add greatly to the beauty of the scenery, which is also embellished with several handsome seats, of which the principal are Seymour Hill, that of W. Charley, Esq.; Woodbourne, of M. Charley, Esq.; Dunmurry House, of W. Hunter, Esq.; Suffolk, of J. McCance, Esq.; Glenville, of W. McCance, Esq.; and Collin House, of W. Roberts, Esq.; besides others which are noticed in the account of the parish of Drumbeg, *which see*. In the village are some extensive flourmills, worked partly by water and partly by steam, and attached to them are large stores for grain and maltkilns. Near these is a large bleach-green, in which 14,000 pieces of fine linen are annually bleached; and at Glenburn, a little lower down upon the same stream, is another, in which 12,000 are annually finished. Quarries of freestone for building are wrought here; there are also quarries of basalt, which in the grounds of Glenburn consists of rude columnar masses with concave and convex joints, similar to those of the Giants' Causeway. Beneath the freestone are some thin strata of coal, which have never been worked. The church of Ballygosh has long since disappeared, and the rectorial tithes of the two townlands which constituted the parish were granted by Jas. I. to Sir Arthur Chichester, and the vicarial tithes to the incumbent of Drumbeg, in the proportions of two-thirds and one-third respectively. There is a place of worship for Presbyterians, formerly in connection with the General, but now with the Remonstrant, Synod of Ulster. Closely adjoining the bridge was discovered, while quarrying the stone for its erection, a natural basaltic wall in a direction from north to south, composed of stones of different sizes and forms, and having in a striking degree the appearance of art. On Collin mountain, to the north-west of the village, is a very conspicuous cairn of considerable extent; it consists of small stones piled together in a conical form, and is now almost covered with green sward.

DUNSEVERICK, or DOONSERE a parish, partly in the barony of CAREY, and partly in that of LOWER

DUNLUCE, county of ANTRIM, and province of ULSTER, 3¼ miles (N. E.) from Bushmills; containing 1813 inhabitants. This parish is situated on the northern coast, which is here characterised by features of grandeur and sublimity. It contains the noble promontories of Pleaskin and Bengore; the latter, situated in 55° 14' 50" (N. Lat.) and 6° 28' (W. Lon.), forms the commencement of that beautiful and majestic range of columnar basalt which is called the Giants' Causeway. The shore is indented with several interesting bays, of which that near Milltown is much frequented during the season; and the small creek of Portanna flows up to the village. According to the Ordnance survey it comprises 4277½ statute acres: the land is fertile and the system of agriculture rapidly improving. There are several quarries of limestone and stone for building; fossil or wood coal, found beneath the basalt and between the strata, is worked to a considerable extent, but it is of very indifferent quality; and near Pleaskin is a very fine quarry of columnar basalt. A profitable salmon fishery is carried on at Port Moon bay, where the fish are taken in great abundance. At Port Ballintrae is a coast-guard station, forming one of the eight which constitute the district of Ballycastle. The living is a perpetual curacy, in the diocese of Connor, and in the alternate patronage of the Rectors of Billy and Ballintoy, out of which parishes it was formed under the act of the 7th and 8th of Geo. IV., 1830. It is endowed with the tithes of the townlands of Lisnaguniog, Feigh, and Carncolp, in the parish of Billy, amounting to £37. 9. 3., and with those of the townlands of Artimacormick, Drimnagee, and Drimnagesson, in the parish of Ballintoy, amounting to £29. 8. 3¾., making the total endowment £66. 17. 6¾. The church, a neat edifice with a square tower, was erected in 1832, at the expense of the late Board of First Fruits. There is a place of worship for Presbyterians. Lochaber school, in which about 100 children are gratuitously instructed, was built in 1827 and is supported by subscription; and there is a pay school, in which are about 30 boys and 20 girls, and a Sunday school. In 1831, many thousand Roman coins of silver were found under a stone near Bengore Head, and fossils and minerals of every variety are found here in profusion. The venerable remains of Dunseverick castle are noticed in the account of Ballintoy, in which parish they are situated.

F

FALLS UPPER, a district of the parish of BELFAST, in the barony of UPPER BELFAST, county of ANTRIM, and province of ULSTER: the population is returned with Belfast. It is a perpetual cure, or chapelry, in the diocese of Connor, endowed with the small tithes, amounting to £50, and in the gift of the vicar of Belfast: the rectorial tithes, amounting to £100, are impropriate in the Marquess of Donegal.

FINVOY, a parish, in the barony of KILCONWAY, county of ANTRIM, and province of ULSTER, 5 miles (S. W.) from Ballymoney, on the road from Ballymoney to Kilrea; containing 6093 inhabitants. This parish, which is bounded on the west by the river Bann, and on the east by the Mainwater, comprises, according to the Ordnance survey, 16,474¼ statute acres, of which about one-third is bog and barren heath, and the re-

View of Belfast from Turf Lodge. Drawn by George Petrie and engraved by William Miller. From P. D. Hardy, Northern tourist, or, stranger's guide to the north and north west of Ireland *(Dublin, 1830).*

mainder, with the exception of about 90 acres in the river Bann and a small lough of about 5 acres, is good land; about 3187 acres are applotted under the tithe act, and valued at £2281 per ann. The surface is varied: the parish is divided into three portions by two bogs which intersect it, and parallel with which are two mountainous ridges, one called the Craigs, and the other Killymorris. The system of agriculture has, within the last few years, been greatly improved; there are some quarries of basalt, which is raised for building and for mending the roads; and coal and iron stone are supposed to exist in several parts, but neither has yet been worked. Bricks are manufactured, for which there is plenty of clay along the banks of the Bann. The principal gentlemen's seats are Moore Lodge, that of G. Moore, Esq.; and Cullytrummin, of Sampson Moore, Esq. In the small village of Dunloy there is a good inn. Fairs are held there on the 15th of Feb., May, Aug., and Nov.; and it is a constabulary police station. In its immediate vicinity is the hill of Dunloy, which, according to the Ordnance survey, has an elevation of 707 feet above the level of the sea at low water. The river Bann is not navigable up to this parish, the approach being obstructed by the falls of Portna. The living is a rectory and perpetual curacy, in the diocese of Connor; the rectory forms part of the union and corps of the prebend of Rasharkin, in the cathedral of Connor; the perpetual curacy, which was instituted in 1808, is in the patronage of the Prebendary. The tithes amount to £450, of which £300 is payable to the rector, and £150 to the perpetual curate. There is neither glebe-house nor glebe. The present church was erected on the site of the original structure, by aid of a gift of

£200 and a loan of £400 from the late Board of First Fruits, in 1810; and the Ecclesiastical Commissioners have lately granted £129 for its repair. In the R. C. divisions the parish is united to that of Rasharkin; the chapel is situated at Killymorris. There is a place of worship for Presbyterians in connection with the Synod of Ulster, of the second class. About 380 children are taught in four public schools, of which the parochial school was founded in 1822; and there are four private schools, in which are about 200 children, and eight Sunday schools. There are several forts, artificial caverns, and druidical remains in various parts of the parish; among the latter is a cromlech of hard black stone, between the upright pillars of which is an entrance to a chamber underneath, which communicates with two other chambers, the whole within a circle of 45 feet in diameter. This interesting relic is situated beyond the summit of the Craig; and at the distance of a furlong from it is a square fort, enclosing an area of 9000 square feet, surrounded with a deep trench. Within 300 yards of the fort are three erect tapering pillars, supposed to be monumental memorials of certain chiefs slain and buried on the spot. The view from the Craig rocks embraces that side of Lough Neagh which is towards the river Bann, and the mountains of Derry in the distance. At Lischeahan *is* a mineral spring, the water of which has the taste and smell of gunpowder.

G

GALGORM, a village, in the parish of AHOGHILL, barony of LOWER TOOME, county of ANTRIM, and province of ULSTER, 1 mile (W.) from Ballymena, on the river Maine ; containing 37 houses and 226 inhabitants. The castle of Galgorm, built by the celebrated Dr. Colville, is a handsome square embattled structure, now the seat of the Earl of Mountcashel: the whole of the rooms are wainscoted with Irish oak.

GLENARM, a post-town, in the parish of TICK-MACREVAN, barony of UPPER GLENARM, county of ANTRIM, and province of ULSTER, 17½ miles (N. W.) from Carrickfergus, and 105¾ (N. by E.) from Dublin ; containing 880 inhabitants. This town, which has a sub-post-office to Larne and Cushendall, is situated in a deep glen, which opens to the sea, and on the Glenarm river, which here empties itself into the bay of that name, and over which are two bridges. It contains 145 houses, and is said to have been incorporated by a charter of King John, in the 4th year of his reign ; but since the conquest of Ulster it has not exercised any municipal privileges. Glenarm castle was for many years the residence of the MacDonnels, Earls of Antrim, of whom Randal MacDonnel, Marquess of Antrim, was

attainted during the protectorate. It was originally built in 1639, and is now the seat of Edmund McDonnel, Esq., by whom, since his marriage with the Countess of Antrim, the present castle was erected on the site of the former structure, of which very little remains. It is a noble quadrangular pile, flanked at the angles with four large towers embellished with minarets terminating in vanes, and surmounted with stately domes ; the entrance is under a large massive gateway ; the hall is of large dimensions and noble appearance, and the state apartments are spacious, lofty, and magnificent. The demesne is richly planted and beautifully embellished with myrtles and other delicate shrubs ; at a small distance to the south is the great deer-park, formerly enriched with stately timber, and watered by a mountain torrent, which afterwards flows through the lawn ; and on the left of the road to Larne is the little park, bounded by a succession of precipitous rocks rising from the shore, and forming a bold headland, round which has been carried the Antrim coast road from Larne to Ballycastle, cut through the solid rock, and 10 feet above high water mark at spring tides, of which a detailed account is given in the article on the county. The town is much resorted to for sea-bathing ; the harbour is small and chiefly frequented by vessels from the opposite coast of Scotland, which bring coal and take

Town and castle of Glenarm. Drawn by T. M. Baynes and engraved by William Le Petit. From G. N. Wright, Ireland illustrated *(London, 1831)*

back grain, limestone, and other produce. Vessels may ride in safety in the bay within a quarter of a mile from the shore, in five or six fathoms of water. Fairs are held on the 26th of May and October, a chief constabulary police force has been stationed here, and there is also a coast-guard station belonging to the district of Carrickfergus. A court leet and baron for the manor of Glenarm, which is co-extensive with the barony, is held every third week, for the recovery of debts to the amount of £10, in which the proceedings are by attachment and civil bill process. Here is a handsome R. C. chapel, and a good school-house was built in 1829 from the lord-lieutenant's fund. Near the castle are some remains of an ancient Franciscan monastery, founded in 1465 by Sir Robert Bisset, and of which the site and revenues were, after the dissolution, granted to Alexander Mac Donnel, ancestor of the Earls of Antrim. Between Larne and Glenarm are the ruins of Cairn castle, situated on a rock in the sea; and near them are the remains of a castle, built by the family of Shaw in 1625.

GLENAVY, or LYNAVY, a post-town and parish, in the barony of UPPER MASSAREENE, county of ANTRIM, and province of ULSTER, 7½ miles (S.) from Lurgan, on the road to Antrim; containing 3390 inhabitants, of which number, 399 are in the town. According to the Ordnance survey it comprises 16,786 statute acres, 9219½ of which are in Lough Neagh and 342½ in Lough Portmore. The soil is well cultivated, and there is very little waste land or bog; there is some basalt. The town contains 68 houses, and is divided into two equal parts by the river Glenavy. It has four quarterly fairs, principally for horned cattle and pigs. Here is a large cotton-mill, and much flax is spun and woven in the cottages. At Glenconway is an extensive bleach-green. From its situation on Lough Neagh, this parish has a communication by water with Belfast and Newry. The principal seats are Goremount, the residence of Mrs. Gore; Ballyminimore, of W. Oakman, Esq.; and Glenconway, of Mrs. Dickson. The living is a vicarage, in the diocese of Connor, united to the vicarages of Camlin and Tullyrusk, and in the patronage of the Marquess of Hertford, who is impropriator of the rectory and proprietor of the parish: the tithes amount to £221. 19. 4., of which £172. 17. 4. is payable to the vicar, and £49. 2. 2. to the impropriator; and the gross value of the benefice is £380 per annum. The glebe-house, in the parish of Camlin, was built in 1819, on a site given by the Marquess of Hertford, at an expense of £1072, of which £500 was a loan and £300 a gift from the late Board of First Fruits. The church was rebuilt in 1814; it is a handsome edifice with a square tower, for the erection of which the Marquess of Hertford subscribed £100 and the late Board gave £200 and lent £250. In the R. C. divisions the parish is the head of a union or district, comprising also Camlin, and Killead, and containing two chapels, one of which is a large building near Glenavy. There is also a place of worship for Primitive Methodists. There are schools at Ballynacoy, Crew, Fourscore Ballyvanen, and Old Park. On Ram's island, in Lough Neagh, are the remains of a round tower; and in the parish are several raths and tumuli. From Crew hill a fine view is obtained of Lough Neagh and of parts of six counties, with several towns and seats.

GLENWHIRRY, an extra-parochial district, in the barony of LOWER ANTRIM, county of ANTRIM, and

province of ULSTER, 6 miles (W. by S.) from Larne, on the road to Broughshane; containing 1358 inhabitants. According to the Ordnance survey it comprises 11,368¼ statute acres. There is a meeting-house for Presbyterians in connection with the Synod of Ulster, of the third class. About 80 children are educated in two private schools, and there is a Sunday school.

GLYNN, a parish, in the barony of LOWER BELFAST, county of ANTRIM, and province of ULSTER, 1½ mile (S.) from Larne; containing 1668 inhabitants, of which number, 379 are in the village. This parish, anciently called Glinus, and also Gleno or Glenco, is beautifully situated in a pleasant glen, through which a mountain stream takes its course into Lough Larne, which forms the entire eastern boundary of the parish; and also on the royal military coast road. The harbour of Larne is very capacious, and may be entered at all times of the tide. In 1597, Sorley Mac Donnel, having assaulted the garrison of Carrickfergus and taken the governor, Sir John Chichester, prisoner, brought him to this place, and beheaded him on a stone that had formed the plinth of an ancient cross, and which then pointed out the boundary of North Clandeboy. The parish comprises 4484½ statute acres, which are generally in a state of high cultivation; the system of agriculture is greatly improved, and there is neither bog nor waste land. Here are some very extensive lime-works, called the Maghramorne Lime Works, the property of John Irving, Esq., from which large quantities of lime are exported to Scotland and the northern parts of England. These are the largest lime-works in the united kingdom: in 1836, there were 459 vessels, of the aggregate burden of 18,040 tons, exclusively employed in the trade; the average export is 16,228 tons, and the demand is annually increasing; the sum paid weekly for labour amounts to £1804. On a chymical analysis by Dr. Thomson, of Glasgow, the stone is found to contain 99 per cent. of pure lime, and it has been ascertained by experience that, whether employed as a manure or a cement for building, it will go twice as far as lime of the ordinary quality. Rail and tram roads have been laid down, which greatly facilitate the operations; there are also convenient wharfs, so that any quantity of the article can be furnished without delay or detention of the shipping. The principal seats are Maghramorne House, a modern mansion, beautifully situated on the bay of Larne, the residence of Mr. Irving, who is also the chief proprietor of the lands in the barony; Glynn House, that of Randall W. Johnston, Esq.; and the Cottage, of Miss McClaverty. The village is pleasantly situated and contains 75 houses neatly built. One of the first bleach-greens established in Ireland was at this place; it was subsequently the site of a cotton-mill, and in 1830 the machinery was applied to the spinning of fine linen yarn, in which about 120 persons are at present employed. The living is a vicarage, in the diocese of Connor, and in the patronage of the Marquess of Donegal, in whom the rectory is impropriate: the vicarial tithes amount to £52. There is no glebe-house or glebe, and the church is a picturesque ruin; the Protestant parishioners attend the different places of worship in Larne. About 35 children are taught in the parochial school, for which a house was built by R. W. Johnston, Esq.; and there are two private schools, in which are about 100 children. A nunnery was founded here at a very remote period, of which St. Darerca, sister of St. Patrick, was abbess; it was called Linn, and is supposed to have been situated at Glynn, near Larne, where some traces of a chapel still exist; the site, with all its possessions, was granted by Jas. I. to Sir Arthur Chichester, by the designation of the "Chapel of Glynn." Here is a powerful vitriolic spring, in which the star stone is found in great perfection.

I

INNISPOLLAN, a grange, in the barony of LOWER GLENARM, county of ANTRIM, and province of ULSTER, 3 miles (N.) from Cushendall, on the road to Ballycastle; containing 155 inhabitants. This place, which is extra-parochial, comprises, according to the Ordnance survey, 933½ statute acres. In the R. C. divisions it forms part of the union or district of Culfeightrin, and has a chapel at Glendon.

INVER, a parish, in the barony of LOWER BELFAST, county of ANTRIM, and province of ULSTER, adjoining the post-town of Larne, and containing 953 inhabitants. This parish is situated on the Larne water, and on the shore of Larne Lough, and is bounded on the east by the sea. It is said to have been at a very early period the site of a priory, of which the only remains are the present parish church. During the disturbances of 1798, many of the insurgents made their escape to this place after their defeat in the battle of Antrim. It comprises, according to the Ordnance survey, 1773 statute acres, which are generally in a state of profitable cultivation; there is neither bog nor waste land. Inver Lodge is the seat of G. Whitla, Esq.; and Inver House, of Archibald Barklie, Esq. Here are some very spacious flour-mills, and adjoining them are extensive premises for bleaching and finishing linen cloth, of which 30,000 webs are annually bleached, exclusively of large quantities finished in their brown state. Iron-stone abounds, but is not worked, though every facility of conveyance is afforded by a safe harbour and good quay room. The living is a vicarage, in the diocese of Connor, forming part of the union of Carrickfergus and of the corps of the deanery of Connor; the rectory is impropriate in the Marquess of Donegal. The tithes amount to £70, of which £40 is payable to the impropriator and £30 to the vicar. The church, formerly that of the priory, has been so disfigured with plaister, as to have lost all originality of character; it has been appropriated to the perpetual curacy of Larne, in the patronage of the Dean. In the R. C. divisions the parish forms part of the union or district of Larne and Carrickfergus. About 70 children are taught in the national school at Ballysnood. There are the remains of a small fort on the banks of the river, near the church.

INVERBEG, a village, in the parish of INVER, barony of LOWER BELFAST, county of ANTRIM, and province of ULSTER; containing 29 houses and 133 inhabitants.

INVERMORE, a village, in the parish of INVER, barony of LOWER BELFAST, county of ANTRIM, and province of ULSTER; containing 41 houses and 230 inhabitants.

ISLAND MAGEE, otherwise ISLAND MAGUY, a parish, in the barony of LOWER BELFAST, county of ANTRIM, and province of ULSTER, 6 miles (N. E. by E.) from Carrickfergus; containing 2610 inhabitants. Edward Bruce landed on this island in 1315; and Sir

Moyses Hill, ancestor of the Marquess of Downshire, took refuge in a cave here when pursued by the Mac Donells, who had slain Sir John Chichester. In 1642 all the R. C. inhabitants were killed by some Scottish soldiers under Munro, on their march to Carrickfergus. The parish forms a peninsula between Larne Lough and the North Sea, and the Isle of Muck or March lies near the coast. According to the Ordnance survey it comprises 7036½ statute acres of excellent land in a high state of cultivation, which produces wheat and beans of the finest quality. Coal is supposed to exist, and basalt used for building and for repairing the roads is abundant. Spinning and the weaving of linen cloth and calico are carried on in various parts of the parish, and some of the inhabitants are employed in fishing. There is a pier at Portmuck, from which much limestone is shipped. There are coast-guard stations at Portmuck and Blackhead, which are included in the district of Carrickfergus. A court is held by the seneschal of the Marquess of Donegal, for the recovery of debts and the determination of pleas to the amount of £20. It is a rectory, in the diocese of Connor, forming part of the union of Carrickfergus: the tithes amount to £400. The church, a small edifice, rebuilt in 1827, on the foundations of an ancient and more extensive structure, is close to the margin of Larne Lough. There are two places of worship for Presbyterians, of the third class, one in connection with the Synod of Ulster, the other with the Seceding Synod. About 270 children are educated in 10 private schools. Near Brown's bay is a rocking stone, weighing about 12 tons; and at Ballyumpage are the remains of a cromlech or druids' altar; there are also the remains of two ancient churches. In the cliffs called the Gobbins are seven caves, into which the tide flows: they are a little above low water mark, under a basaltic rock, 210 feet high, intersected by layers of ochreous basalt, about an inch thick, and of a deep vermillion colour. Near the entrance to the peninsula are the remains of Castle Chichester, occupying a beautiful situation on a bold shore. A spring of pure but weak saline water rises near Red Hill. The ancient rent of this island was two goshawks and a pair of gloves.

K

KELLS, a parish, in the barony of LOWER ANTRIM, county of ANTRIM, and province of ULSTER, 5½ miles (N.) from Antrim, on the road from Ballymena to Randalstown: the population is included in the return for the parish of Connor, into which this place (which in the civil divisions is not recognized as a parish) is generally considered to have merged. In the early part of the ninth century, a cell existed here, on the site of which a priory was erected some time before the arrival of the English, by O'Brien Carrog, who dedicated it to the Blessed Virgin; and it existed till 1442, when it was surrendered, with all its possessions. The village has a neat appearance; it is a constabulary police station, and has a penny post to Antrim. Fairs are held on Jan. 10th, March 1st, June 10th, and Sept. 12th. The parish is in the diocese of Connor, and is wholly impropriate in the Earl of Mountcashel, who allows the incumbent of the adjoining parish of Connor £3 per annum for discharging the clerical duties.

A dolmen, called here 'a druid's altar', Island Magee. From The Dublin Penny Journal, *vol. 1, 1832.*

KILBRIDE, a parish, in the barony of UPPER ANTRIM, county of ANTRIM, and province of ULSTER, 2¼ miles (W. N. W.) from Ballyclare, on the road from Ballymena to Doagh; containing 1849 inhabitants. This parish comprises, according to the Ordnance survey, 5641 statute acres. It is a rectory and vicarage, in the diocese of Connor, and part of the union of Donegore: the tithes amount to £373. 3. 4½. There is no church; divine service is performed in a school-house every Sunday. About 240 children are taught in four private schools, and there are three Sunday schools.

KILDOLLAGH, or KILDALLOCK, a parish, partly in the barony of UPPER DUNLUCE, county of ANTRIM, but chiefly in the North-west Liberties of COLERAINE, county of LONDONDERRY, and province of ULSTER, 2 miles (S. E.) from Coleraine, on the river Bann; containing 982 inhabitants. According to the Ordnance survey it comprises 2006 statute acres, of which 1984 are in Londonderry: the land is fertile and well drained, fenced, and cultivated. It is a rectory, in the diocese of Connor, forming part of the union of Rasharkin. About 40 children are educated in a private school, and there is a Sunday school. Near the village of Loughans are the ruins of the ancient church; also the foundations of the castle of McQuillan, where a sanguinary battle was fought, in 1534, between the rival septs of O'Kane and McQuillan. Not far distant is a lofty fort, containing a large cave.

KILLAGAN, a parish, partly in the barony of UPPER DUNLUCE, but chiefly in that of KILCONWAY, county of ANTRIM, and province of ULSTER, 8 miles (S. E.) from Ballymoney, on the road to Belfast, and also on that from Ballymena to Ballycastle; containing 1451 inhabitants. This parish comprises, according to the Ordnance survey, 3838 statute acres, of which 1406¼ are in the barony of Upper Dunluce, and 2431¾ in that of Kilconway: it is in a good state of cultivation, considerable improvement having been made in the system of agriculture. A large expanse of water, called Mount-Hamilton Lough, has lately been drained, and the land brought into profitable cultivation. In the village of Clogh Mills are some flax and corn mills, and the weaving of linen is carried on by many of the inhabitants in their own houses. It is a rectory, in the diocese of Connor, forming part of the union and corps of the prebend of Connor in the cathedral of St. Saviour; the tithes amount to £115. About 100 children are taught in two public schools, and there is also a Sunday school. On a gentle eminence, near the centre of the parish, are some remains of Mount Hamilton castle, in front of which was the lake before mentioned. There is also a large circular earthwork, called Mount Hamilton Fort, in which Pictish coins, military weapons, arrow heads of flint, and other relics of antiquity, have been discovered; and in the bog was found, in 1831, a firkin of butter in a fossilised state.

KILLEAD, or KILLAGH, a parish, in the barony of LOWER MASSEREENE, county of ANTRIM, and province of ULSTER, 4½ miles (S.) from Antrim, on the road to Lurgan; containing 7183 inhabitants. This extensive parish is for a distance of eight miles bounded on the west by Lough Neagh, and is divided into the districts of Upper and Lower Kilmakevit, and Upper and Lower Killelough; it comprises, according to the Ordnance survey, 42,836½ statute acres, including 789¼ in the Grange of Carmany, and 19,794½ in Lough Neagh. The land is in a high state of cultivation, and there is neither bog nor waste land; the whole surface is drained, fenced, and managed on the Scottish system; the principal crop is wheat, for which the soil is peculiarly adapted, and which was cultivated here with great success when scarcely known in any other part of the county. The farm-houses are large and well-built, and have excellent farm-yards and homesteads attached to them, and with the comfortable cottages of the peasantry, and the numerous orchards, gardens, plantations, and hedgerows, give to this district a rich and cheerful appearance. The principal gentlemen's seats are Langford Lodge, the handsome mansion of the Hon. Col. Pakenham; Glendarragh, of Langford Heyland, Esq., Benneagh, of J. Macaulay, Esq.; Glenoak, of R. Macauley, Esq.; and Tully House, of J. Murray, Esq. The weaving of linen is carried on to some extent in various parts of the parish. The living is a vicarage, in the diocese of Connor, and in the patronage of the Earl of Massareene; the rectory is impropriate in J. Whitla, Esq., and nine others. The rectorial tithes amount to £830. 18. 3., and the vicarial to £700. The church is a plain modern structure, nearly in the centre of the parish. The glebe-house is an elegant residence, erected in 1824 by the present incumbent, at an expense of £2000; the glebe comprises about ten acres. At Gartree, formerly a separate parish, but since the Reformation included in this parish, of which it is the principal burial-place, a very handsome church was erected in 1831, under the auspices of Col. Pakenham, aided by a loan of £900 from the late Board of First Fruits: the Ecclesiastical Commissioners have lately granted £315 for its repair. At the entrance to the churchyard is a triumphal arch, erected in 1832, at the expense of the parishioners, in honour of Capt. Armstrong, to whose memory it bears a long inscription. It is endowed with £100 per annum by Col. Pakenham, the patron, who has built a handsome residence for the chaplain, and serves as a chapel of ease to the parochial church. In the R. C. divisions this parish forms part of the union or district of Glenavy; the chapel, a small neat building, was erected in 1824. There are places of worship for Presbyterians in connection with the Synod of Ulster of the first class, and for Seceders; to the former, which is situated at Tully, is attached a very extensive burial-ground, in which is a costly monument, in the Grecian style, to the memory of S. Cunningham, Esq., of the island of St. Vincent's, a native of this parish. About 600 children are taught in the public schools, of which one at Ballyhill was built in 1809, by Mr. Johnson, by whom it is partly supported: one in the churchyard, built in 1802, is supported by the vicar; and one built by Col. Pakenham is supported by him and his lady, at whose expense also many of the children of both sexes are entirely clothed. There are also ten private schools, in which are about 300 children. Lady Massareene bequeathed £100, and Mr. Cunningham £200, to purchase land and divide the rents among the poor; a small farm in Ballygenniff was accordingly purchased, and is let for £16 per annum. There are numerous mounds and forts, some defended by a single and others by a double fosse; two of them have arched excavations. There are also several ruins of churches, and many relics of antiquity have been discovered in the neighbourhood. Clotworthy, Earl of Massareene, was interred in the parish church.

KILLYGLEN, a parish, in the barony of UPPER GLENARM, county of ANTRIM, and province of ULSTER, 2 miles (W. N. W.) from Larne, on the road from that place to Glenarm; containing 524 inhabitants. This parish, which in the Ordnance survey is called a grange belonging to Killegan parish, comprises 2295½ statute acres. It is a rectory, in the diocese of Connor, forming part of the union and corps of the prebend of Connor: the tithes amount to £62. 2. 5½. In the R. C. divisions it is part of the union or district of Larne. About 30 children are educated in a private school.

KILRAUGHTS, or CILRAGHTS, a parish, in the barony of UPPER DUNLUCE, county of ANTRIM, and province of ULSTER, 4 miles (E.) from Ballymoney, on the roads leading respectively from Coleraine to Belfast and from Ballymena to Bushmills; containing 1837 inhabitants. This parish comprises, according to the Ordnance survey, 5132¼ statute acres, of which very little is waste; the system of agriculture is in a very unimproved state. The land is of excellent quality, and is generally occupied by small farmers, who devote a portion of their time to weaving; consequently the due cultivation of the soil is neglected. There is only a small portion of bog, not more than sufficient to afford a moderate supply of fuel. The living is a rectory, in the diocese of Connor, forming part of the union and corps of the prebend of Rasharkin in the cathedral of Connor, and in the patronage of the Bishop; the tithes amount to £150. The church is a ruin, situated on an eminence; attached to it is a burial-ground, which is still used. There are places of worship for Presbyterians in connection with the Synod of Ulster, of the second class, for Seceders of the second class, and for Covenanters. About 45 children are taught in the parochial school, which is aided by the rector; the schoolhouse was built by subscription in 1824; there are two private schools, in which are about 70 children, also two Sunday schools.

KILROOT, or KILROI, a parish, in the barony of LOWER BELFAST, county of ANTRIM, and province of ULSTER, 2¼ miles (E. N. E.) from Carrickfergus, on the road to Larne; containing 536 inhabitants. At Kilroot Point, the French general Thurot, with three ships and 600 men, landed in 1760 and attacked Carrickfergus, which being at the time unprovided with a regular garrison, was obliged to capitulate. He also threatened to lay siege to Belfast, but on the approach of the forces which were advancing to expel him, he re-embarked his troops at this place, and set sail for France. The parish, which is situated on the bay of Carrickfergus, comprises, according to the Ordnance survey, 2418 statute acres; the land is in general in a good state of cultivation, and the most improved system of husbandry prevails. Castle Dobbs, the residence of R. Dobbs, Esq., and Bella Hill, the property of Marriott Dalway, Esq., are the principal seats: there are some interesting ruins of the ancient mansion of Castle Dobbs. Basalt and limestone exist in great abundance: of the former a regular quarry of the columnar formation has been opened; the tops of the columns, which are of four, five, and six sides, are only a few inches below the surface; all dip to the northward, and are nearly as perfect as those of the Giants' Causeway, resembling in some degree those massive columns called the Giants' Organ; between them are thin layers of decomposed rock; the ends of the joints are in some almost flat, and in others concave and convex. There is an extensive bleach-green belonging to Michael Andrews, Esq., of Ardoyne, in which the elegant royal damasks from the Ardoyne manufactory are finished, to the number of more than 10,000 pieces annually, affording constant employment to 25 persons. A constabulary police force is stationed here. The living is a vicarage, in the diocese of Connor, united by charter of Jas. I. to the rectory of Ballynure and the vicarage of Templecorran, together forming the union and corps of the prebend of Kilroot in the cathedral of Connor, and in the patronage of the Bishop; the rectory is impropriate in the Marquess of Donegal. The tithes amount to £151. 6. 7., of which £101 is payable to the impropriator, and £50. 6. 7. to the vicar; those of the entire benefice amount to £560. There is neither glebe-house nor glebe. The church has been in ruins for more than 200 years; the church of the union is at Ballynure. In the R. C. divisions the parish forms part of the union or district of Carrickfergus and Larne. A school for girls was built and is supported by Mrs. Dobbs; and a school-house was built in 1836, which is in connection with the New Board of Education. A nitrous spring rises in a bed of marly clay in the parish, the water of which has an aperient quality. Dean Swift held the prebend of Kilroot, which was his first preferment.

KILWAUGHTER, a parish, in the barony of UPPER GLENARM, county of ANTRIM, and province of ULSTER, 1 mile (W. S. W.) from Larne, on the road to Ballymena; containing 2016 inhabitants. This parish comprises 9803½ statute acres, of which 11½ are under water, about one-third is arable, and a very large portion mountain and waste land, particularly Agnew Hill, which has an elevation of 1558 feet above the level of the sea. The lands near the castle are in a high state of cultivation; there is some bog, and limestone and basalt are abundant. Kilwaughter Castle, the elegant mansion of E. J. Agnew, Esq., proprietor of nine-tenths of the parish, and for several centuries the residence of that family, is situated within a beautiful and extensive demesne. In the plantation above the castle is a place called Dhu Hole, a fissure in the limestone rock, into which falls a river that is nowhere seen again till it enters Lough Larne. There are some extensive cotton-mills in the parish, that formerly employed more than 1000 persons, but are now unoccupied; linen cloth is woven in some parts. It is a rectory, in the diocese of Connor, forming part of the union and corps of the prebend of Cairncastle in the cathedral of Connor. A perpetual curacy has been recently instituted, called the curacy of Cairncastle and Kilwaughter, which is endowed with the tithes of the latter parish, amounting to £90. The church is at Cairncastle; the glebe, in this parish, was purchased by the late Board of First Fruits, which also built an excellent glebe-house, in 1813. There is a small R. C. chapel at Craiganorn. About 200 children are taught in three public schools. The

late Mr. Agnew bequeathed £10 per annum to the poor. There are some slight remains of the old church in the castle demesne.

KIRKINRIOLA, or KIRCONRIOLA, a parish, in the barony of LOWER TOOME, county of ANTRIM, and province of ULSTER, on the road from Belfast to Londonderry; containing, with the post-town of Ballymena, (which is separately described), 7297 inhabitants. This parish, which is also called Kilconriola and Ballymena, comprises, according to the Ordnance survey, 6390 statute acres, in a very indifferent state of cultivation. The soil is light and sandy, and in some parts intermixed with stones, and consequently unproductive without great labour and expense; the farms are small, and are chiefly in the occupation of persons who, dividing their attention between agriculture and the spinning of yarn and weaving of linen, expend but little capital on the land, and pay but little attention to its improvement. There are considerable tracts of waste land and a large extent of bog. In the valley of the river Braid are indications of coal, but no mines have yet been opened; and there are extensive quarries of stone in several parts of the parish, from which has been raised all the stone for building the houses and bridges in the town and neighbourhood. The principal seats are Ballymena Castle, the residence of P. Cannon, Esq.; the Green, of A. Gihon, Esq.: Hugomont, of H. Harrison, Esq.; Brigadie, of J. Tracey, Esq.; and Ballygarry, of D. Curell, Esq. It is an impropriate curacy, in the diocese of Connor, forming part of the union of Ballyclugg; the rectory is impropriate, by purchase from the Earl of Mountcashel, in William Adair, Esq. The tithes amount to £223. 10. 4., the whole payable to the impropriator, who is proprietor of the parish, and charges them in the rent of the lands. The stipend of the curate is £71. 16. per annum, of which £31. 10. is paid by the impropriator, and £40. 6. from Primate Boulter's augmentation fund. The glebe-house, towards the erection of which the late Board of First Fruits granted a loan of £73. 16. 11., in 1823, is near the church; the glebe comprises six acres, valued at £15 per annum. The church of the union was built in 1712, at the extremity of the parish, near Ballyclugg, and repaired in 1822, for which purpose a loan of £100 was granted by the late Board of First Fruits. In the R. C. divisions it is the head of a union or district, called Ballymena, and comprising also the parish of Ballyclugg; there are chapels at Ballymena and Crebilly respectively: there are places of worship for Presbyterians in connection with the Synod of Ulster, of the first and second classes, one in connection with the Seceding Synod of the third class, and one for Wesleyan Methodists. Guy's free school is supported by a bequest of the late John Guy, Esq.; the school-house was built at an expense of between £400 and £500, and the master has a house and garden rent-free; there also ten other public schools, the master of one of which, the diocesan school, receives a salary of £120 per annum: they afford instruction to about 850 children. In ten private schools about 400 children are taught, and there are nine Sunday schools. There are some remains of the ancient parish church, which appears to have been a spacious and handsome structure, but they are diminishing rapidly by the removal of the materials for gravestones. There are several ancient encampments in the parish, of which the most conspicuous is on the high grounds above Ballingarry, near which, in the townland of Bottom, is a fine circular

Lambeg House. Drawn by Joseph Molloy and engraved by E. K. Proctor. From Belfast Scenery *(Belfast and London, 1832).*

fortress, surrounded by a fosse and vallum. Near the glebe-house is a mass of rock, 30 feet in circumference and 8 feet high, called the Standing stone, of which no tradition is extant ; and near Ballymena, on the Braide water opposite the castle, is a very remarkable moat rising from the brink of the river to a great height, and now covered with a plantation.

L

LAMBEG, a parish, partly in the baronies of UPPER BELFAST and UPPER MASSAREENE, county of ANTRIM, but chiefly in the barony of UPPER CASTLEREAGH, county of DOWN, and province of ULSTER, 2½ miles (N.) from Lisburn, on the old road from Belfast to Dublin ; containing 1537 inhabitants, of which number, 175 are in the village. The parish, which is pleasantly situated on the river Lagan, comprises, according to the Ordnance survey, 1567 statute acres, of which 376¾ are in the county of Antrim. The land is good and the system of agriculture improved ; and the surrounding scenery is pleasingly diversified. Lambeg House, the property and residence of A. Williamson, Esq., is a handsome modern mansion, formerly belonging to J. Williamson, Esq., author of an able treatise on the linen trade, and framer of the laws by which it is now regulated throughout Ireland ; he was much persecuted for framing those laws, and was driven from his house and his native country by an infuriated mob. Chrome Hill, also a spacious modern mansion, was erected by R. Nevin, Esq., late of Manchester, who established here some extensive works for printing muslin, in which he first applied with success his invention of the " Ba Chrome," now universally used, and also introduced the oxyde of chrome into the ornamental department of the china manufacture, from which circumstance he named his estate. The village is about a mile north of Lisburn, with which and also with Belfast it is connected by houses continued along the road between those towns. The blanket manufacture established by the Wolfenden family, who settled in this part of the country about two centuries since, is still carried on. On the river Lagan are two large bleach-greens ; and further down the stream is the extensive printing establishment of Mr. Nevin, the buildings of which are capacious and furnished with every modern improvement in machinery. The living is a perpetual curacy, in the diocese of Connor, and in the patronage of the Bishop, to whom the

70

rectory is appropriate as mensal, but the whole of the tithes, amounting to £103. 19. 2¾., are given by him to the curate.　The church occupies the site of an ancient monastery, said to have been founded in the 15th century by Mac Donell for Franciscan friars of the third order; it is a small but handsome edifice in the Grecian style, with a tower at the west end.　There is a place of worship for Presbyterians in connection with the Synod of Ulster; also a national school, in which are about 90 children, and a private school of about 120 children.　From a part of the churchyard being called the Nuns' Garden, it has been supposed that there was a nunnery here, but no account of such an establishment is extant.

LARNE, a sea-port, market and post-town, and a parish, in the barony of UPPER GLENARM, county of ANTRIM, and province of ULSTER, 11 miles (N.) from Carrickfergus, and 97 (N. by E.) from Dublin, on the road from Belfast to Ballycastle; containing 3182 inhabitants, of which number, 2616 are in the town. This place is situated on the shore of Lough Larne, which was formerly called Olderfleet, and gave name to a castle built on the extreme point of the promontory of Curraan, which forms the small bay adjacent to the town.　This fortress, under the protection of which the town arose, is supposed to have been erected by a Scottish family named Bisset, to whom a settlement on this part of the coast was granted by Hen. III., and to have been subsequently improved by the English.

Edward Bruce landed here in 1315 with an army of 6000 men for the conquest of Ireland; and during the same reign, Hugh Bisset forfeited his lands here by taking part in the rebellion.　These were subsequently claimed in right of the same family, by James Mac Donnell, Lord of Cantire, and after his death were granted by Queen Elizabeth during her pleasure, to his son Angus, on condition that he should carry arms only under the King of England, and pay annually a certain number of hawks and cattle.　Olderfleet castle was at that time considered so important a defence against the Scots that, in 1569, it was entrusted to Sir Moyses Hill, but was dismantled in 1598.　Jas. I., in 1603, granted the entire headland to Sir Randal Mac Donnell, surnamed Sorley-Boy; but in 1612 gave the castle and lands to Sir Arthur Chichester, together with the right of ferry between this place and Island Magee.　During the disturbances of 1798, the town was attacked by the insurgent army from Ballymena, but the assailants were repulsed by the Tay fencibles, assisted by the yeomanry and inhabitants.

The town is beautifully situated on the shore of Lough Larne, on the eastern coast, and is divided into the old and new towns, containing together 482 houses, most of which are well built, and of very neat appearance; the streets in the old town are narrow and indifferently paved; the new town consists of one long and regular street, in which the houses are of stone

View of Larne. Drawn by T. M. Baynes and engraved by William Le Petit. From G. N. Wright, Ireland illustrated *(London, 1831).*

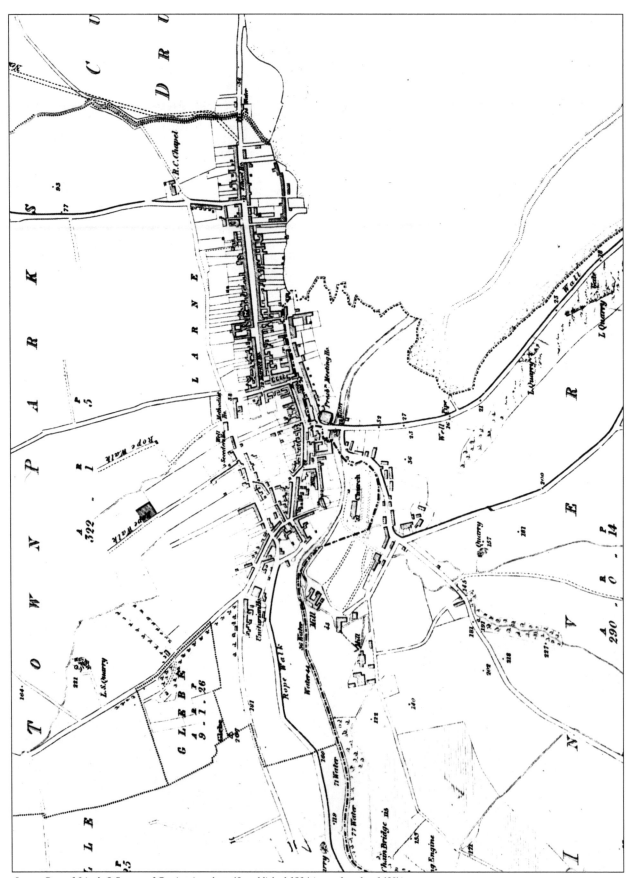

Larne. Part of 6 inch O.S. map of Co. Antrim, sheet 40, published 1834 (reproduced at 140%).

and handsomely built. There are two public libraries, supported by subscription, both containing good collections. During the last century a very extensive trade was carried on in salt, of which large quantities prepared here from rock salt imported from Liverpool were sent from this port to Denmark, Norway, Sweden, Russia, and Prussia; the duties paid thereon, on the average, amounted to £18,000 per annum. About the middle of the last century this was the only port in the North of Ireland from which emigrant vessels sailed. The present trade consists chiefly in the exportation of oats, beans, flour, and, occasionally, black cattle, and a very considerable quantity of lime; and the importation of coal, slates, wheat, and North American timber. The number of vessels that entered inwards during the year ending Jan. 5th, 1835, was 340, of the aggregate burden of 13,517 tons, and of which 298 were from British ports and 42 employed in the coasting trade; and during the same year, 113 vessels, of the aggregate burden of 4329 tons, cleared out from this port, of which 64 were bound to British ports and 49 were coasters. The port, which is a member of that of Belfast, has an excellent harbour for small vessels, for which there is good anchorage between the Curraan, and the peninsula of Island Magee, in 2 or 2½ fathoms, quite land-locked; great numbers of vessels from Scotland anchor off this place, while waiting for their cargoes of lime from the Maghramorne works. There are some good quays on both sides of the lough about a mile from the town, the water being too shallow to float vessels further up. The royal military road along the coast passes through the town. The market is on Tuesday; a great market is held on the first Monday of every month, and there are fairs on Dec. 1st and July 31st, principally for black cattle, a few inferior horses and pigs. A constabulary police force has been established in the town, and there is also a coast-guard station belonging to the Carrickfergus district. A court for the manor of Glenarm is held here every six weeks; and petty sessions are held every alternate week.

The parish comprises, according to the Ordnance survey, 2210 statute acres of good arable and pasture land; the system of agriculture is slowly improving, and there is neither waste land nor bog. Limestone abounds, and is quarried both for building and agricultural purposes; at Ballycraigey, about a mile to the north of the town, is a quarry of felspar, worked occasionally for building; and at Bankhead a fine stratum of coal has been discovered, but is not worked. The principal seats are Gardenmore, the elegant villa of S. Darcus, Esq.; the Curraan, the residence of M. McNeill, Esq.; and the glebe-house, of the Rev. S. Gwynn. The living is a perpetual curacy, in the diocese of Connor, and in the patronage of the Dean; the tithes amount to £135. 11. 11., of which £123. 15. 7. is payable to the curate, who receives also £23. 8. from Primate Boulter's fund. The glebe-house was built in 1824, by a gift of £450 and a loan of £50 from the late Board of First Fruits; the glebe comprises 3¼ acres. The church, previously to its alteration in 1819, had some interesting details of ancient architecture. In the R. C. divisions the parish forms part of the union or district of Carrickfergus and Larne; a chapel was erected here in 1832 by subscription. There are places of worship for Presbyterians in connection with the Synod of Ulster and the Seceding Synod, each of the second class, and with the Presbytery of Antrim of the

first class, also for Wesleyan Methodists. About 150 children are taught in the national school of the parish, and a dispensary is supported by subscription. There are some remains of the ancient castle of Olderfleet on the promontory of Curraan; and on the sea side, about a mile north of the town, is a cavern called the Black Cave, passing under the projecting base of a huge rock; the length of the cave, which is open at both ends, is 60 feet, and its height from 3 to 30 feet; the sides are formed of basaltic columns of large dimensions. On the shore of the lough, near the town, are some singular petrifactions of a blue colour, apparently the result of a spring issuing from a bank at high water mark. In a short road leading from the east to the north of the town is a chalybeate spring, at present little used.

LAYDE, a grange, in the barony of LOWER GLENARM, county of ANTRIM, and province of ULSTER, 4½ miles (W.) from Cushendall; containing 444 inhabitants. It comprises, according to the Ordnance survey, 7834 statute acres; and is extra-parochial, never having paid church cess or tithes: there being no provision for the cure of souls, the members of the Established Church attend the parish church of Layde.

LAYDE, a parish, in the barony of LOWER GLENARM, county of ANTRIM, and province of ULSTER; containing, with the post-town of Cushendall (which is separately described), 4056 inhabitants. This parish, called also Cushendall, from its post-town, and Newtown Glens, from its situation in the centre of the Glyns, was the residence of the Mac Auleys of the Glyns, who joined the standard of Mac Donnel at the celebrated battle of Aura, in 1569, after which the combined armies spent some days in festivity on the mountain of Trostan, on which they raised a cairn, still called "Coslin Sorley Boy." According to the Ordnance survey it comprises, exclusively of the Granges of Layde and Innispollan, 20,476¼ statute acres, one-third of which is arable, and the remainder chiefly in pasture; the surface is undulating and in some parts mountainous; in the low grounds are some good meadow lands, the valleys are well cultivated, and the mountainous districts afford tolerable pasturage. Here are quarries of coarse freestone and of white limestone, which is burnt for manure. Salmon and many other kinds of fish are found in the rivers, and on the coast of this parish, which is skirted by the coast road from Belfast to the Giants' Causeway, and is intersected by the royal military road. On the former road is a splendid viaduct over the river Glendon, which connects this parish with Culfeightrin and the barony of Glenarm with that of Carey. Mount Edward is the residence of Gen. Cuppage; and Glenville, of the Rev. W. McAuley. The living is a rectory, in the diocese of Connor, and in the patronage of the Bishop; the tithes amount to £235. 7. 7½.; the glebe comprises 4 acres. A church was built about a mile from Cushendall in 1800, but having gone to ruin, another was built in the town in 1832. In the R. C. divisions the parish is the head of a union or district, called Cushendall, including this parish and Ardclinis, and containing chapels at Cushendall and Redbay. The parochial school is partly supported by the rector; and F. Turnley, Esq., has built a good school-house for a national school. In these and three other public schools about 340 children are educated, and about 45 are taught in a private school; there are also four Sunday schools, and a dispensary.

Lisburn town hall and cathedral. Drawn by H.E.Delap and engraved by R.Clayton. From The Dublin Penny Journal, *vol. 4, 1836.*

The ancient church is in ruins, but the cemetery is still used. The poet Ossian is said to have been born here.

LISBURN, an unincorporated borough, market-town, and parish, partly in the barony of UPPER MASSAREENE, county of ANTRIM, and partly in the barony of UPPER CASTLEREAGH, but chiefly in that of LOWER IVEAGH, county of DOWN, and province of ULSTER, 6 miles (S. W. by S.) from Belfast, and 73 (N.) from Dublin; containing 13,249 inhabitants, of which number, 5218 are in the borough, 5941 in that part of the parish which is in the county of Down, and 2090 in that which is in the county of Antrim. This place was, in the reign of Jas. I. and long after, called Lisnegarvey; and though now a populous and flourishing town, it was at that time a very inconsiderable village. Its rapid increase in population and importance may be attributed to Edward, Viscount Conway, to whom, in 1627, Charles I. granted the remainder of the manor of Killultagh (a portion of which had been previously given by Jas. I. to his ancestor, Sir Fulk Conway), who, on obtaining possession of this grant, built a castle here, which became the head of the manor. The same grant conferred the privileges of courts leet and baron, view of frank pledge, manorial courts for debts not exceeding £2, a court of record every three weeks for sums not exceeding £20, a weekly market, and two annual fairs. Soon after the erection of the castle, some English and Welsh families were induced by the proprietor to settle here, and a town consisting of more than fifty houses soon arose. On the breaking out of the war in 1641, a body of 1000 men assembled and preserved the town for some time from the attempts of the insurgents, and held their detached parties in check; but on the 28th of November in that year, the garrison consisting only of five newly raised companies and Lord Conway's troop of horse, the insurgent army commanded by Sir Phelim O'Nial, Sir Conn Magennis, and General Plunket, on their march to Carrickfergus, advanced to attack the town. Sir Arthur Tyringham, however, arriving with a small reinforcement, and being aided by Sir George Rawdon, repulsed the columns of the enemy as they successively advanced to the assault, and by a galling fire from the streets committed great slaughter among them. At nightfall further reinforcements arrived from Carrickfergus and Belfast; and the insurgents despairing of success, set fire to the town, which in a few hours was reduced to ashes; a sanguinary conflict being maintained in the burning town till nearly midnight, when the insurgents were finally put to flight, leaving behind them a number of slain equal to three times the entire number of the garrison, of whom only from 20 to 30 were killed. In 1644, General Monroe made an attempt to obtain possession of the town, but was frustrated by the vigilance and resolution of the garrison; and on the 6th of December, 1648, that general, with the Scottish forces under his command, was signally defeated on the plains of "Lisnegarvey," by Col. Venables and Sir Charles Coote, two of Cromwell's commanders, to the former of whom the castle was surrendered in 1650. On the landing of the Duke of Schomberg, near Bangor, in 1689, a considerable body of forces in the interest of Jas. II. assembled at this place, but afterwards abandoned it without any attempt for its defence, and Wm. III. passed through the town shortly before the battle of the Boyne. Chas. II., to reward the fidelity of the inhabitants to his father and to himself, had

erected the church of Lisburn into a cathedral for the united dioceses of Down and Connor, and had granted the townsmen the privilege of sending two representatives to the Irish parliament; but what more especially contributed to the improvement and commercial importance of the town was the settlement here, after the revocation of the edict of Nantz, of many Huguenot families, who introduced the manufacture of linen, and brought with them improved machinery from Holland. The skill and industry of these new settlers were liberally encouraged by the government, which granted large sums of money for the erection of suitable buildings for carrying on the manufactures, &c., and, by giving an example to others engaged in the same trade, soon raised the quality of the manufactures to a degree of excellence previously unknown. In 1707, the town and castle were burned to the ground; the latter has never been rebuilt, but the present town soon arose from the ruins of the former, and gradually increased in extent; it has been greatly improved at various times, and especially within the last few years by the spirited exertions of the agent of the Marquess of Hertford, who is owner in fee of the whole town, and of a considerable part of the surrounding country; and it is now one of the handsomest inland towns in the province of Ulster.

The town is situated on the north-western bank of the river Lagan, which separates the counties of Antrim and Down, and on the high road from Dublin to Belfast: it consists principally of one long irregular line of street, extending nearly from east to west, from which several smaller streets branch off; and contains, according to the last census, 992 houses, of which 675 are roofed with slate, and the remainder with thatch; all the houses in the principal streets are well built, and amply supplied with excellent water conveyed by pipes from works in the neighbourhood. The great terrace of the castle, which is still remaining, has been made an agreeable promenade; it is sheltered from the north by Castle-street, and is kept in the best order at the expense of the Marquess of Hertford. On the opposite side of the river is a small suburb, not included in the ancient limits of the borough, but within the parish and the new electoral boundaries. A new line of road has been made at a great expense at the entrance from Dublin on the south-west, and also at the entrances from Belfast and Armagh, by which the town has been much improved. The manufacture of linens and cambrics, which are sold in their brown state every market day at the linen-hall, a neat and commodious building erected for the purpose, is still carried on to a considerable extent, and maintains its high reputation for the superior quality of these articles; and the diapers and damasks of this place have long been distinguished for their unrivalled beauty of pattern and fineness of texture. On a small island in the river Lagan are extensive chymical works for the preparation of acids, chlorides, &c., for the supply of the several bleach-yards, of which some of the largest in the kingdom are adjacent to the town, the principal being at Lambeg, Colin, Seymour Hill, Suffolk, and Chrome Hill, where 189,000 pieces are annually bleached and finished, principally for the London market. There are also extensive establishments for the printing, bleaching, and dyeing of muslins; and near the town are an extensive thread manufactory and a large flour-mill. The trade is much facilitated by the Lagan navigation between Lough Neagh

Lisburn. Part of 6 inch O.S. map of Co. Antrim, sheet 67, published 1834 (reproduced at 140%).

76

and Belfast, which joins the river Lagan a little above the town, by which, with the aid of several collateral cuts, the navigation is continued to Belfast. The market is on Tuesday, and is the largest and best in this part of the country for every description of provisions; it is also much frequented on account of the quantities of linen and other articles which, in addition to its supply of provisions, are brought for sale; there is a cattle market on the same day. The fairs are annually held on July 21st and Oct. 5th, and are chiefly for horses, cattle, sheep, lambs, and pigs, of which the supply is very large. The market-house is a handsome building surmounted by a cupola, and, in addition to the accommodation it affords to the market, contains a suite of assembly-rooms. There are also very extensive shambles, corn-stores, sheds, and weigh-houses, erected by the proprietor of the town, and well-enclosed market-places for cattle, sheep, and pigs.

By the charter of Chas. II. conferring the elective franchise, the inhabitants not being a body corporate, and consequently having no municipal officer, the seneschal of the manor of Kilultagh was appointed returning officer for the borough; and the right of election was vested in the inhabitants generally, every pot-walloper being entitled to vote; but by an act of the 35th of Geo. III., cap. 29, it was restricted to the £5 householders, of whom, previously to the late act for amending the representation, there were only 141, and of these only 81 were qualified to vote. By the 2nd of Wm. IV., cap. 88, the right of election was confirmed in the £5 householders; and the boundary of the borough, which was very indistinct, was enlarged and clearly defined, and now comprises an area of 1325 acres, the limits of which are minutely described in the Appendix. The number of voters registered up to March 1st, 1836, was 134; the seneschal is still the returning officer. Manorial courts are held by the seneschal every third Wednesday, at which debts to the amount of 40s. are recoverable; and there is a court of record, with jurisdiction to the amount of £20 late currency. Courts leet are also held twice in the year, when a leet grand jury is sworn, by whom a petty constable is appointed for each of the 17 constablewicks into which the manor is divided; presentments for payment of salaries, repairs of roads, and other works are made; and all the municipal functions of the borough are exercised. Petty sessions are also held in the town every Tuesday; and here is a station of the constabulary police. A large and handsome edifice now used as the court-house of the manor, and for holding the petty sessions and other public meetings, was originally built and supported by Government as a chapel for the Huguenot emigrants, whose descendants having attached themselves to the Established Church, the minister's stipend has been discontinued, and the building appropriated to the above purposes. The manor gaol of the borough, under the custody of the marshal of the manor court, has, since the 7th of Geo. IV., been disused as a place of confinement, and is now used as a place of custody for goods attached by the court till bailed.

The parish, which is also called Blaris, comprises, according to the Ordnance survey, 10,697 statute acres, of which 2827¼ are in the barony of Upper Massareene, county of Antrim, and 3064 in Upper Castlereagh, and 4805¾ in Lower Iveagh, county of Down. The lands are very fertile, and the system of agriculture is highly improved; for the last twenty years, wheat has been the staple crop, and oats, formerly the principal produce, are now grown only for the sake of a due rotation of crops. The Maze race-course, described in the article on Hillsborough near which town it is situated, is in this parish. The surrounding scenery is enlivened by numerous gentlemen's seats, among which are Ballymacash, the residence of Edw. Johnson, Esq.; Brookhill, of James Watson, Esq.; Larchfield, of Wm. Mussenden, Esq.; Lambeg House, of Robert Williamson, Esq.; Seymour Hill, of Wm. Charley, Esq.; Chrome Hill, of Richard Niven, Esq.; Ingram Lodge, of J. Richardson, Esq.; Suffolk, of the late J. Mᶜ Cance, Esq.; and Colin, of Matthew Roberts, Esq.; besides many other elegant houses near the town. The living is a rectory, in the diocese of Connor, and in the patronage of the Marquess of Hertford. The tithes amount to £700: there is a glebe-house but no glebe attached to the living. The church is a spacious and handsome building, with a tower, to which an octagonal spire was added in 1807, at the expense of the late Marquess of Hertford; a fine organ has been presented to it by the present Marquess; and in its improvement considerable sums have been expended, including a recent grant of £256 from the Ecclesiastical Commissioners. It contains a handsome monument to Lieut. Dobbs, a native of the town, who was killed in an engagement with Paul Jones off this coast; and an elegant monument has recently been erected at the expense of the bishop and clergy of the diocese, to the memory of the celebrated Dr. Jeremy Taylor, Bishop of Down and Connor, who died here in 1667, and was buried in a vault in the church of Dromore, which he had built. In the churchyard are several monuments to many of the Huguenots who settled here under the patronage of Wm. III. and Queen Anne. It is the cathedral church of the united dioceses of Down and Connor; the visitations are held in it, and all the business belonging to the see is transacted in the town. There are no chapels of ease within the parish, but divine service is performed in the school-houses of Newport, Maze, and Broomhedge, in rotation. In the R. C. divisions the parish is the head of a union or district, also called Blaris, comprising the parishes of Lisburn and Hillsborough, in each of which is a chapel. There is a meeting-house for Presbyterians of the Synod of Ulster, of the first class, also two for Wesleyan Methodists, and one for the Society of Friends.

To the north of the town is the Ulster Provincial School for the Society of Friends, founded in 1794 by Mr. John Handcock, who bequeathed a sum of money for the erection of the premises; 50 children, who are eligible at eight years of age and remain till fourteen, are boarded, clothed, educated, and apprenticed; each scholar pays £3. 12. per annum, and the remainder of the expense, which averages about £14 per annum each, is defrayed by contributions from the society. A free school for boys was founded in 1810, and aided by the Association for Discountenancing Vice; and there is a similar school for girls, built and supported by subscription: the late George Whitla, Esq., bequeathed £100 to each, the interest of which is applied in procuring clothing for some of the poorest children. There are also two other schools for both sexes, one of which is aided by the same society, and the other is supported by subscription. An infants' school, also supported by subscription, was established in 1832, and a building was erected for its use at an expense of £120, towards defraying which the Marquess of Hertford contributed

£50. The number of boys on the books of these schools is about 400, and of girls, 300; and in the private pay schools are about 360 boys and 240 girls. An almshouse for eight poor women was founded under the will of Mr. Williams, in 1826; and six almshouses, for as many poor widows, were also founded by a member of the Trail family, and are now wholly supported by William Trail, Esq.; they were rebuilt on a more convenient site in 1830, at the expense of the Marquess of Hertford. The several charitable bequests amount in the aggregate to £2750, invested in government securities, the interest of which sum is distributed in winter among the poor, according to the wills of the respective donors. A Humane Society for the restoration of suspended animation has been established here; and in an airy part of the town is situated the County Infirmary, supported equally by subscriptions and grand jury presentments. On the White Mountain, about two miles to the north of the town, are the ruins of Castle Robin, erected by Sir Robert Norton in the reign of Elizabeth; the walls now remaining are 84 feet long, 36 feet wide, and 40 feet high, and near them is a large mount. Among the distinguished individuals born here may be noticed Dr. Edw. Smith, Bishop of Down and Connor, in 1665. Lisburn confers the titles of Earl and Viscount on the family of Vaughan.

LOUGHGUILE, or LOUGHGEEL, a parish, partly in the barony of KILCONWAY, but chiefly in that of UPPER DUNLUCE, county of ANTRIM, and province of ULSTER, 6½ miles (E. S. E.) from Ballymoney, on the road from Ballymena to Ballycastle; containing 6379 inhabitants. This place is celebrated for a battle which was fought on the Aura mountain, between the Mac Quillans and Mac Donnells, in which the former were defeated; and near the intrenchments that were thrown up on the occasion, and of which there are still some remains, is a large cairn, where the slain on both sides are said to have been interred. The parish is situated on Lough Guile and intersected by the river Bush, which rises in the Cambrick mountain, and after a bold and devious course of 13 miles falls into the sea at Bushmills. It comprises, according to the Ordnance survey, 30,165 statute acres, of which 6466¼ are in the barony of Kilconway, and 23,689¾ are in Upper Dunluce; 59½ are water, and of the land, about one-third is wild and boggy pasture, and the remainder chiefly arable land. The surface is boldly undulating, rising in some parts into lofty eminences, of which Mount Aura has an elevation of 1530 feet. The soil is principally light and gravelly, but in the valleys extremely fertile: the system of agriculture has greatly improved since the decline of the linen manufacture, and excellent crops are raised. There are some extensive tracts of limestone, which is quarried and burnt into lime, in which a considerable trade is carried on; and there is an ample supply of bog turf. Lisanour Castle, situated on the shores of the Lough, was originally built by Sir Philip Savage in the reign of John, and in 1723 was purchased by the ancestors of the Macartney family, of whom George, Earl Macartney, was born and for some time resided here. The last remains of the ancient building were removed in 1829, on the erection of the present mansion, the seat of George Macartney, Esq., which is beautifully situated in a fertile valley romantically interspersed with woods and lakes, and adorned with extensive and flourishing plantations; near the margin of one of the lakes is an elegant cottage in the later English style, richly embellished, and forming a picturesque feature in the scenery of the vale. Fairs are held here on the 19th of Feb., June, Aug., and Nov., chiefly for horses, cattle, pigs, and linen yarn. A constabulary police force is stationed here, and petty sessions are held on alternate Tuesdays. On the death of Dr. Trail, the last chancellor of Connor, and under Bishop Mant's act for dissolving the union attached to the chancellorship of that see, the living, previously a vicarage, became a rectory and vicarage, in the diocese of Connor, and in the patronage of the Bishop: the tithes amount to £515. The church, a small plain edifice with a tower surmounted by a spire, was rebuilt in 1733, chiefly at the expense of the late Earl Macartney. The R. C. parish is co-extensive with that of the Established Church; the chapel is a spacious edifice, built in 1785, near the entrance of Lisanour Castle. At Magheraboy is a place of worship for Seceders. About 300 children are taught in four public schools, of which a female school and Sunday school are supported by Mrs. Macartney; and there are seven private schools, in which are about 280 children. A dispensary affords medicine and advice to the poor, who are visited at their own dwellings when unable to attend. There are several Danish forts in the parish.

M

MAGHERAGALL, or MARAGALL, a parish, in the barony of UPPER MASSEREENE, county of ANTRIM, and province of ULSTER, 2½ miles (W. by N.) from Lisburn, on the road from Hillsborough to Antrim, and close by the Lagan canal; containing 3102 inhabitants. During the war of 1641, this place was the rendezvous of the insurgent forces, consisting of 8000 men, under Sir Phelim O'Nial and Sir Con Magennis, previous to their attack on Lisburn; whence, after their defeat, they returned to Brookhill, in this parish, then the seat of Sir G. Rawdon, which they burned to the ground, as well as a church, and slaughtered many of the inhabitants of Ballyclough and its vicinity. The parish comprises, according to the Ordnance survey, 6555½ statute acres, principally in tillage; the system of agriculture has been greatly improved. In the lower parts the land is generally good, and produces excellent crops, but in the upper part it is inferior. It is stated that the first application of lime, as manure, in the county, took place here, in 1740, at Brook Hill, the residence of J. Watson, Esq. There are about 50 acres of bog, but no waste land. Limestone for building and agricultural purposes is abundant and very good; basalt is also found. The weaving of linen and cotton is carried on for the Lisburn market, and for the manufacturers of Belfast. The principal seats are Brook Hill, the residence of J. Watson, Esq., in whose demesne a small river disappears, and, after passing under the hill, re-appears; and Springfield, of Capt. Houghton. The living is a vicarage, in the diocese of Connor, and in the patronage of the Bishop; the rectory is appropriate to the see of Down and Connor. The tithes amount to £300, of which £200 is paid to the bishop, and £100 to the vicar, who also receives £46. 4. from Primate Boulter's augmentation fund: there is no glebe-house or glebe. The church was rebuilt in 1830, by a loan of

£1000 from the late Board of First Fruits; it is a neat edifice, with a large tower. There are places of worship for Seceders, of the second class, and Wesleyan Methodists. About 270 children are educated in the parochial and two national schools; the former is partly supported by the incumbent, and the school-house was built in 1826, chiefly at the expense of the Marquess of Hertford. There are also five private schools, in which are about 180 children. Remains of the old church, which was destroyed in the civil war, exist near Brookhill, and have been converted into a stable: many human bones have been turned up by the plough; and silver and copper coins of the reigns of Elizabeth, Jas. I., and Chas. I., have been found on the estate of Mr. Watson, and are in his possession. In the plantations are two circular forts, in a perfect state, the smaller appearing to have been an outpost to the larger. Opposite to these are several large stones, the remains of a cromlech, here called the Giant's Cave, on ploughing the ground near which, in 1837, several urns were found curiously engraved and containing human bones. The late Commodore Watson was proprietor of Brook Hill, where he resided for a short period before his return to India, where he died of his wounds.

MAGHERAMESK, a parish, in the barony of UPPER MASSEREENE, county of ANTRIM, and province of ULSTER, 1 mile (N.N.E.) from Moira, on the road to Belfast; containing 1700 inhabitants. In this parish was the fortress of Innisloghlin, the strong hold of the O'Nials, supposed to have been built to defend the frequently contested pass of Kilwarlin, over which Spencer's bridge, now connecting the counties of Down and Antrim, has been erected. It was the last refuge of Hugh, Earl of Tyrone, and was besieged in 1602 by Sir Arthur Chichester and Sir H. Danvers, to whom it was surrendered on the 10th of Aug.; upon this occasion, great quantities of plate and valuable property fell into the hands of the victors. The parish, which is bounded on the west by Lough Neagh, comprises, according to the Ordnance survey, 3149¼ statute acres of good arable land in an excellent state of cultivation; the system of agriculture is highly improved, and there is neither waste land nor bog. Trummery House, for many years the residence of the Spencer family, is now only a farm-house. The weaving of linen and cotton is carried on here for the manufacturers of Belfast, and many persons are employed in the extensive limestone quarries; at Megabuy hill has been found a gypsum of superior purity, resembling talc. The summit level of the Lagan canal from Lough Neagh to Belfast is in the parish.

The living is a vicarage, in the diocese of Connor, united from time immemorial with the vicarages of Aghagallen and Aghalee, and in the patronage of the Marquess of Hertford, in whom the rectory is impropriate. The tithes amount to £128. 4., of which £29. 4. is payable to the impropriator and the remainder to the vicar; the glebe-house and the glebe, which comprises 13 statute acres, valued at £16. 5. per ann., are in the parish of Aghalee; the gross value of the benefice, tithes and glebe inclusive, is £334. 5. The church of the union is at Aghalee. There is a place of worship for the Society of Friends, a national school in which are about 60 children, and a private school in which are about 30. Of the ancient fortress of Innisloghlin there is scarcely a vestige: the ground was occupied by a farmer, who, in 1803, levelled the bul-

warks, filled up the intrenchments, and left only a small fragment of the castle standing; in levelling the ground were found many cannon balls, several antique rings of gold, and various other valuable articles. In the townland of Trummery, between Lisburn and Moira, are the extensive ruins of the ancient parish church; close to the western gable of which were the remains of one of the ancient round towers, about 60 feet high and of the same diameter throughout, with a conical roof of stone; it was levelled with the ground in 1828, and nothing but the scattered fragments remain. Adjoining these ruins is a doon or rath nearly perfect.

MASSEREENE, a village, in the grange of MUCKAMORE, barony of LOWER MASSEREENE, county of ANTRIM, and province of ULSTER, contiguous to the town of Antrim; containing 319 inhabitants. This place is situated on the Six-Mile-water, by which it is separated from Antrim; and though now only a small village, forming a suburb to that town, it is the head of, and gives name to, one of the largest and most fertile baronies in the county. In 1426, a priory for Franciscan friars was founded here by one of the O'Nial family, which, in 1621, was granted by Jas. I. to Sir Arthur Chichester, Baron of Belfast. The village contains 70 houses, and commands a fine view of the castle of Antrim, on the opposite side of the river. The whole western extremity of this district is washed by the waters of Lough Neagh, and comprises a large tract of fertile land in a very high state of cultivation, together with Massereene deer-park, which is enclosed with a stone wall five miles in circumference. Near the village, on the shore of the river, is a very copious chalybeate spring, strongly impregnated with iron, sulphur, muriate of soda, and fixed air, which has been found highly beneficial in chronic diseases; and on the shore of Lough Neagh is a lofty cliff, called Martin's bank, from which issue several saline springs, so powerfully impregnated as to deposite crystallised salt in large quantities, by the natural evaporation caused by the heat of the sun; no attempt has hitherto been made to establish any salt-works at this place, which does not appear to have attracted an adequate degree of attention. Massereene gives the title of Viscount to the family of Foster, of Antrim Castle.

MOLUSK, or MOBLUSK, a parish, in the barony of LOWER BELFAST, county of ANTRIM, and province of ULSTER, 8 miles (N. W. by N.) from Belfast, on the road to Antrim; containing 766 inhabitants. This place is said to have formerly belonged to the preceptory of the Knights Templars in the adjoining parish of Templepatrick, who had an establishment here also, of which there are no vestiges. Moblusk comprises 928¾ statute acres, according to the Ordnance survey, two-thirds of which are good land, the remainder being inferior; agriculture has of late much improved, a judicious mode of drainage having been adopted, and considerable portions of bog reclaimed and brought under cultivation: good crops of corn and potatoes are produced. Near the village there is an extensive establishment, called Hyde Park Print-field, belonging to Messrs. Batt, where great quantities of muslin are finished for the English and foreign markets, and in which more than 200 persons are employed. The parish is in the diocese of Connor, and is a rectory, forming part of the union of Carrickfergus and of the corps of the deanery of Connor. The tithes amount to £25. 11. 9., but as the inhabitants are exclusively Presbyterians, no tithes have been levied for many years; it is, however, the intention of the dean to erect a church and to collect the tithes. There does not appear to have been a church since the Reformation, but the burial-ground shews where the edifice originally stood. Nearly adjoining the village is a Presbyterian meeting-house. A school-house has been erected by Messrs. Batt, in which, chiefly by their assistance, 46 children are gratuitously taught: and at Glenoe is a National school, in which are about 80 children. Remains of large encampments and fortifications are observable in the parish and on its borders. There are several large stones standing erect, and under some of a similar description which were removed for improvements in the land, were found urns, or the fragments of baked clay, containing ashes, or black unctuous earth.

MOSSIDE, a village, in the grange of DRUMTALLAGH, barony of CAREY, county of ANTRIM, and province of ULSTER; containing 50 houses and 231 inhabitants.

MUCKAMORE, a grange, in the barony of LOWER MASSAREENE, county of ANTRIM, and province of ULSTER, 1 mile (S. E.) from Antrim; containing 1798 inhabitants. This place, anciently *Mach-airi-mor*, or the " great field of adoration," is situated on the Sixmile-Water; and comprises, according to the Ordnance survey, 3921¼ statute acres, exclusively of 1519 acres covered by Lough Neagh. It probably derived its name from its having been, during the times of Druidical superstition, the place selected for the performance of the religious rites of that people; a rude pillar consisting of a single stone, now called the " hole stone," or " old stone," is supposed to commemorate the fact. A monastery was founded here in 550, by Colman Elo, commonly, from the great number of churches that he had founded, called St. Columbkill. This establishment acquired great celebrity, and notwithstanding the internal wars which distracted the country, continued to flourish till the 32nd of Hen. VIII., when it was delivered up to the king's commissioners by Bryan Doyomahallon, its last abbot. Soon after the conquest of Ulster, in 1172, De Courcy visited this monastery and confirmed to the monks their former possessions and extended their ancient privileges, to which were added a grant of free warren, with an annual fair and a monthly market by Hen. VI., in 1430. In the 18th of Jas. I., it was granted by letters patent to Sir Roger Langford, from whom it descended to the Earls of Massereene, under whom it is held on lease for lives renewable in perpetuity. Only a very small portion of this once splendid pile is now remaining; but the extensive cemetery is still the burial-place of the surrounding district. Its situation was one of the finest that could have been selected, comprehending every advantage of wood and water, and every variety of hill and dale, with a pleasingly undulating surface, and a soil of exuberant fertility. The whole of the grange, which is extra-parochial, is in the highest state of cultivation, and is drained, fenced, planted, and stocked upon the English system. Muckamore House, the residence of S. Thompson, Esq.; Greenmount, of W. Thompson, Esq.; the Lodge, of F. Whittle, Esq.; and New Lodge, of the Rev. A. C. Macartney, are all handsome mansions delightfully situated in grounds tastefully and elegantly laid out. Close to the ruins of the abbey, and on the Six-mile-Water, is a very extensive bleach-green, belonging to W. Chaine, Esq., at which more than 80,000 pieces of linen are annually finished for the London market; there are also, on the

same river, another bleach-green on a smaller scale, an extensive paper-manufactory, and one of the most complete flour-mills in the county, in which 2200 tons of grain are annually ground: these works afford employment to the labouring population of the liberty, and also to many from the town of Antrim. The fair granted by Hen. VI. is held in the village of Oldstone, on the 12th of June, and is the largest horse fair in the province. The members of the Established Church attend divine service in the church of Antrim. About 80 children are educated in a school at Oldstone, aided by an annual donation from Mr. Thompson; and about 30 children in a private school. There are also two Sunday schools. Within the liberty are several raths and forts, two of the first of which are very extensive and in a perfect state; and there are also several remains of cromlechs. Among the ruins of the abbey, two silver candlesticks and other valuable relics are said to have been discovered some years since.

N

NEWTOWN-CROMMELIN, a parish, in the barony of KILCONWAY, county of ANTRIM, and province of ULSTER, 6 miles (N.) from Broughshane, on the road to Ballycastle; containing 727 inhabitants. It comprises, according to the Ordnance survey, 3445½ statute acres of land, which is in general of an inferior description, nearly two-thirds consisting of mountain and bog. Here is a station of the constabulary police, and fairs are held on the second Tuesday in every month. The living is a perpetual cure, in the diocese of Connor, and in the gift of the Incumbent of Dunaghy. The tithes amount to £30; and the gross income of the curacy, augmented by £66 per annum from Primate Boulter's fund, and including the glebe of eight acres, valued at £8 per annum, is £104. The glebe-house was built in 1831, at an expense of £500, of which £450 was a gift and £50 a loan from the late Board of First Fruits. The church was erected about the same period, by aid of a gift of £800 from the Board. About 270 children are educated in the schools of the parish, of which one for boys is supported by an annual allowance of £26 from the Methodist Missionary Society, and one for girls is aided by a small annual payment from a London Society; there are also a private school and two Sunday schools.

NILTEEN, or NALTEEN, a grange, in the barony of UPPER ANTRIM, county of ANTRIM, and province of ULSTER, 3½ miles (E.) from Antrim, on the Six-mile Water; containing 1109 inhabitants. According to the Ordnance survey, it comprises 2737¾ statute acres, all superior arable land. It is one of the four denominations which constitute the union of Donegore, in the diocese of Connor; the vicarial tithes, payable to the incumbent of Donegore, amount to £124. 0. 11½.; the rectorial tithes, payable to Jas. Moore, Esq., of Clover Hill, to £248. 1. 11. Within the grange are three pay schools, in which about 65 boys and 40 girls are taught; there is also a Sunday school.

P

PARK-GATE, a village, in the parish of DONEGORE, barony of UPPER ANTRIM, county of ANTRIM, and province of ULSTER, 4½ miles (E.) from Antrim; containing 35 houses and 162 inhabitants. It is a station of the constabulary police; petty sessions are held on alternate Tuesdays, and fairs on the 7th of Feb., May, and Aug., and on the 4th of November.

PORTRUSH, a sea-port, in the parish of BALLYWILLAN, barony of LOWER DUNLUCE, county of ANTRIM, and province of ULSTER, 5 miles (N. E.) from Coleraine, to which it has a penny-post; containing 337 inhabitants. It is situated at the north-western extremity of the county, on a peninsula of basalt jutting a mile into the sea toward the Skerries, having on the west a small

Seal of the Harbour Company.

but deep bay. According to the early annalists, this was the chief landing-place in the territory of the Rowte or McQuillan's country; it was also chosen by Sir John Perrot, as the landing-place of his artillery at the siege of Dunluce castle. On the plantation of Ulster by Jas. I., it was made a creek to Coleraine, but it latterly has absorbed all its trade, as the accumulation of sand on the bar of the latter port has rendered it very dangerous. A large artificial harbour has been just finished at Portrush, the entrance to which is 27 feet deep at low water, which has not only secured to it this advantage but has considerably increased its trade. The number of vessels now trading hither is 120, of the aggregate burden of 10,260 tons. The principal trade is with Liverpool, Whitehaven, the Clyde and Campbeltown. The chief imports are timber, coal, iron, barilla and general merchandise; the exports, linen cloth, provisions, grain, live stock, poultry, eggs and salmon, the export of which last is very great during the season, which commences in May and ends in September; the numbers of salmon taken off the shore have been much increased by an improved kind of net, but the principal supply is from the Bann and Bush rivers. The grain shipped in 1834 exceeded 6000 tons; the butter, 8166 firkins. Steam-boats ply weekly to Liverpool and Glasgow, and three times a week to Londonderry, Moville and Ennishowen. The town, owing to these causes, is rapidly improving. Many villas and lodges have been built in it or its immediate neighbourhood; and the beauty of its situation, commanding an extensive and varied range of scenery, makes it a favourite place of resort for strangers, particularly during the bathing season. A chapel of ease is about to be built in it, the parish church being a mile distant: there is a meeting-house for Wesleyan Methodists. It is a station for the constabulary police and for the coast-guard. A male and female school, founded by the late Dr. Adam Clarke, and supported by the Irish Missionary Society, is kept in a large and handsome brick edifice with a cupola and bell. A handsome hotel is now in progress. Close to the town is a beautiful and extensive strand, and at its southern extremity is a range of cliffs of white limestone, in which are several extensive caves; near it are some hills formed wholly of sand drifted by the northern winds; some of these are of recent formation, as the rich vegetable soil, bearing evident marks of cultivation, can be traced beneath them. After a violent storm in 1827, which swept away some of the sand, the remains of an ancient town were exposed to view, shewing the foundations of the houses, in which were found domestic utensils, moose deer's horns, spear heads of brass, and other military weapons. In the immediate neighbourhood is also a rock in which are imbedded large and perfect specimens of the cornu ammonis: various other species of fossils are frequently discovered. A new line of road from this place to Portstewart was made along the cliffs close to the shore, and a railroad from it to Coleraine is in contemplation.

R

RACAVAN, or RATHCAVAN, a parish, in the barony of LOWER ANTRIM, county of ANTRIM, and province of ULSTER, on the road from Larne to Ballymena; containing, with the post-town of Broughshane (which is separately described), 4479 inhabitants. This parish, which is also called Rathcoon, is situated on the river Braid, and according to the Ordnance survey comprises, including a small detached portion, 17,563 statute acres, of which 12,271 are applotted under the tithe act, and valued at £5176 per annum. The surface is boldly varied; there are large tracts of mountain, bog, and waste; the remainder is arable land of a light gravelly soil. There are several basaltic quarries in operation; greenstone is found in great abundance; and near the base of Slemish, a detached mountain of greenstone, gold is said to have been found. Race View, the seat of R. Harrison Esq., is in the parish. There are four extensive bleach-greens, with beetling-engines and other apparatus, in which together more than 100,000 webs of linen are finished annually; there is also a large mill for spinning linen yarn, and the weaving of linen cloth is extensively carried on in various parts of the parish. A large fair is held at Broughshane on the 17th of August, for horses, cattle, and pigs; and great numbers of carcases of pigs are sold in the market every Tuesday, to the agents of the Belfast merchants. The parish is within the jurisdiction of the manorial court of Buckna, held every month at Broughshane, for the recovery of debts not exceeding £20.

The living is a rectory, in the diocese of Connor, forming part of the union of Skerry, or the Braid; the tithes amount to £316. 16. 1. The church at Broughshane has been built within the last 50 years. There is a place of worship for Presbyterians in connection with the Synod of Ulster, of the first class, a spacious handsome building with a cupola, containing a bell; also for Covenanters at Craigamuoy. About 100 children are taught in the national school at Broughshane; and there are four private schools, in which are about 800 children, and two Sunday schools. Here is an excellent institution for the accommodation of the poor, and a clothing society, affording clothing to 50 males and 50 females annually; both are supported by subscription. Mr. Jamieson, in 1829, bequeathed £600 to the poor, but the legacy has not been yet paid over for that purpose. There is a small ancient churchyard at some distance from the main road, and difficult of access; it is of triangular form and well walled, and is now used exclusively as a burial-place for Presbyterians.

RALOO, or RALLOO, a parish, in the barony of LOWER BELFAST, county of ANTRIM, and province of ULSTER, 5¼ miles (N.) from Carrickfergus; containing 2171 inhabitants. It comprises, according to the Ordnance survey, 6105¾ statute acres of land, of which about one-fourth is of good and one-fourth of medium quality, and the remainder boggy and mountainous. It is a rectory, in the diocese of Connor, constituting part of the union of Carrickfergus and corps of the deanery of Connor: the tithes amount to £148. 12. In the R. C. divisions it is part of the union or district of Larne and Carrickfergus. At Toreagh, Ballyvallagh, and Loughmorn, are schools under the National Board, in which about 180 children are educated; and there are three private schools, in which are about 100 children.

RAMOAN, or RATHMORAN, a parish, in the barony of CAREY, county of ANTRIM, and province of ULSTER; containing, with the post-town of Ballycastle (which is separately described), 4739 inhabitants. This place, called also *Rathmona*, signifying "the fort in the bog," is situated on the sea-shore, and forms the western boundary of Ballycastle bay. The coast, consisting of bold, precipitous cliffs, is here too abrupt to afford a convenient landing-place, except the quay at Ballycastle, which was constructed at considerable expense, though now in a dilapidated state. The parish comprises, according to the Ordnance survey, 12,066½ statute acres, principally under cultivation; the system of agriculture is highly improved, but the lands in several parts being very much exposed, the wheat does not ripen well. The quality of the land differs much, but is in general productive, and the extensive mountain of Knocklaide affords good pasturage: it is one of the highest in the county, half being within this parish, and the other half in that of Armoy; its summit is 1685 feet above the level of the sea at low water. There are considerable tracts of bog near the Coleraine road, and of waste land in the line towards the Giants' Causeway, and near the base of Knocklaide. Coal of excellent quality is found here, but no mines have been opened, though the collieries in the adjoining parish of Culfeightrim, usually known as the Ballycastle collieries, were formerly worked to a considerable extent. Superior freestone, in colour and grain equal to Portland stone, is quarried here, but not to any great extent. The spinning of linen yarn, and the weaving of cloth, are carried on in some of the farmhouses. A market and fairs, and courts leet and baron, are held at Ballycastle. Clare Park is the elegant seat of Chas. McGildowney, Esq.; Glenbank, of Mrs. Cuppage; and the glebe-house, of the Rev. Leslie Creery.

The living was formerly a vicarage, united to that of Culfeightrim, the rectories of which, since 1609, were appropriate to the chancellorship of Connor, till 1831, when, on the decease of Dr. Trail, the last chancellor, it became a rectory and vicarage, in the diocese of Connor, under the provisions of the act of the 5th of Geo. IV., cap. 80, and now constitutes the corps of the chancellorship, with cure of souls, in the patronage of the Bishop. The tithes amount to £400: the glebe-house was built in 1809, at an expense of £480, of which £369 was a

gift, and £110 a loan, from the late Board of First Fruits; the glebe comprises 26 acres of good arable land, valued at £39 per annum. The church is a small edifice, and was rebuilt in 1812, at an expense of £369, a loan from the same Board: it contains some very ancient monuments. There is also an endowed church, or chapel, at Ballycastle. In the R. C. divisions the parish is called Ballycastle; it contains two chapels, one in the town, the other at Glenslush. There are two places of worship for Presbyterians, in connection with the Synod of Ulster, one of which is in the town, and the other near the church; both are of the third class: there is also a Methodist meeting-house. About 400 children are educated in five public schools, of which the parochial school is principally supported by the rector; and in five private schools are about 180 children. There are also six Sunday schools. At Ballycastle are almshouses founded by Hugh Boyd, Esq., who also endowed a charter school, now discontinued, near the church, with 12 acres of land. On the summit of Knocklaide is a tumulus called *Cairn-an-Truagh*, said traditionally to be the burial-place of three Danish princesses. There are several raths in the parish, some terminating in a pointed apex, and others flat on the top like a truncated cone; of the latter sort, one, within a quarter of a mile of the town, is called *Dun-a-Mallaght*, the "cursed fort." The castle of Doonaninney stands on a bold headland, 300 feet above the level of the sea, commanding the channel and the isle of Rathlin: two miles westward are the noble and romantic ruins of Kinbane, or Kenbann, castle, built on a projecting cliff of limestone rock, running out several hundred feet into the sea, under some bold headlands, which rise 280 feet above the ruins. In the town of Ballycastle are the remains of the edifice which gave name to the place; an uninteresting gable is all that exists: about two miles hence, on the Glenslush water, are the ruins of a very extraordinary castle, called *Goban-Saor*, which once was the residence of the powerful chieftain O'Cahan: and immediately adjoining the quay of Ballycastle are the interesting ruins of the abbey of Bonamargy, founded by Mac Donnell, in 1509, which was perhaps the latest erected in Ireland for Franciscan monks; the chapel is in tolerable preservation, being the burial-place of the Antrim family. According to Archdall, St. Patrick founded a religious house here, called Rath-Moane, in which he placed St. Ereclasius. Vast quantities of beautiful pebbles are found along the shore, among which are chalcedony, opal, dentrites, and belemnites. On the lands of Drumans, on the side of the great mountain of Knocklaide, is a spring, the waters of which are strongly chalybeate, and may be conveyed to distant places without any diminution of their effect.

RAM'S ISLAND, in the parish of GLENAVY, barony of UPPER MASSEREENE, county of ANTRIM, and province of ULSTER; the population is returned with the parish. This small island, which is situated about two miles from the eastern shore of Lough Neagh, comprises, according to the Ordnance survey, 6a. 3r. 23p.: it is partially planted with fruit trees and otherwise improved and ornamented, and with the remains of its ancient round tower forms an interesting object from the shores of the lake. The tower, of which 43 feet still remain, is divided into three stories, and has an entrance on the south-west nearly level with the ground; in the second story is a window facing the south-east, and in the third is another facing the north. About 5½ feet from the

Lord O'Neill's cottage, Ram's Island, Lough Neagh. From The Dublin Penny Journal, *vol. 2, 1833.*

ground are the remains of some letters or characters cut on the stones in the interior, but so obliterated by time as to be now illegible.

RANDALSTOWN, a market and post-town (formerly a parliamentary borough), in the parish of DRUM-MAUL, barony of UPPER TOOME, county of ANTRIM, and province of ULSTER, 17¾ miles (N. W. by W.) from Belfast, and 97¼ (N.) from Dublin, at the junction of the mail coach roads from Coleraine and Magherafelt to Belfast; containing 618 inhabitants. This place, which is situated on the river Maine, was from that circumstance called Mainwater, and also Iron-Works, from the forges and furnaces formerly in extensive operation, and of which there are still some remains. In the war of the Revolution the town was the head-quarters of the Earl of Antrim's forces, who marched hence for the siege of Londonderry; and in the disturbances of 1798, a body of the insurgent forces attacked it, burned the market-house, and continued their devastations till the approach of Cols. Clavering and Durham, on the evening of the same day, when they retreated to Toome bridge. In 1683, Chas. II., in consideration of a fine of £200, granted to Rose, Marchioness of Antrim, the manor of Edenduffcarrick, with all its rights and privileges, and constituted the town of Iron-Works a free borough, with power to return two members to parliament, to be chosen by the majority of the inhabitants,

on precept to the seneschal of the manor issued by the sheriffs of Antrim. The borough continued to return two members till the Union, when the franchise was abolished.

The town is pleasantly situated on the western bank of the river Maine, over which is a handsome bridge of nine arches, and contains 113 houses, neatly built and of pleasing appearance. The barracks for the staff of the county militia, whose head-quarters and depôt are here, are well built; there is a good inn near the bridge. The chief trade is the spinning of cotton and the weaving of calico, for which there are extensive mills; in these, more than 600 persons are employed; and there is a large bleach-green. The market is on Wednesday and is abundantly supplied with wheat, flour, meal, and pork, great quantities of wheat and pork being sent to Belfast; there is also a market for linen and linen yarn on the first Wednesday in every month; and fairs are held on July 16th and Nov. 1st, chiefly for cattle and pigs. The market-house, in which are an assembly-room and rooms for holding the various courts, is a neat and well-arranged building. There is a constabulary police station in the town, and petty sessions are held on alternate Thursdays. A court baron for the manor, which is the property of Earl O'Neill, is held before the seneschal every month, at which debts not exceeding £20 are recoverable; and a court leet annually, at

83

which a weigh-master, a market jury and constables are appointed, and some small presentments made for the repair of the court-house and other purposes. The parish church, a handsome structure in the early English style, with an octagonal spire, is situated in the town ; in which are also a spacious and well-built R. C. chapel, two Presbyterian places of worship, and a dispensary. In the immediate vicinity is Shane's Castle, park, and demesne, the property, and, previously to the destruction of the mansion by an accidental fire in 1816, the residence of Earl O'Neill, which is noticed more particularly in the article on Drummaul.

RASHARKIN, a parish, in the barony of KILCONWAY, county of ANTRIM, and province of ULSTER, 2¼ miles (E.) from Kilrea, on the road to Ballymena; containing 7481 inhabitants. This parish, called also Rath-Arkin and Magherasharkin, lies on the border of the county of Londonderry, from which it is separated by the river Bann : it is 6 miles long and 5 broad, and comprises, according to the Ordnance survey, 19,337¾ statute acres, of which a very large quantity is mountain waste land, or bog; the remainder is of a light soil, but of excellent quality for flax, potatoes, oats and clover ; the system of agriculture in some parts is very good, in others the reverse. The linen manufacture is carried on to a considerable extent, the cloth being sold at Ballymena ; and there are two bleach-greens, one at Dunroin, belonging to John Cunningham, Esq., in which about 34,000 webs are annually bleached ; the other at Dunminning, belonging to Tho. Birnie, Esq., which bleaches about 20,000 webs, principally for the English market. These gentlemen have elegant residences attached to their respective establishments. At Killymurris is a very extensive vein of coal, chiefly of the kind called cannel, which is very productive, though by no means skilfully wrought : there are some quarries of basalt, from which the stone is raised for building and road-making. The Bann is navigable from Lough Neagh to Portna, where there is a convenient wharf, at which considerable business is done at times. A fair for cattle and pedlery is held annually in the village of Rasharkin, which is also a chief constabulary police station. The living is a vicarage, in the diocese of Connor, united by charter of Jas. I. to the rectories of Finvoy and Kilraghts and Kildallock grange, which together form the corps of the prebend of Rasharkin in the cathedral of Connor, and in the patronage of the Bishop. The rectory is impropriate ; one portion of the rectorial tithes, amounting to £55. 15. 8., belongs to Robert Harvey, Esq. ; two other portions, amounting to £101. 16. 8., belong, one moiety to Sir Tho. Staples, Bart., and the other to Edw. Caulfield, Esq. ; the residue, amounting to £46. 3. 1., has been appropriated to the use of Castle-Dawson chapelry ; the total of the rectorial tithes is £203. 15. 5. The vicarial tithes payable to the incumbent are £222. 7., and the aggregate value of the union, including the glebe, is £811. 17. per annum. The parishes of Rasharkin and Finvoy are held with cure of souls, those of Kilraghts and Kildallock without cure. The glebe-house, having been found by the present incumbent in a dilapidated and uninhabitable state on his admission to the benefice, has been put into complete repair by him, at an expense of £3692, without having any demand on his successor for the repayment of any portion thereof : the glebe consists of 50a. 0r. 34½p. statute measure, valued at 18s. 6d. per acre. The church is a small but very beautiful edifice on a commanding situation. In the R. C.

divisions the parish is united with that of Finvoy ; both have chapels : that of Rasharkin is in the village, in which there are also two places of worship for Presbyterians. A parochial school is chiefly supported by the rector : at Dromore are two schools under the direction of the Rev. Mr. Wilson ; a male and female school at Dunminny were built and are supported, the former by Mr. Birnie and the latter by Miss Birnie ; a school at Glenback is in connection with the Board of National Education, another is in connection with the London Hibernian Society, and there are two others, aided by grants from individuals. In these schools about 130 boys and 120 girls are instructed : besides whom, 418 boys and 160 girls are educated in 13 private schools : there are also 8 Sunday schools. There are several raths in the parish : one of these, at Lisnacannon, is of very large dimensions ; it has two fosses and three ramparts, and covers nearly an acre and a half of ground. Several silver coins, of the reigns of Stephen, John and Rich. III., and of Robert and David Bruce, were found here ; and an artificial cavern was discovered near the church. The body of a man who had committed suicide in 1776, and had been buried in a bog in the mountain, was found in 1827, without the smallest signs of decomposition.

RASHEE, a parish, in the barony of UPPER ANTRIM, county of ANTRIM, and province of ULSTER, 2 miles (N. W.) from Ballyclare, on the road from Larne to Broughshane : the population is returned with the parish of Ballyeaston. This parish comprises, according to the Ordnance survey, 6460½ statute acres. It is a rectory, in the diocese of Connor, one portion of it forming part of the union and corps of the prebend of Carncastle, and the remainder constituting part of the perpetual cure of Ballyeaston.—See BALLYEASTON and CARNCASTLE.

RATHLIN, an island and parish, in the barony of CAREY, county of ANTRIM, and province of ULSTER, 6½ miles (N.) from Ballycastle ; containing 1039 inhabitants. This island, which is situated off the northern coast of Antrim, nearly opposite to the town of Ballycastle, in lat. 54° 36' (N.), and lon. 9° 15' (W.), and which is regarded as the *Ricnia* of Pliny and the *Ricina* of Ptolemy, has received various appellations from different writers. By the Irish historians it is called *Recarn*, or *Recrain* ; by Buchanan, *Raclinda* ; by Mackenzie, *Rachri* ; by Ware, *Raghlin* ; and *Raghery* by Hamilton, who derives that name from *Ragh Erin*, signifying the " fort of Erin." Its present name, which has been adopted by all modern writers, is but a slight modification of that given to it by Ware. St. Comgall is said to have landed in this island with the intention of founding a cell, but was expelled by a band of soldiers. In the sixth century, however, a church was founded here by St. Columba, who placed it under the superintendence of St. Colman. But the foundation of this religious establishment is by some writers attributed to Lugard Laither, who was abbot about the year 590, and by others to St. Legene, abbot of Hy, by whom it was repaired about the year 630. In 790, a body of Danish pirates, in their first descent upon the coast, laid waste the whole island and destroyed the monastery, which was soon afterwards restored ; it was again destroyed in 973, by the Danes, who martyred the abbot, St. Feradach ; since which time no subsequent notice of it occurs. King John granted the island to Alan of Galway ; and Robert Bruce, when driven from

Scotland by the success of Baliol, his competitor for the crown, took refuge here, where he fortified himself in a castle, of which a fragment still remaining bears his name. In 1558, the Earl of Sussex, then Lord-Deputy, attacked the Scots who had taken possession of the island and expelled them with great slaughter; and so much did the place suffer from the repeated ravages of the English and Scots, that it is stated in a manuscript history of the country to have been totally uninhabited in 1580.

The island is about six miles and a half in length, and about a mile and a half in breadth near the centre; the eastern portion curves towards the main land, from the nearest point of which it is about three miles distant, forming a small enclosure which is called Church bay. It comprises, according to the Ordnance survey, 3398¾ statute acres, including 30½ acres under water: about three-fourths consist of rocks and stony pasture, and the remainder of arable land of medium quality. It is fully exposed to the northern ocean, and the tides running here with great impetuosity, the sea is often so rough as frequently to deter tourists from visiting it. The western side is rocky and mountainous, and the appearance of the coast strikingly magnificent; brown rocks and still darker masses of basaltic pillars are in some places contrasted with chalk cliffs: on the northern side the precipices towards the sea rise to the height of 450 feet without any projecting base. The soil is a light mould, intermixed with fragments of basalt and limestone; the valleys are rich and well cultivated, and arable land, meadows, and a variety of rocky pastures are scattered over the whole island. The substratum of nearly the whole island is basalt and limestone, and on the eastern side especially it forms beautiful ranges of columns, differing from those of the Giants' Causeway only in their dimensions, and in the greater variety of their arrangement, being found in the same places perpendicular, horizontal, and curved. Considerable beds of hard chalk extend for some distance along the southern shore, and in some places, as near Church bay, where they are intersected by basaltic dikes, the hard chalk or limestone is found to possess phosphoric qualities; beds of puzzolana are also found here, and on the shores a substance resembling pumice stone. Mr. Hamilton traces a vein of coal and iron-stone passing under the sea from the mines at Ballycastle to this island, which he thinks has been separated from the opposite coast by some convulsion of nature. Barley of excellent quality and cattle are sent off from this place; the former is chiefly purchased by Scottish merchants. Kelp was formerly made in great quantities; its manufacture was the chief source of wealth to the inhabitants, but since the bleachers have discontinued the use of it, there is very little demand; the chief markets for it are Campbelltown and Glasgow. There are two storehouses, one for kelp and one for barley, erected by the Rev. Mr. Gage, proprietor of the island, for the purpose of collecting the produce of his tenantry; there is also a mill for grinding oats. The horses, cattle, and sheep are all small. Church bay, though affording good anchorage, is entirely exposed to the violence of the western winds, during the prevalence of which no vessel can ride here in safety; the only other havens are some small creeks on the eastern side, of which the principal is Port Ushet, where the small craft belonging to the island shelter

during the winter. The inhabitants of this part of the island are principally fishermen, who make short voyages and carry on a little trade by way of barter; they all speak the English language; but in the western part of the island the Irish language is universal, and the inhabitants, from want of intercourse with strangers, have many peculiarities; they are a simple, laborious, and honest people, entertaining an ardent affection for their island, which alone they regard as their country, and speak of Ireland as of a foreign land. They are very dexterous in seeking for the nests of sea fowl, for which purpose they swing themselves down the face of the precipices by means of a rope secured to a stake on the summit. Both Catholics and Protestants generally live together in the greatest harmony, undisturbed by the difference of religion; they frequently intermarry; scarcely was an individual ever known to emigrate formerly, but many young men have gone to America of late years. There is neither any town nor regular village; the dwellings of the inhabitants are irregularly scattered throughout the island. The proprietor, the Rev. R. Gage, is constantly resident and acts as magistrate. A coast-guard station for one officer and six men, one of the eight that constitute the district of Ballycastle, has been established here.

The living is a rectory, in the diocese of Connor, and in the patronage of the Bishop; the tithes amount to £60, which is augmented with £27.14. from Primate Boulter's fund. The glebe-house has been condemned as unfit for residence, and the curate has a house and garden rent-free provided by the incumbent, who pays him a stipend of £60. The glebe comprises 15 acres, valued at £18.15. per ann., making the gross income of the benefice £106.9. The church, towards the erection of which the late Board of First Fruits contributed a gift of £800, is a neat small edifice with a square tower, erected in 1815. The R. C. chapel is a plain building. About 180 children are taught in three public schools. There are some slight remains of the ruined fortress called Bruce's castle, of the original foundation of which there is nothing upon record. Nearly in the centre of the island are some small tumuli; in one of these was found a stone coffin, near which was an earthen vessel, and a considerable number of human bones; and on the small plain where these tumuli are placed have been found brazen swords, spear-heads, and a large fibula, which are deposited in the museum of Trinity College, Dublin. Near the Black Rock, on the south of Church bay, are four remarkable caverns, which, though penetrating a basaltic mass and at a point remote from any calcareous formation, have calcareous stalactites depending from the roof, which by their continual dropping have deposited an incrustation, about an inch in thickness, on the floor beneath.

REDBAY, a hamlet, in the parish of LAYDE, barony of LOWER GLENARM, county of ANTRIM, and province of ULSTER, 1¼ mile (S.) from Cushendall: the population is returned with the parish. This place is situated on the eastern coast, and on the new coast road from Glenarm to the Giants' Causeway; the shore is bold, and above the bay are some lofty cliffs of romantic appearance, on one of which are the interesting remains of Redbay castle, said to have been erected in the reign of Elizabeth. Underneath this castle is a spacious and singular cavern, of which the sides and the roof are formed of rounded silicious stones imbedded in a matrix of sandstone, commonly called pudding-stone, and differing entirely from those of the rocks in the vicinity; the opening is towards the sea, and through the arch which forms the entrance is a fine view of the sea, especially at high water, when it is agitated. In the vicinity is a small R. C. chapel belonging to the union or district of Cushendall.

ROUGHFORT, a village, in the parish of TEMPLE-PATRICK, barony of LOWER BELFAST, county of ANTRIM, and province of ULSTER; containing 195 inhabitants. Fairs are held on May 31st and Nov. 29th.

S

SHILVODAN, a grange, in the barony of UPPER TOOME, county of ANTRIM, and province of ULSTER, 4½ miles (N.) from Antrim, on the road to Ballymena; comprising, according to the Ordnance survey, 3546½ statute acres of land, partly consisting of mountain.

SKERRY, SKIRRIE, or SQUIRRE, a parish, in the barony of LOWER ANTRIM, county of ANTRIM, and province of ULSTER, 3 miles (N. E.) from Ballymena, on the river Braid, and on the roads leading respectively from Glenarm and Larne to Ballymena; containing 4405 inhabitants. According to the Ordnance survey it comprises 26,176 statute acres. The surface is mountainous, and the soil varied; the lower lands are fertile and well cultivated, but in other places the ground is entirely neglected; there are large tracts of bog, producing abundance of fuel, and of waste and mountain land, affording rough pasturage. The principal seats are Knockboy, the residence of A. Davison, Esq.; Bushyfield, of the Rev. R. Stewart; Nowhead, of J. Logan, Esq.; White Hall, of J. White, Esq.; Tullymore, of the Hon. J. B. R. O'Neill; Glencairn, of the Rev. W. Crawford; and Claggan, the splendid hunting seat of Earl O'Neill. Coal and ironstone have been discovered, but neither has been yet worked; basalt of every description is obtained in abundance, and greenstone is found in some places. At Knockboy is an extensive mill for spinning linen yarn and flax, and the weaving of linen cloth is carried on in almost every house. An annual fair is held at Tullymore, on Nov. 17th, for cattle, horses pigs, and pedlery. The living is a rectory, in the diocese of Connor, united from time immemorial with the rectory of Racavan, and in the patronage of the Marquess of Donegal: the tithes amount to £399. 7. 8., and of the entire benefice, which is popularly called the union of the Braid, to £716. 3. 9. The ancient church has been long in ruins; the present, situated in the town of Broughshane, and which is the church of the union, is a small edifice in the Grecian style of architecture, with a handsome spire; it was erected by Charles, ancestor of the present Earl O'Neill, probably about the year 1765, on condition of the parishioners keeping it in repair; a gallery was added to it, and a vestry built at the expense of the parish in 1829. In the church is a beautiful marble font, the gift of the Rev. Mr. Crawford. In the R. C. divisions the parish, with Dunaghy, is called the parish of Glenravel. There is an excellent parochial school-house, in which also divine service is performed on alternate Sundays; and there are also schools at Ballycloghan, Correen, Knockboy, Tullymore, Longmore, and Ballymena, chiefly supported by the resident gentry. The late Alex. Davison, Esq., bequeathed

£100 towards the education of poor children. The ruins of the ancient church, in which were interred many of the ancestors of Earl O'Neill, are situated on the summit of a conical hill, and form a conspicuous object for many miles round; and there are numerous forts, raths, and artificial caverns in the parish. It is said that small particles of gold have been found in the rills running from the hills where the greenstone is obtained; and in the valley of the river Artoags, near the bridge, are some fine basaltic columns of four, five, six, and seven sides, exactly like those of the Giants' causeway. Above the bridge, on the same stream, is a picturesque waterfall; and about a mile from Claggan is a curious cave, formed of large stones in appearance similar to those forming druidical monuments, from which the townland on which it is situated is supposed to have derived its name; several of the stones have been removed by the peasantry, and the plough has contributed to deface this monument of ancient times.

SOLAR, a parish, in the barony of UPPER GLENARM, county of ANTRIM, and province of ULSTER, on the road from Larne to Cushendall; containing 259 inhabitants. It is bounded on the east by the sea, and is a rectory, in the diocese of Connor, forming part of the union and corps of the prebend of Connor: the tithes amount to £19. 17.

STRAIDKELLY, or STRAIGHTKELLY, a village, in the parish of TICKMACREVAN, barony of LOWER GLENARM, county of ANTRIM, and province of ULSTER, 1½ mile (N. W. by N.) from Glenarm, on the old coast road to Belfast; containing 25 houses and 172 inhabitants. It is situated on the hill of Cloony, over which the old road passes at an elevation of nearly 200 feet above the level of the sea, while the new military road takes nearly a level course along the shore round the base of the hill, being not more than 15 feet above high water mark.

STRANOCUM, a village, in the parish of BALLYMONEY, barony of UPPER DUNLUCE, county of ANTRIM, and province of ULSTER; containing 29 houses, and 132 inhabitants. Fairs are held on April 20th and Dec. 29th.

T

TEMPLECORRAN, or BROAD ISLAND, a parish, in the barony of LOWER BELFAST, county of ANTRIM, and province of ULSTER, 5 miles (N. E.) from Carrickfergus, on the road from Belfast to Larne, and on Lough Larne; containing, with the village of Ballycarry (which is separately described), 1338 inhabitants. In 1597 a battle was fought at the highly romantic vale called Old Mill Glen, near Ballycarry, between the Mac Quillans and Mac Donnells, in which the former were defeated; and in November of the same year another took place on the same spot between the Mac Donnells and Sir John Chichester, in which the latter was slain and his army cut to pieces. This parish, which is also called, after the name of the village, Ballycarry, comprises, according to the Ordnance survey, 4744¼ statute acres, in a high state of cultivation. The system of husbandry is in a very improved state, and has been much promoted by the present proprietor, who is a

Templecorran church. Parish of Kilroot. Drawn by Andrew Nicholl and engraved by J. Bastin. From S. C. Hall, Ireland: its scenery, character, & c., *vol. 3, (London, 1841).*

practical and spirited agriculturist. Limestone and basalt are found in great abundance. Red Hall, the seat of G. Kerr, Esq., is an elegant mansion with a fine demesne. The spinning of yarn and the weaving of linen cloth are carried on. A court is held for the manor of Broad Island by the seneschal of Marriot Dalway, Esq., for the recovery of debts and determination of pleas to the amount of £20; its jurisdiction extends over this parish and that of Kilroot. Fairs are held at Ballycarry.

It is a vicarage, in the diocese of Connor, forming part of the union of Ballynure and of the corps of the prebend of Kilroot in the cathedral of Connor; the rectory is impropriate in D. Kerr, Esq. The tithes amount to £347. 1. 6., of which £231. 7. 8. is payable to the impropriator, and the remainder to the vicar. The church, originally a spacious and handsome cruciform structure, is now a ruin; it was at one time occupied by the Presbyterians, since whose ejectment it has not been used as a place of worship. There are chapels for Presbyterians, Independents, and Methodists; the first is in connection with the Remonstrant Synod, and of the first class. There are two national schools, situated at Ballycarry and Windygap, in which are about 120 children; and a private school of 10 girls. R. G. Kerr, Esq., in 1825, bequeathed £200 in trust to the vicar and the senior Presbyterian minister, to divide the interest among the poor. There is a curious hollow cave, called the Salt Hole, into which rushes a large stream of water which is not found again; and in the grounds of Red Hall is a glen of very extraordinary character. The Rev. Mr. Bryce, minister of the first Presbyterian congregation established in Ireland, lived and was buried here: and over the remains of a poet, known only as the Bard of Ballycarry, a monument has been raised.

TEMPLEOUGHTER, a parish, in the barony of UPPER GLENARM, county of ANTRIM, and province of ULSTER, adjoining the post-town of Glenarm, and on the Glenarm water: the population is returned with the parish of Ticmacrevan, by which this parish is entirely enclosed; nearly two-thirds of it are barren mountain. It is ecclesiastically consolidated with Ticmacrevan, *which see.* A small fragment of the ancient church is

still remaining on the lawn in front of the castle of Glenarm, near the principal entrance. The church of the union was built about 55 years since by act of council within the limits of this parish, and in a situation convenient for both parishes.

TEMPLEPATRICK, a parish, partly in the barony of LOWER, but chiefly in that of UPPER, BELFAST, county of ANTRIM, and province of ULSTER, 4 miles (E. by S.) from Antrim, on the road from Belfast to Londonderry; containing 4217 inhabitants, of which number, 314 are in the village. This place is said to have derived its name from a preceptory of Knights Templars established here at a very early period, but of its foundation or its history nothing is recorded. The parish, in form nearly triangular, comprising also within its limits the ancient parishes of Carn Graney or Grame, Ballyrobert, and Umgall, was granted, in the reign of Jas. I., to Sir Arthur Chichester, and afterwards regranted to Roger Norton. At the hamlet of *Dunadry,* or *Dunetherg,* "the Middle Fortress," one mile from Templepatrick, a sharp action took place in 1648 between the English and Scotch forces, in which the celebrated Owen O'Conolly, who commanded the former, was mortally wounded. The parish comprises, according to the Ordnance survey, 13,261½ statute acres, a considerable portion of which is mountain land, though affording good pasturage for sheep; there is but a small tract of bog, scarcely yielding sufficient fuel for the use of the inhabitants. The system of agriculture is beginning to improve under the auspices of Lord Templetown, the proprietor, who has subdivided the larger townlands, increased the size of the farms, drained and brought into cultivation great quantities of waste land, laid out the whole valley from the castle to the Six-mile-water as lawn and pasture ground, upon which large numbers of cattle are fed, planted a great number of trees and whitethorn hedges, and made many other improvements. Near the village is the venerable mansion of Castle Upton, formerly called Norton Castle, after Sir Robert Norton, by whom it was founded in the reign of Elizabeth, and now the seat of Viscount Templetown: it occupies the site of the ancient preceptory, and is in the castellated style of architecture; it is at present being restored from the partial dilapidations it had suffered from time to time. The weaving of linen and calico, and the making of hosiery are carried on in several of the farmhouses; and in and near the village are extensive limeworks, supplied with limestone raised on the spot; there are also numerous quarries of basaltic stone, which is obtained in abundance. Though there are no fairs in the parish, two of the largest in the county are held on its borders, one at Park Gate, a mile to the north, and the other at Oldstone, two miles to the west. This parish appears to have been one of the earliest Presbyterian settlements in Ireland; on the introduction of a Scottish colony into Ulster, Josias Welsh, grandson of the Scottish reformer, John Knox, is said to have obtained possession of the church, from which he was ejected in 1631 by the bishop of Down and Connor, for nonconformity; he was, however, reinstated by Archbishop Ussher, and died in 1634.

The living is a vicarage, in the diocese of Connor, and in the patronage of the Marquess of Donegal, in whom the rectory is impropriate: the tithes amount to £365, of which £70 is payable to the impropriator, and the remainder to the vicar. There was no church from the time of the Reformation till the year 1827, when the present church, a small edifice with a tower at the west end, was erected on an elevated site, at an expense of £830 British, a gift from the late Board of First Fruits. There are three places of worship for Presbyterians, one in connection with the Synod of Ulster, of the third class, one with the Remonstrant Synod, of the second class, and one with the Seceding Synod. There are four national schools, situated at Lyle Hill, Ballypaliday, Ballintoag, and Molusk; and a school at Carn Graney, founded in 1811 by the trustees of Erasmus Smith's charity, and partly supported by them and partly by the Hon. Col. Pakenham, in which five schools are about 230 children; and five private schools, in which about 190 children are taught. Of the ancient preceptory nothing remains except what is included within the walls of Castle Upton (the crypt under which is in a perfect state, and the finely-groined roof in good preservation), and the cemetery of the ancient temple church, in which are the tomb of the Rev. Josias Welsh, and the mausoleum of the Templetown family. In a field at a short distance from the mail road to Antrim is *Cairn Graine*, a remarkably fine monument of antiquity : it consists of ten large tabular stones, supported on upright pillars in the manner of a cromlech, but ranged in a straight line of 41 feet in length in a direction from north-east to south-west; the stone at the north-eastern extremity is rather low, and every succeeding one increases in elevation towards the south-western extremity, where the tabular stone is of very large dimensions and supported on five upright pillars. Various conjectures have been entertained as to the origin of this interesting relic; the name literally implies "the Heap of the Sun." Not far from this heap is one of the mounds or forts so frequently found in this country; it appears to have been very extensive and of great elevation, but has been much diminished and disfigured by the removal of the sand, of which, intermixed with common field stones, it was originally formed. Near Dunadry is a very perfect circle of large stones, and there are several other raths in the parish. This place gives the titles of Viscount and Baron Templetown to the Upton family.

TICKMACREVAN, or GLENARM, a parish in the barony of UPPER GLENARM, county of ANTRIM, and province of ULSTER; containing, with the parish of Templeoughter, the post-town of Glenarm, and the village of Straidkelly (each separately described), 3859 inhabitants. It comprises, according to the Ordnance survey, an area of 20,506¾ statute acres; and is situated on the Glenarm water, which rises in Slemish mountain and discharges itself into the sea at the town, where it is of considerable size. A very large portion of the parish is mountain, bog, and waste, but the remainder is in a high state of cultivation under the most improved system of agriculture, and produces wheat, beans and barley in great abundance and of excellent quality. Limestone of many varieties is found here; some kinds contain echenites, belemnites, and other similar fossils; and large masses of ponderous iron ore and decomposed basalt used in making Roman cement, are found imbedded among the limestone rocks; one species of it is remarkable for its quality of setting instantly when immersed in water. Great quantities of limestone are exported from Glenarm, the quay of which is

much resorted to by Scotch vessels in this trade, which bring coal and general merchandise in exchange. Close to the town of Glenarm is a coal mine, which has not been worked to advantage; there are also indications of that mineral in other parts of the parish. Glenarm Castle, the residence of Edw. M°Donnell, Esq., which is in this parish, is described in the account of the town. The glebe-house is the residence of the Rev. Ross Jebb; and there are several elegant bathing-lodges at Carnlough, belonging to Alex. M°Manus, Esq., and others, which have tended much to induce visitors from the inland parts to resort hither during the summer months.

The living was a rectory and vicarage, the former annexed, in 1609, to the chancellorship of Connor, and the latter episcopally united, in 1768, to the rectory of Templeoughter, (which is completely enclosed within it); but on the death of Dr. Trail, the late chancellor, in 1830, the two parishes were consolidated under the provisions of Dr. Mant's act, into a single rectory, in the diocese of Connor, and placed under the patronage of the Bishop. The tithes, including those of Templeoughter, amount to £240 : the glebe-house, which is situated about 1½ mile from the church, near the seashore, was built in 1813 by aid of a gift of £450 and a loan of £46 from the late Board of First Fruits; the glebe of the union comprises 23a. 0r. 30p. valued at £46. 7. 6. per ann. : the total value of the benefice amounts to £286. 7. 6. The church, which occupies the site of an ancient monastery close to the shore near the town, was built in 1768, at the expense of the noble family of M°Donnell, and was enlarged in 1822 by a loan of £300 from the late Board of First Fruits : it is a plain building with a tower and spire. The R. C. parish, which is called Glenarm, is co-extensive with the consolidated rectory of Tickmacrevan, and has two chapels, one at Glenarm, and the other at Carnlough, about two miles north-west of it. There are places of worship for Presbyterians, one of which is in connection with the Remonstrant Synod and of the third class, and a meeting-house for Wesleyan Methodists. Besides the schools noticed in the account of Glenarm, there are those of Cornabarna, Carnlough, Longfalls, and the Park, for the gratuitous education of poor children, in all of which there are 200 boys and 114 girls; there are also 4 private and 4 Sunday schools. Some remains of the ancient monastery, built in 1465 by Robt. Bisset, a Scotchman, for Franciscan friars of the third order, are still to be seen on the shore near the town; also those of the ancient church, a mile west of the town.

TOOME, a post-town, in the parish of DUNEANE, barony of UPPER TOOME, county of ANTRIM, and province of ULSTER, 22½ miles (W. N. W.) from Belfast, on the road to Londonderry, and 102½ (N. by W.) from Dublin; containing 122 inhabitants. This place, which gives name to the barony, had at a very early period a ford or ferry across the river Bann, which formed the only pass from one part of Ulster to the other, and on the first invasion of the English was considered to be of so much importance that De Courcey erected a castle here for its protection. It has been the scene of many sanguinary contests, its name being conspicuous in the history of all the insurrections that have occurred in this part of the country. In the parliamentary war the castle was surprised and taken by the R. C. bishop of Clogher, in 1650, but was soon after taken by Col. Venables, an officer in Oliver Cromwell's army, by whose orders it was subsequently dismantled. In the disturbances of 1798, a body of insurgents, after their defeat at Antrim, retreated from Randalstown to this place and posted themselves on the eastern side of the river, where they remained for two days, and on the approach of Gen. Knox, who was marching hither with 1500 of the yeomanry, to prevent the disaffected of Derry from joining them, they broke down one of the arches of the bridge, with a view to interrupt his progress. The town, which contains only about 20 houses, is situated on the eastern bank of the river Bann, over which in its short course from Lough Beg into Lough Neagh is a handsome bridge, erected at the sole expense of the late Earl O'Neill. It has a sub-post-office to Randalstown and Castledawson, and is a constabulary police station. In the court-house are held petty sessions every fortnight, and the court for the manor of Mullaghgane. Near the spot where the river unites with Lough Neagh is a good wharf with a commodious quay. Fairs are held on March 28th and Dec. 4th, and a pleasure fair is held at the bridge on Easter-Monday. The remains of the castle have fallen from the cliff and are scattered on the strand of Lough Neagh; many cannon balls have been found near its site.

TULLAGHORE, TULLACHGOR, or TULLOGH-GOR, a parish, in the barony of UPPER DUNLUCE, county of ANTRIM, and province of ULSTER, adjoining the town of Ballymoney : the population is returned with the parish of that name, into which Tullaghore has merged. It comprises, according to the Ordnance survey, 432¼ statute acres. Here is said to have been formerly a religious house, over which St. Nehemias presided in the time of St. Patrick.

TULLYRUSK, a parish, in the barony of UPPER MASSAREENE, county of ANTRIM, and province of ULSTER, 3 miles (E.) from Glenavy, on the road from Lisburn to Antrim; containing 2360 inhabitants. It comprises, according to the Ordnance survey, 4779½ statute acres, chiefly under pasture; the land in the lower part is tolerably good, but in the southern part there is much unimproved and barren mountain : there are about 100 acres of bog at the Brown moss. The climate, from the position of the parish between Lough Neagh and Belfast Lough, is moist and chilly. The rivers Crumlin and Glenavy bound it to the east and west. The weaving of linens and cottons for the Belfast market is carried on to some extent in the farm-houses. Knockairn is the residence of Fortescue Gregg, Esq. It is a vicarage, in the diocese of Connor, forming part of the union of Glenavy; the rectory is impropriate in the Marquess of Hertford. The tithes amount to £71. 1. 11., of which £15. 15. is payable to the impropriator, and £55. 6. 11. to the vicar. In the registry of Connor this parish is called a grange, and in the terrier and regal visitation book a chapelry; having been, probably, either a Bishop's mensal or a dependency on one of the great monasteries. The church of Tullyrusk stood in the townland of that name, near the verge of the parish; from the portions of its foundations still remaining, its dimensions appear to have been 62 feet by 17. Adjoining it is a large and well-enclosed cemetery, in which the Protestant

dissenters and Roman Catholics chiefly bury. There are four private schools, in which about 140 children are educated; and two Sunday schools. Several raths and tumuli occur in various parts. The crystals commonly called Lough Neagh pebbles are found in great quantities on turning up the land by the plough, although the lake whence they take their name is three miles distant, and the elevation of the land where they are found is many hundred feet above the level of its surface.

U

UMGALL, a grange, in the parish of TEMPLEPATRICK, barony of UPPER BELFAST, county of ANTRIM, and province of ULSTER, 6 miles (N. W.) from Belfast : the population is returned with the parish. It is situated upon the road from Belfast to Antrim, and comprises, according to the Ordnance survey, 753½ statute acres.

W

WHITEABBEY, a village, in the parish of CARMONEY, barony of LOWER BELFAST, county of ANTRIM, and province of ULSTER, 4 miles (N.) from Belfast, on the shore of Belfast Lough; containing 71 houses and 391 inhabitants. It takes its name from an old abbey, whose picturesque ruins consist of a chapel, the remains of which denote the early English style of architecture, but at what time or by whom founded is not known.

WHITEHOUSE, a village, in the parish of CARNMONEY, barony of LOWER BELFAST, county of ANTRIM, and province of ULSTER, 3 miles (N.) from Belfast, on the road to Carrickfergus; containing 132 inhabitants. It is situated on the shore of Belfast lough, and is principally occupied by the proprietors and work-people of the cotton factories, to which it owes its origin: the first cotton-mill established in Ireland was erected here, in 1784, by Mr. Nicholas Grimshaw, whose sons still carry on the manufacture in all its branches; the buildings are very extensive, and the spinning of yarn and weaving of cotton and muslin afford employment to above 1000 persons. Here are also some very large print-works, erected by another of Mr. Grimshaw's sons, in which more than 200 persons are employed. The village is neatly built, and its inhabitants are in comfortable circumstances. It has a penny post to Belfast and Carrickfergus; petty sessions are held every three weeks, and there is a coast-guard station, being one of eight in the district of Carrickfergus. Fairs are held on the first Tuesday in May and Nov., principally for cattle.

Merville, as seen from the shore, Whitehouse. Drawn by Joseph Molloy and engraved by E. K. Proctor. From Belfast scenery *(Belfast and London, 1832).*

Acknowledgements

Grateful acknowledgements are due to the following institutions for permission to use illustrations from books in their possession: the Linen Hall Library for the views on pages vi, 30, 37, 38, 56, and 63; the National Museums and Galleries of Northern Ireland, Ulster Folk and Transport Museum, for the views on pages 36, 37, 38 and 41. The original O.S. maps are from the map library of the school of geography at QUB.

For their valuable assistance thanks must be expressed to Dr Eugene Mc Kendry, Mr Roger Dixon, Dr Nollaig O Muraille, Mrs Fionnuala Carson Williams, Mr John Killen, Mrs Norah Essie, Ms Maura Pringle, Mrs Angelique Bell, Mr Patrick Mc Williams and Mr John Hamill.